1991

The Frontier Experience and the American Dream

The Frontier Experience and the American Dream

ESSAYS ON AMERICAN LITERATURE

EDITED BY

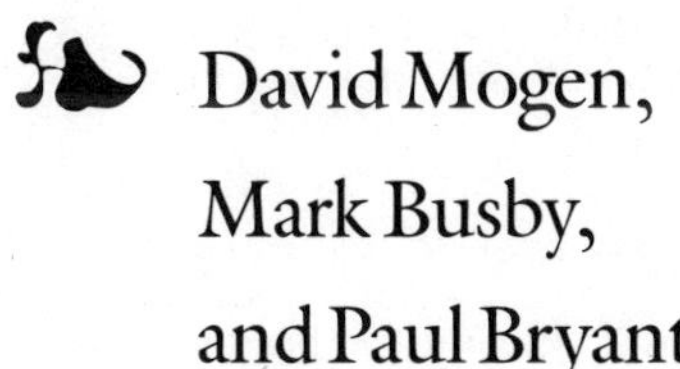

David Mogen,

Mark Busby,

and Paul Bryant

TEXAS A&M UNIVERSITY PRESS
College Station

First Edition

The paper used in this book meets the minimum requirements of the American National Standard for Permanence of Paper for Printed Library Materials, Z39.48-1984. Binding materials have been chosen for durability.

LIBRARY OF CONGRESS CATALOGING-IN-PUBLICATION DATA

The Frontier experience and the American dream : essays on American literature / edited by David Mogen, Mark Busby, and Paul Bryant. – 1st ed.

p. cm.

Includes index.

ISBN 0-89096-398-3 (alk. paper)

1. American literature–History and criticism. 2. Frontier and pioneer life in literature. 3. Myth in literature. 4. Canon (Literature) I. Mogen, David, 1945– . II. Busby, Mark, 1945– . III. Bryant, Paul, 1928– .

PS169.F7F76 1989

810′.9′15–dc19 88-35474

CIP

Contents

Acknowledgments

David Mogen acknowledges the support of the College of Arts, Humanities, and Social Sciences at Colorado State University, for typing and formatting the original manuscript and for helping fund indexing and proofreading. He also acknowledges his wife, Elizabeth, for her generous encouragement and support.

Mark Busby would like to thank Hamlin Hill and the Department of English and the Interdisciplinary Group for Historical Literary Study at Texas A&M University for support, Larry Reynolds for his careful reading of the introduction, Josh Busby for his enthusiasm, and Linda Busby, who remains his best editor.

Paul Bryant would like to acknowledge with gratitude the assistance of the Radford University Foundation in the preparation of this volume.

Acknowledgments

The Frontier Experience and the American Dream

Introduction: Frontier Writing as a "Great Tradition" of American Literature

MARK BUSBY, DAVID MOGEN, AND PAUL BRYANT

Frontier Mythology and American Literary Tradition

This collection of essays reconsiders the American literary tradition from colonial times to the present by focusing on the imaginative impact of the frontier experience. Our thesis is that historically the existence of a frontier of settlement, and of unsettled and even unknown lands beyond, has generated in the American literary imagination a set of images, attitudes, and assumptions that have shaped our literature into a peculiarly American mold. The frontier experience has so profoundly altered our cultural history that it affects our sense of ourselves even today, and thus far its central importance to our literary tradition has not been fully recognized. Though much has been written about the central role played by frontier mythology in American culture, the relationship between this mythology and our literary heritage demands further clarification.

These essays explore the aesthetic implications of the frontier experience and the American dream as they inform both works long considered American classics and others that have been excluded from the canon. Additionally, we enter the dialogue currently under way among scholars of American literature, particularly in "The Extra" section of *American Literature,* about the nature of American literary history, canon formation, and reevaluation.[1] Ultimately, we believe that this book will help refocus and restructure the American literature curriculum.

Although frontier mythology can function to reduce history and experience to stereotypes and clichés, historically our artists have also used it to create a distinguished body of American writing. However, we still do not have an aesthetics of frontier literature sufficiently sophisticated to interpret and illuminate this tradition. Richard Slotkin's analysis of the relationships among history, mythology, and cultural symbols, or "icons," describes how American frontier mythology metaphorically encodes key cultural values into our language:

> Myths are stories, drawn from history, that have acquired through usage over many generations a symbolizing function that is central to the cultural functioning of the society that produced them. Historical experience is preserved in the form of narrative; and through periodic retellings those narratives become traditionalized. These formal qualities and structures are increasingly conventionalized and abstracted, until they are reduced to a set of powerfully evocative and resonant "icons"–like the landing of the Pilgrims, the rally of the Minutemen at Lexington, the Alamo, the Last Stand, Pearl Harbor, in which history becomes a cliché. At the same time that their form is being simplified and abstracted, the range of reference of these stories is being expanded. Each new context in which the story is told adds meaning to it, because the telling implies a metaphoric connection between the storied past and the present–as, for example, in the frequent invocation of Pearl Harbor in discussions of the need to prepare for nuclear preemptive strikes; or the invocation of "Munich-style appeasement" when discussing the possibilities for negotiating with our adversaries.
>
> In the end myths become part of the language, as a deeply encoded set of metaphors that may contain all of the "lessons" we have learned from our history and all of the essential elements of our world view.[2]

Slotkin's formulation suggests the Janus-faced role played by mythology, which can both limit and expand the meanings of experience: through mythology "history becomes cliché," but mythology also transforms history into symbol, providing artists a meaningful medium with which to interpret our heritage and to give it new forms. Essentially, we are both advancing Slotkin's line of inquiry into areas he does not cover and examining its aesthetic implications–especially the symbolic vocabulary of frontier mythology. Our key assertions are these:

(1) that historically, frontier mythology has created a symbolic vocabulary that has been employed to express and interpret the American Dream, to articulate, examine, and criticize American values;

(2) that frontier mythology is intrinsically *dialectical,* or, to use Mikhail Bakhtin's word, *dialogic,* insofar as traditionally Anglo, masculine purveyors of the American dream have called forth responses by women, minority writers, and others who write from differing perspectives;

(3) that understanding how frontier mythology shapes our literary tradition highlights the continuity in that tradition, as well as the continuity between American imaginative writing and its broader cultural context;

(4) that understanding the dialectical and dialogical nature of this literary tradition will help open up the literary canon, by revealing how different regions, ethnic groups, classes, and genders have adapted frontier archetypes and enriched the American Dream, giving it new patterns and meanings.

We do not wish to suggest that frontier mythology provides the *only* significant context for an understanding of American literature. As Russell Reising notes in his study of theories of American literature, theorists such as F. O. Matthiessen, Lionel Trilling, Perry Miller, and others "claim to have defined an American tradition, if not *the* tradition." We agree with Reising that "the very idea of a comprehensive theory of American literature, like that of the great American novel, may be an impossibility" (p. 17). But we believe that this mythical approach to American literature provides perspective and enhances understanding–just as does, for example, highlighting the Puritan background.

Our thesis bears some relationship to Frederick Jackson Turner's Frontier Hypothesis, but whereas Turner deals with social history we are concerned with the literary imagination. Our study is not based primarily on traditional historiographical sources of evidence but on the archetypal images, myths, and symbols of our literature. Turner's theories have, of course, been rethought and to some extent rejected in recent years, but their influence upon decades of American historiography suggests the power of his central idea that the American frontier experience had a profound effect on the development of American civilization.

Though today an extensive tradition of criticism defines different aspects of the "Americanness" of American literature, we still lack a comprehensive overview of the implicit theme of these studies–that we have a Great Tradition of American literature whose continuity fundamentally derives, not from European literary movements, but from the imaginative impact of the frontier experience. By illustrating how mythology derived from the frontier experience historically shapes and criticizes versions of the "American Dream," we hope to show how neither the established canon nor critical analyses of that canon have adequately recognized some of the distinctive qualities of American literature.

The concept of the "frontier," as it will be considered in this study, is not merely a physical line defined by Bureau of the Census population-density data in different historical eras. Rather, it consists as well of a group of images, ideas, and expectations that came into focus during the European Renaissance and found its most dramatic expression in the development of American civilization. It begins with a sense of wonder at the infinite possibilities in the expanding world of the Renaissance explorers, for the frontier as the margin of the known opened the possibility of wonders in the unknown. The frontier as the limit of the settled and developed offered the possibility of new land, new resources, seemingly inexhaustible, yet to be gained. The frontier as the limit of existing society demarcated the line beyond which beckoned freedom from existing social and political restraints. In effect, the frontier was the gateway through which one might escape from time into space, from bounds to boundlessness, and from the works of corrupt and corrupting humanity to the works of God in uncorrupted nature.

In these terms, the effects of the frontier did not end with the 1890 census, as Turner suggested. From F. Scott Fitzgerald's emphasis in *The Great Gatsby* on the importance of the ability to dream and the capacity for wonder, to the need still for "a blank spot on the map," expressed by Aldo Leopold in *A Sand County Almanac* and by Wallace Stegner in his "Wilderness Letter," the sense of a border beyond which "civilization" does not dominate remains a vital concept in American thought. The action need not occur there (*Death of a Salesman* happens in Brooklyn), the characters need not ever have been there, but the sense that such a place exists, or at least should exist, creates the imaginative context in which many American writers work.

What we have just described is the dominant expression of frontier mythology—one that began as an idea in the earlier explorers' imaginations before America was discovered. But we also need to look at the frontier from the other side of the border—from the point of view of those who were either excluded from or ousted by the dream of possibility and promise that flowered before Dutch sailors' eyes and those of other settling Europeans. Native Americans, Mexican-Americans, blacks, and to a great extent, even the women who accompanied or followed the male settlers, were left out of the initial dream. As a result, their literature reveals that it too has been greatly affected by the same symbolic structures and images, though often in an inverted way. Many of these writers enter the dialogue of American literature to portray the frontier experience from their perspective as threatening and exclusive.

We therefore agree with R. W. B. Lewis's assessment of the social and dynamic nature of literary activity and the culture of which literature is a product. In *The American Adam* Lewis finds

> an analogy between the history of a culture or of its thought and literature—and the unfolding course of a dialogue: a dialogue more or less philosophic in nature and, like Plato's, containing a number of voices. Every culture seems, as it advances toward maturity, to produce its own determining debate over the ideas that preoccupy it. . . . The debate, indeed, may be said to *be* the culture, at least on its loftiest levels; for a culture achieves identity not so much through the ascendancy of one particular set of convictions as through the emergence of its peculiar and distinctive dialogue. . . . Intellectual history, properly con-

ducted, exposes not only the dominant ideas of a period, or of a nation, but more important, the dominant clashes over ideas. Or to put it more austerely: the historian [or critic] looks not only for the major terms of discourse, but also for major pairs of opposed terms which, by their very opposition, carry discourse forward. The historian looks, too, for the coloration or discoloration of ideas received from the sometimes bruising contact of opposites.[3]

Lewis's analysis stresses the dialectical nature of the process, concentrating on the struggle from thesis to antithesis to synthesis. Many of the essayists in this collection also emphasize dialectical elements, such as the civilization/wilderness dichotomy. But it is also profitable to apply Mikhail Bakhtin's concept of dialogue, since it accounts for diversity on a more fundamental level. For Bakhtin discourse is a social process. Language contains the implications of previous users and anticipates response. In *The Dialogic Imagination* Bakhtin writes:

The linguistic significance of a given utterance is understood against the background of language, while its actual meaning is understood against the background of other concrete utterances on the same theme, a background made up of contradictory opinions, points of view and value judgments—that is, precisely that background that, as we see, complicates the path of any word toward its object.[4]

In *Mikhail Bakhtin: The Dialogical Principle* Tzevetan Todorov explains that Bakhtin applied the concept to all discourse:

The most important feature of the utterance, or at least the most neglected, is its *dialogism,* that is, its intertextual dimension. . . . Intentional or not, all discourse is in dialogue with prior discourses on the same subject, as well as with discourses yet to come, whose reactions it foresees and anticipates. A single voice can make itself heard only by blending into the complex choir of other voices already in place. This is true not only of literature but of all discourse. . . .[5]

The dialogue with which we are concerned presents conflicting interpretations of the frontier experience. That many voices have engaged in the dialogue means, as Emory Elliott notes, that a

contemporary history of our literature must seek to represent the contributions of a full range of writers, including women, members of racial and ethnic minority groups, and artists who work in literary forms that have come to be recognized as literary art only in the last few decades, such as film, the literary journal, scientific writing, journalism, and the autobiography. The proliferation of critical methodologies and expansion of the canon over the last twenty years would seem to make pluralism of method and diversity of material the primary goals of a contemporary literary history. (P. 614)

Several writers here will attempt to demonstrate that Lawrence Buell overly limits the field when he asserts that "the wilderness tradition in American narrative will have to be redescribed as essentially a male tradition" (p. 112). We try to demonstrate that women writers enter into the discussion as well, though, of course, with a different–sometimes harshly critical–perspective.

In proposing that the frontier idea structures a Great Tradition in American literature, we are considering this idea in its widest extension, to include metaphorical extrapolations from historical experience into mythical archetypes, symbols, and narrative patterns. Thus we are not as concerned with revealing new literal frontier elements in American writing (Richard Slotkin, Edwin Fussell, Annette Kolodny, and others have done much of this already) so much as we are with revealing how this mythical context illuminates the main traditions of American writing. Additionally, we are concerned with the realignment of the literary tradition to which this reinterpretation necessarily leads. Though this collection of essays applies our interpretive approach to many aspects of American writing, it is by no means comprehensive. We believe that this mythical approach might be extended to many areas that are beyond the scope of this study, providing a context in which to reappraise much of our literary tradition.

For example, while our generally recognized classics remain important, this interpretive approach to them suggests why many writers in the genteel tradition are sometimes more derivative than central. And it leads to reconsideration of works traditionally discounted as merely regional or "colorful" or ethnic. Obviously, this approach highlights the importance of such forms as colonial captivity narratives which, as Richard Slotkin and Annette Kolodny have both demonstrated, constitute the first major tradition of indigenous American narrative. Exploration narratives, such as those of Cabeza de Vaca (reminding us that the Puritans were not the only source of American mythology, any more than New England is the only region with a colonial past), Daniel Boone, and Lewis and Clark, may prove a significant tradition. Indeed, there is a whole panoply of non-fiction prose works–by settlers, explorers, soldiers, naturalists, trappers, and other sojourners on the frontier–that may deserve a more prominent place in our literary history.

This mythic approach promises to alter interpretive emphases and help redetermine the canon in specific periods and genres. A Southern writer such as William Gillmore Simms may prove more interesting in this context than in that of antebellum politics, just as a political novel such as *Uncle Tom's Cabin* or an autobiography such as Frederick Douglass's *Narrative* may appear more aesthetically powerful when interpreted as a mythic statement about the values identified with the American Dream. Women writers, writings by and about native Americans, blacks, Hispanics, and Jews, and genres such as the Western or science fiction—all can be seen to contribute, often ironically, to the central consideration of what the Myth of America means, what values it emphasizes, what values it tends to ignore. Rather than portraying our Great Tradition as a static canon of "fine writing," we conceive it as a dramatic interplay of diverse voices shaping our frontier heritage into differing conceptions of the American Dream.

Exploring the Territory: The Design of this Study

The essays in this collection have been grouped into five categories: the opening section of theoretical essays is followed by a collection of period studies, then by a group of essays on regional adaptations of the frontier mythology, followed by those on multicultural perspectives, and, finally, by those on various genres. We approach the groupings with large strokes, but we do not pretend to cover the areas comprehensively. Rather, we have selected representative subjects from the wide range of possibilities to demonstrate how this mythical approach applies to widely diverse aspects of American literature.

The three general essays describe various aspects of frontier mythology's impact on American culture and literature. David Mogen identifies the primary elements of the frontier paradigm: "the conflict between an Old World and a New World, the ironic drama of the frontier figure negotiating between them, the theme of wilderness metamorphosis . . . , and the often ironic triumph of 'progress.'" Langdon Elsbree points to the dialogic nature of American literature by demonstrating the significance of a counter-paradigm, one in which a single individual does not forge an isolated self but where the action focuses instead on "establishing, consecrating a home." Finally, Wayne Ude examines the effect of the frontier experience on style and notes how North American writers use "Magical Realism," a technique usually associated with South American literature.

The period studies attempt to redress one of the difficulties in many American literary theories that has held sway since the impact of New Criticism, a militant ahistoricism. To understand American literature and American culture requires a conscious sense of historical factors. Within this context, Charlotte McClure discusses Emily Dickinson and the American Renaissance, Jim Folsom examines the significance of frontier themes in the literature written when the frontier seemed about to disappear, and Mark Busby demonstrates the continued importance of frontier themes in post–World War II and post-Vietnam literature—long after Turner declared the end of the frontier.

The three essays included in the section entitled "Regional Adaptations" illustrate how different regional cultures have adapted a national frontier mythology to define their own regional heritage and values. Ritchie Watson provides a transition from the period studies section, for he concentrates on the mythology of a specific period and a specific region, focusing on the importance of the frontier yeoman figure as it challenged the cavalier in antebellum Southern fiction. Deb Wylder examines Western writers in general, but he is concerned with the variety in Western writing. Not only does he discuss the traditional "Western," that is, writing by Western writers concerned with cowboys in the West, but he also treats two other subgenres of western writing: mountain-man and Indian literature. Gerald Haslam narrows the focus to literature of California, a state that has, as John Steinbeck's *The Grapes of Wrath* makes clear, often represented the last best hope of achieving the American Dream.

The next section of the book contains essays concerned with the frontier heritage as interpreted in minority and women's literature. Mick McAllister concentrates on native-American literature and demonstrates how the positive suggestions of westering's linearity conflict with tribal emphases on returning home. Joan Penzenstadler surveys the various transformations of the frontier image in Chicano literature, discussing not only the more widely known Hispanic writers like Tomás Rivera and Rolando Hinojosa but also a number of lesser-known figures and novels written in Spanish. Then in an essay that is somewhat of a departure from the rest of the collection, noted Chicano writer Rudolfo Anaya, author of the prize-winning novel *Bless Me, Ultima,* discusses how a minority writer senses his connection with the Anglo tradition. Finally, Melody Graulich demonstrates how women writers have responded with a combination of sensitivity and skepticism to elements of frontier mythology.

Clearly, this multi-cultural approach to frontier mythology could be applied to many other cultural perspectives as well. For instance, although we include no individual essay on black writers, in his section on contemporary fiction Mark Busby discusses Ralph Ellison and Alice Walker, and we believe that a number of other important black writers such as Langston Hughes ("What happens to a dream deferred?"), David Bradley, Toni Morrison, Ishmael Reed, and Sherley Anne Williams have been strongly influenced by frontier mythology and the promise of the American Dream. Even Frederick Douglass's *Narrative* may be profitably seen as following the frontier paradigm, as young Douglass undergoes a transformation in the wilderness after a violent confrontation with Covey. Likewise, although we include no essay on Asian-American writers, such writers as Maxine Hong Kingston, Frank Chin, and David Henry Hwang also demonstrate the strength of frontier mythology in both positive and negative ways.

The essays in the last section of this collection deal with the influence of frontier mythology on specific genres. Paul Bryant analyzes the influence of American nature writing on our perception of the frontier and the western wilderness. Through focusing on the conflicting values associated with "home," Linda Ben-Zvi demonstrates how modern American drama, particularly works by Eugene O'Neill and Arthur Miller, continues our mythological dialectic about gender roles. John Lenihan extends the critical approach into film criticism, focusing specifically on Sam Peckinpah's work and indicating how a number of other post-1960 films were influenced by elements of frontier mythology. The essay on film is appropriate, we think, because of the significance of the frontier narrative paradigm to literature and film. John Clark Pratt demonstrates the importance of frontier elements in a number of works about the Vietnam War. Finally, in "Frontiers in Space," Gary Wolfe analyzes adaptations of frontier myths in science fiction. Although we include no essays on other art forms besides film, we believe that painting, sculpture, dance, and photography can also be profitably viewed from the perspective we have defined.

Throughout this collection contributors indicate how the canon might be revised, but they also avoid Christopher Lasch's charge that the "American Studies" approach "perpetuates a nationalistic mythology of American uniqueness"[6] that defuses criticism of the American system. A number of writers in this anthology point out both the inherent strengths and weaknesses of the frontier heritage. In fact, such criticism is a requisite element of our mythological dialectic. We hope to demonstrate that since American frontier mythology develops as a symbolic language for defining and examining fundamental issues of value, it expresses a dynamic dialogue about what America has been, is, and should be.

NOTES

1. The announcement of new literary histories by Cambridge and Columbia University presses led to Annette Kolodny's "The Integrity of Memory: Creating a New Literary History of the United States," *American Literature* 57 (1985): 291–307. Responses that followed were William C. Spengemann's "American Things/Literary Things: The Problem of American Literary History," *American Literature* 57 (1985): 456–81; Emory Elliott, "New Literary History: Past and Present," *American Literature* 57 (1985): 611–21 (subsequent reference in the text is to this edition). Sacvan Bercovitch, "America as Canon and Contest: Literary History in a Time of Dissensus," *American Literature* 58 (1986): 99–108; Lawrence Buell, "Literary History Without Sexism? Feminist Studies and Canonical Reception," *American Literature* 59 (1987): 102–14 (subsequent reference in the text is to this edition). Emory Elliott, "The Politics of Literary History," *American Literature* 59 (1987): 268–76. See also Nina Baym, "Melodramas of Beset Manhood: How Theories of American Fiction Exclude Women Authors," *American Quarterly* 33 (1981): 123–39; Sacvan Berco-

vitch, ed., *Reconstructing American Literary History* (Cambridge, Mass.: Harvard Univ. Press, 1986); Paul Lauter, "Race and Gender in the Shaping of the American Literary Canon: A Case Study from the Twenties," *Feminist Studies* 9 (1983): 435–63; Russell Reising, *The Unusable Past* (New York: Methuen, 1986); subsequent reference in the text is to this edition.

2. Richard Slotkin, *The Fatal Environment: The Myth of the Frontier in the Age of Industrialization, 1800–1890* (New York: Atheneum, 1985), p. 16.

3. R. W. B. Lewis, *The American Adam* (Chicago: Univ. of Chicago Press, 1955), pp. 1–2.

4. M. M. Bakhtin, *The Dialogic Imagination* (Austin: Univ. of Texas Press, 1981), p. 281.

5. Tzvetan Todorov, *Mikhail Bakhtin: The Dialogical Principle* (Minneapolis: Univ. of Minnesota Press, 1984), p. x.

6. Christopher Lasch, "The Cultural Cold War: A Short History of the Congress for Cultural Freedom," in *Toward a New Past: Dissenting Essays in American History,* ed. Bartram Bernstein (New York: Pantheon Books, 1968), pp. 322–59.

PART ONE
General

The Frontier Archetype and the Myth of America: Patterns That Shape the American Dream

DAVID MOGEN

Much attention has been devoted recently to redesigning the American literature curriculum by opening up the canon. But this result would be achieved most coherently by focusing on the mythical dialectic in American writing, on how our literature symbolically criticizes and reshapes images representing American ideals. Our curriculum and our American literature anthologies do not adequately dramatize the most fundamental patterns that structure our literary tradition. We still have not integrated into our pedagogical structures several ideas that inform much of our best scholarship: (1) because of our frontier heritage there is a central mythology in American culture; (2) our cultural mythology based on the frontier experience is national in scope as well as regional; (3) this national frontier mythology fundamentally structures a major tradition of American writing that ironically examines and defines the American Dream.

Today none of these assertions are startling or even, perhaps, terribly controversial. Indeed, they are supported and documented by much of the theoretical writing about American literature of the last three decades. This was not always so, of course. It is instructive to reread Howard Mumford Jones's *Theory of American Literature* to remember that in 1948, when it was written, American literature in general had only recently established itself as a valid field of literary study. Within the context of the Modern Language Association, bothering to theorize at all about such stuff was still vaguely radical. We are not so far from the colonial mentality as we think. And Jones himself dismisses Turner's frontier thesis as an "extraordinary vogue" of the 1920s, whose faddishness was irrefutably exposed when critics discovered parallels between Turner's concerns and those of Henry James: "Indeed, when a frontier influence was discovered by some enthusiasts in the international novels of Henry James, a useful hypothesis had been reduced to absurdity."[1] Thus, one era's "absurdity" becomes another's central concern. Today, the parallels between the historical patterns Turner identifies and the central themes of American writing may seem self-evident. Indeed, just as Freud's analysis of the dynamics of the psyche was shaped by the patterns of Greek tragedy, so Turner's interpretation of American history was shaped by our best writers.[2] And this reflexive relationship does not invalidate either Freud or Turner. Rather, it illustrates how imaginative literature gives shape and meaning to our experience.

Since the publication of Henry Nash Smith's *Virgin Land* in 1950, followed by R. W. B. Lewis's *The American Adam* in 1955, the landscape of American literary studies has changed drastically. Rather than implicitly defending their territory against outsiders, as Jones was still doing, scholars have been excitedly exploring its interior. As a result, we now have a wealth of major and minor interpretations of American literature, all illustrating how its peculiar "Americanness" is expressed in certain fundamental narrative patterns and symbols. My purpose here is not to explore new ground, for the initial mapping has already been done. Rather, I wish to call attention to the large contours of the land we survey. Certain of its features can only be seen from a particular height. Perhaps the time has come when historical distance gives us a vertical perspective; from our new vantage points in jet planes and space shuttles we finally can see patterns that a man on horseback could only sense. We may have lost the smell of the sage, but we do have a wider field of vision. At last we can see how the solitary figure in the wilderness appears against the backdrop of the nation as a whole—even of the world at large.

As has often been noted, the frontier line in American history has two dimensions, one in space and one in time. From our present vantage point, nearing the end of the century after Turner declared our frontier history ended, we can clearly see why the cowboy is not merely a Western hero but an American hero—why, indeed, the two terms "Western" and "American" are oddly synonymous, regional rivalries aside. Spatially, the cowboy is a hero of the big sky country in which he rides. But historically he has a complex relationship to past, present, and future. He descends from Hannah Duston and Mary Rowlandson, our first frontier heroes, captive in the wilderness; from Goodman Brown (still too conventionally "good" to accept his vagabond frontier instincts), from Daniel Boone and Leatherstocking, from Ishmael and Huck Finn—all of whom are captive in civilization and at home only in the wilderness. And if the cowboy has an extensive ancestry, by now he also has spawned an impressive and somewhat incongruous lineage in the twentieth century. His modern descendants are a motley band, upholding the code in ignoble times, striking out for unprecedented new frontiers; they include Jay Gatsby and Jake Barnes, Ántonia and Sister Carrie, McMurphy and Chief Bromden, tough private eyes and countless space pioneers.

The cowboy's elaborate genealogy indicates why he has never been merely a regional hero but instead is a national hero with an international audience. His story is significant because within the context of American literary tradition he represents the values of our last frontier, and his fate is ultimately an emblem of the last pure experience of the American Dream. Frontier stories implicitly dramatize a central cultural mythology about the contradictory values represented in that dream, and the frontier setting has always functioned as a symbolic territory expressing our aspirations and our deepest fears, as well as our ironic sense of the tragedy brought by "progress." Details about the cowboy West are eloquent symbols because they, like the cowboy himself, represent the final stage in the conquest of the New World. Western landscape itself is haunted with meaning, a stark setting eloquently suited, because of its vast contrasts and overwhelming presence, to dramatize the essential American story, the ironic, ambivalent drama of the frontier hero's encounter with a New World.

This approach to Western story clarifies certain aspects of the long-standing debate about the importance of historical "authenticity" in Westerns. If wit can fully dramatize the absurdity of surrendering literary judgments to the reductionist guidelines of history buffs, Don D. Walker has already completed the job in "Who Is Going to Ride Point?" in which he points out that indiscriminate enthusiasm for historical "accuracy" in Western fiction invites sagas about the trials of "a working hand who divided his time between mowing hay, fighting screwworms, and looking after sucking calves."[3] The interesting questions about the cowboy, of course, do not concern how he actually spent his time so much as why his occupation appears so glamorous that we care. Why is a cowboy's life more romantic than a dairy farmer's? The answers cannot be found in exhaustive accounts of historical detail (though in proper hands such detail can be profound) but in the cultural mythology that incorporates them, that gives them significance—the frontier mythology that was first transformed into narrative in exploration narratives and colonial captivity narratives, which has structured a major tradition of American writing from these first truly American stories to today.

Deftly placing the concerns of historical reductionists in perspective, Walker concludes with a whimsical but suggestive image of a new kind of literary camaraderie: "Let DeVoto and Dobie and others ride off into the sunset of critical memory," he suggests, before concluding regretfully, "I do not know that we can ask old Henry James to put on his chaps, [but] the literary art of the West needs all of the craft and sophistication and philosophical seriousness it can muster" (p. 30). The startling thought of inviting Henry James to cowcamp recalls the fact that, after all, it was James's Eastern aristocratic acquaintance, Owen Wister, who first successfully captured the glamour of beans and coffee and gab around a Western campfire. And James himself admired Wister's accomplishment, just as one suspects he would admire the artistry of Eugene Manlove Rhodes's Western classic "*Paso! Por Aqui,*" which is brilliant, not just because Rhodes knows in detail the technique required to rope and ride a steer on the open range but because he also can evoke the mythic context which makes such knowledge eloquent. Indeed, the debate between East and West which opens the story derives from James himself rather than from cowcamp.

Walker's suggestion that Western writers might learn more from riding the trail with Henry James than from reading J. Frank Dobie's work highlights qualities that distinguish the most powerful Western writing from historical trivia and from formulaic melodrama. But his initial question concerning literary values in the Western invites a line of speculation he does not pursue. "In any standard anthology of American literature," he asks, "how many selections can be said to come from Western literature?" (p. 24). The answer, of course, is very few, and Walker's emphasis suggests that this is as it should be, that more than the parochialism of the Eastern literary establishment is involved, since very little writing about the West can actually hold its own by the standards appropriate to such an anthology. Though his emphasis is honest and healthy, he perhaps overstates the case. Indeed, when one is thinking of what Western selections to include in an anthology representing the best of the American literary tradition, material that is passing fair would be inappropriate. Still, existing anthologies do *not* adequately represent the best Western writing: perhaps a piece by Wister should be there, something by Cather, and Van Tilburg Clark, and Waters; and if we include a section on contemporary writing we can comfortably include some of the most highly regarded stylists of our time–Hugo and Stafford and Snyder, Silko and Abbey and Welch, to name a few.

But the question lurking in the background whenever one begins making such lists quickly becomes, "What *is* a Western?" Is Brautigan "Western" when he sets his fables in Montana? Is Ishmael Reed when he writes a jive epic set in a Western Never-Neverland? Is Roger Zelazny when he moves to Arizona and writes science fiction based on Navajo mythology? Is Ray Bradbury when he writes the elegy for our next last frontier on Mars? The term "Western" is potentially as ambiguous as is the term from which it derives, for "the West" in American culture signifies a region located in history and in the imagination as well as in geography. And historically every American region has experienced its own frontier era, creating its own "Western" heritage. More significantly, the term "the West" implies the American Dream evoked symbolically by the setting.

Rather than rehashing an old argument about literary values in the "Western," I am intrigued by the possibilities opened up by reversing the thrust of Walker's response to his central question. He asks of the hypothetical American literature anthology, "How many selections can be said to come from Western literature?" But rephrasing the question suggests more interesting possibilities for comprehending American literary tradition: "How many selections can be said to come from *frontier* literature?" To which question one answer might be—"Ideally, *most* of them. And most writings which are not frontier literature are probably not of great interest, either as literature or as cultural documents. Indeed, perhaps we can now visualize a truly *American* American literature anthology, which would focus on frontier writing as a Great Tradition." Given adequate explanation of key terms, Henry James just might agree. For such an approach would not imply he should have given up his expatriate home for the open range, but would assert instead that James himself is one of our most prominent frontier writers, who dramatized in his international settings the fundamental archetypes of American frontier mythology—the conflicting values of the Old World and the New—which Wister himself merely borrowed to dramatize another conflict of East and West.[4] And James would not be placed in unfamiliar company either, since he would still appear after Whitman and Melville and Hawthorne and Thoreau and Poe and Brockden Brown—frontier writers all—though he might encounter some new personalities from exploration narratives, captivity narratives, and early Daniel Boone narratives.

Perhaps James would dismiss this argument as a spurious verbal trick, which it is, of course, insofar as it simply substitutes the mythical meaning of the term "frontier" for historical and regional ones. But if it is granted that frontier mythology in its furthest extension is the mythical territory in which we debate the meanings of the American Dream, this concept of an American literature anthology presenting frontier writing as a central tradition of American literature is not only practical but long overdue. The actual selections need not differ dramatically from those of more conventional anthologies (though the principle of selection would help remove derivative writers and encourage reconsideration of materials traditionally regarded as merely "colorful," or "regional," or "ethnic"). And the fact is that such an anthology would illuminate the actual dynamics of American literary development. Writing about the cowboy West would appear as a special variant of the frontier mythology that informs all American culture. The continuity that connects Mary Rowlandson to Christopher Newman to the Virginian to McMurphy would be clear.

An anthology presenting this great tradition of American literature in the context of frontier mythology would not only clarify why the Western subject is so fraught with meaning, it would also present our classical American writers in a more penetrating and interesting context—the context in which D. H. Lawrence read them, as revolutionaries opening up new possibilities of consciousness by exploring and shaping a dynamic new mythology. By placing our literature in this context, such an anthology would also illuminate why imaginative writers have been and continue to be profoundly important, both as a source of pleasure and as a source of wisdom: they create and critically examine the subliminal symbols that shape our perceptions. Such an approach would dramatize the relationship between *The Virginian* and the latent appeal of Marlboro ads, between the symbolism of *Moby Dick* and the charms and dangers of the Reagan administration, between *The Last of the Mohicans* and current debates about relationships with other cultures, between Puritan symbols of the wilderness and ecological questions.

Presenting this central tradition of American literature as an expression of frontier mythology would not exclude any other approach, of course, nor would it suggest that literary studies reveal easy answers to any of the complex problems we face. But it would illuminate the ways in which our best literature has forged and expressed a sense of cultural identity. For American mythology does not provide answers about values and deep-seated conflicts; rather, it provides the symbolic language with which we discuss them. Several critical studies already illustrate how discussion of literary texts in this context can assimilate rhetorical, historical, and psychological analysis, illuminating both the inner structures of specific works and their relationship to the mythic tradition in which they participate. Particularly interesting in this context are Viola Sach's *The Myth of America,* Will Wright's *Six-Guns and Society,* John Cawelti's *The Six-Gun Mystique,* David W. Noble's *The Eternal Adam and the New World Garden,* and Harold Simonson's *The Closed Frontier.*

Furthermore, these overtly mythical analyses are only one expression of the major impulse of American literary studies since the fifties, which has been to investigate the broad patterns of theme, narrative structure, and symbolism that illustrate the "Americanness" of our national literature. Numerous significant critical works document the fact that frontier mythology is a central rather than a peripheral preoccupation of American literature: Richard Slotkin's *Regeneration through Violence* and *The Fatal Environment,* Annette Kolodny's *The Lay of the Land* and *The Land before Her,* Edwin Fussell's *Frontier: American Literature and the American West,* Leslie Fiedler's *Love and Death in the American Novel* and *The Return of the Vanishing American,* Henry Nash Smith's *Virgin Land.* Other major interpretations of American literature focus on central themes and stylistic characteristics that can also be interpreted as reactions to the imaginative impact of the frontier experience: R. W. B. Lewis's *The American Adam,* Richard Chase's *The American Novel and Its Tradition,* Leo Marx's *The Machine in the Garden,* D. H. Lawrence's *Studies in American Literature.*

Implicit in this extensive tradition of commentary is the fact that we have a Great Tradition of American Literature, beginning with the first exploration and captivity narratives and extending through the American Renaissance into the present, a tradition which elaborates a central national mythology. Indeed, most significant American literature is structured in some form by the basic archetypes of this mythology–the conflict between an Old World and a New World, the ironic drama of the frontier figure negotiating between them, the theme of wilderness metamorphosis (emergence of the "American Adam/Eve") and the triumph of "progress." Recognition of these fundamental patterns of symbolism and narrative structure reveals the historical continuity that connects the earliest indigenous American literature to contemporary American writing; but it also explains the often-noted similarities of theme and symbolism in apparently disparate genres–Westerns (literature of lost frontiers), detective fiction (literature of contemporary, usually urban, frontiers), and science fiction (literature of new frontiers).

In this sense, frontier mythology is a central preoccupation in American literature–in Hawthorne and James as well as in Cooper and Wister, in Kesey and Mailer as well as in Abbey and Silko. If American literature courses and anthologies were restructured to illustrate the continuity of this Great Tradition, they would be more coherent, more clearly focused, and more interesting. They would also clearly emphasize the crucial role imaginative literature plays in shaping our perceptions of fundamental philosophical, ethical, and political questions. It is no accident that American presidential campaigns are invariably attempts by opposing parties to identify with the most positive aspects of our frontier heritage–for, in fact, the frontier mythology created and ironically examined in our imaginative literature provides the symbolic language with which we continue to debate the answer to Crevecoeur's question "What is an American?" Which are the most truly "American" values?

Our national mythology based on frontier experience is the vehicle with which we examine the ironies and contradictory values expressed in that curious phrase, "The American Dream"–which, after all, has been the implicit subject of many of our best writers since our diverse ancestors arrived on their many different errands into the wilderness.

Though a steadily expanding library of studies describes the ambiguous and ambivalent meanings of "The Myth of America" and "The American Dream," the dynamic, interdependent relationship between the Myth and the Dream still awaits clarification. Though all aspects of American culture reveal this relationship, the structural patterns of American literature dramatize it most clearly. The Myth consists of key symbols and narrative patterns, expressions of an Archetype forged in the national frontier experience, which artists employ to visualize and debate the nature of the Dream. Like all mythically based art-forms, American literature historically articulates cultural ideals, symbolically dramatizing cultural conflicts. Thus, our central myth-system shapes and transforms images of the American Dream. Symbolically, much of our literature examines that most peculiar of American institutions–the conviction that as a nation we embody, or should embody, a unique and fateful mission, that as Americans we are manifestly destined not just to achieve prosperity and power but to represent the best hope of mankind.

The dangers of such a cultural mythology should be as apparent as its apparent idealism. In common usage, the two phrases "The Myth of America" and "The American Dream" often evoke a vaporous and unexamined conviction of special destiny. They can express smug tribalism, the spirit of self-congratulatory "patriotism" that came into vogue in the campaign rhetoric of 1984. Indeed, the Myth and the Dream may yet become assimilated into an American form of newspeak, helping us to cheerily embrace new generations of "Peacemakers" as we righteously battle the evil empire. In this context both the Myth of America and the American Dream express the simple conviction that America represents an ideal, that we as a people are unique in both our aspirations and our accomplishments.

Yet if these terms can reinforce a superficial and arrogant parochialism, they also provide a key to understanding our most profound and searching self-expressions. For by their nature, the terms invite debate and irony. The term "dream" suggests unrealized ideals, after all, perhaps even a potentially destructive habit of escapism. And "myth" suggests falsehood and illusion, commonly held misconceptions, stories perpetuating the mystique of entrenched power structures. By their very nature, the Myth and the Dream invite a dialectic about which ideals they truly represent, about whether an ideal vision of America has been or can be realized, about the ironic contradictions implicit in the very pursuit of the ideal. When Richard Hofstadter described America as a nation founded in perfection and aspiring to progress, he stated the ironic theme of many of our best writers.

Though the Myth and the Dream are sometimes employed as synonymous terms, they more naturally suggest a complementary relationship between stories and values, a relationship that structures fundamental patterns of thought in our culture. In literary terms, the American Dream provides the theme of our national letters. The Myth of America is the medium in which that theme is expressed. Interpretation of the Dream is the "message"; the

Myth is the symbolic language that expresses the message. Interpretations of the Dream vary dramatically, of course, with the writer and the times. And the Myth itself has adapted to transform the meanings of the Dream. Neither the Myth nor the Dream have minimized conflict in an often violently contentious history. Indeed, ongoing debate about the meanings of the Dream expresses the difficulty we have defining a coherent national identity.

Yet if defining the American Dream provides a focus more for debate than for a unifying set of ideals, it provides at least a potentially unifying sense of identity. And if the Myth's most notable characteristics are ambivalence and ambiguity, it at least provides a common symbolic language in which to debate. We may never agree upon the meaning of the Dream, but the last forty years of American scholarship have revealed continuity in the Myth. For instance, once R. W. B. Lewis discovered the nineteenth-century American Adam, investigators like Richard Slotkin could begin constructing his genealogy, piecing together the evolution of the missing links between traditional heroes and this new figure in the American wilderness. Just as an evolutionary perspective portrays the biblical Adam as a development from previous life-forms, so it reveals the American Adam descended from heroes of captivity narratives and legends of Daniel Boone. Now Annette Kolodny and others chronicle the history of the American Eve. And descendants of these early heroes, like Gatsby, continue to imagine they spring forth from their own Platonic conceptions of themselves, whether they settle in West Egg or on Bradbury's Mars. By now we can see that our traditional hero is this self-made figure who knows no tradition, that whole tribes descended from the nineteenth-century Adam populate both our most formulaic visions of cowboys and space travelers and our most ironic literary creations. The history of the American Adam represents nearly four centuries of symbolic response to Crevecoeur's question: "What is an American?"

This whimsical retelling of the story of Adam or Eve simply sketches in one of the most obvious patterns in our literature—the role of the hero. But the significance of the hero's fate depends upon mythical context, and other fundamental patterns in the Myth define the hero's relationship to the Dream represented in the hero's destiny. Richard Slotkin provides the most helpful theoretical descriptions of the Myth, and his formulation in *Regeneration through Violence* defines its major "structural elements": "As artifacts, myths appear to be built of three basic structural elements: a protagonist or hero, with whom the human audience is presumed to identify in some way; a universe in which the hero may act, which is presumably a reflection of the audience's conception of the world and the gods; and a narrative, in which the interaction of the hero and universe is described."[5]

Our mythic hero, in other words, acts out a mythic story in a mythic universe. Symbolically, the hero struggles to resolve conflicts that mirror those of the audience. In American cultural mythology, these basic "structural elements"–setting, hero, and narrative–define a symbolic territory in which the hero's fate reflects upon the meaning of the American Dream. And I have chosen the word "territory" deliberately, to evoke the archetype that structures the Myth, the concept of the frontier. For once the structural elements of the Myth are defined, the influence of the Frontier Archetype becomes evident. The basic elements are these:

1. *Setting:* Opposition between an Old World ("civilization") and a New World (associated with "nature" and/or "wilderness"), which also contains a transition area ("frontier"). Often symbolic rather than historical or geographical, these opposed worlds adapt, transform, and yet preserve the basic pattern of the Frontier Archetype.
2. *Hero:* A frontier figure (or figures, often with wilderness and/or civilized companions) who moves between these worlds.
3. *Narrative:* As "progress" triumphs, the hero's destiny resolves or dramatizes conflicts between the Old World and the New World–triumphantly, ironically, tragically, or comically–usually through some version of failed or achieved *metamorphosis* (either emergence of the American Adam/Eve or integration of this figure with an apparent opposite).

The key elements of this Myth of America are sufficiently adaptable to define the Dream in any time or place, from any historical, regional, or ideological perspective. Though we frequently identify a more limited "myth of the frontier" with historical settings and the expansionist ideals of Manifest Destiny, this more pervasive Frontier Archetype limits neither setting nor doctrine. The Old World and the New World archetypes generate an expandable set of opposing terms, adaptable to any time and any scale: thus, symbolic opposition between the Old World and the New World has been evoked by the settlement and the wilderness (captivity narratives and Hawthorne's wilderness stories); by shore and sea (*Moby Dick*); by Concord and Walden Pond (*Walden*); by Europe and America (Henry James); by East and West (*The Virginian* and most Westerns); by Europe, Virginia, Black Hawk and the prairie (*My Ántonia*); by East Egg and West Egg (*The Great Gatsby*); by Paris and Spain (*The Sun Also Rises*); by a hospital ward and anywhere else (*One Flew Over the Cuckoo's Nest*); by South and North (*Black Boy* and *The Invisible Man*); by Earth and Mars (*The Martian Chronicles*). Schematically, this Frontier Archetype can be represented as seen in Fig. 1.[6]

Clearly, identification of many of these locations with the archetypal values associated with "civilization," "frontier," "nature," and "wilderness" depends to a great extent on literary context: such "New Worlds" as Thoreau's Walden Pond, Hemingway's Spain, and Ellison's New York City have primarily symbolic associations with the historical "West." Also, the valences

The Frontier Archetype

"Civilization" "Frontier"/"Nature"/"Wilderness"

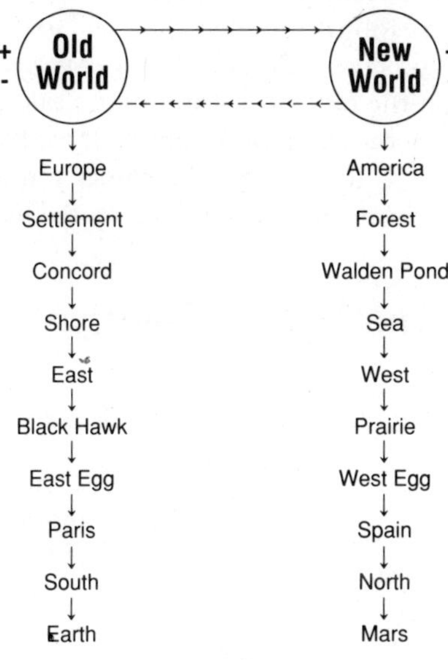

Figure 1

("+" and "–") represent the fact that the values associated with these places are both dependent on literary context and are intrinsically ambivalent. Though the primary impulse in American tradition identifies key American values with the New World, this tradition has often been reversed, so that frontier experience represents the worst as well as the best of our cultural heritage. And the frontier story is ambivalent and implicitly ironic in any case, since its meaning depends upon how "conquering" the West is portrayed—as triumphant, tragic, comic, lyrical, or absurd.

If the Frontier Archetype structures the basic settings of frontier literature, the Myth of America utilizes this inherently symbolic environment as a background for narrative. Just as the Frontier Archetype provides an adaptable and potentially expressive pattern of symbolism, so the metamorphosis drama of the frontier hero, like Whitman's persona in *Song of Myself,* can contain multitudes, whose separate destinies are emblems of hope, irony, comedy, and despair: the hero returns affirming the awful power of the Lord (Mary Rowlandson) or fanatically disillusioned because he rejected his wilderness initiation (Goodman Brown); the hero disastrously marries Old World sterility (Isabel Archer) or triumphantly unites the best of the Old

World and the New (the Virginian and Ántonia); the hero strikes out for new territory (Huck Finn), or he is betrayed by his ideal (Gatsby), or she renounces the ideal to avoid betraying it (Lady Brett), or he withdraws from the quest to realize the Dream (Ellison's *Invisible Man*), or he revitalizes the Dream through Sacred Hoop ceremonies designed to defeat witchcraft posing as civilization and "progress" (Tayo in Silko's *Ceremony*). Indeed, the grandmother's comment on the old tribal stories in *Ceremony* applies equally to the recurring patterns of the Myth of America: "It seems like I already heard these stories before . . . only thing is, the names sound different."[7] Schematically, the Myth of America can be represented as seen in Fig. 2.

The Myth of America

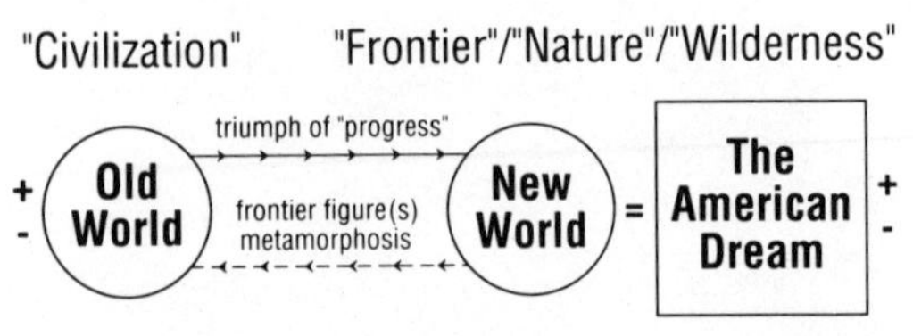

Figure 2

From a larger perspective, the Myth of America can be interpreted as a variant of the universal monomyth Joseph Campbell describes in *The Hero with a Thousand Faces*. Even in myth, Americans can only adapt tradition, not escape it entirely. And indeed, even our Adamic heroes (except, perhaps, Whitman's persona) learn the lessons of earlier heroes: that however expansive their possibilities seem, they still are bounded. Yet if the Myth of America is only one expression of the universal monomyth, it is still a variant that uniquely emphasizes the possibility of rebirth, of exploring the limits of freedom. Rather than bringing their knowledge home, our heroes more typically ride into the sunset, after blazing a trail for others to follow. Delineating the archetypal pattern of the Myth throws into relief the central values evoked by the phrase, "The American Dream": we define ourselves most fundamentally by reference to our frontier heritage, which symbolically represents the ambiguous implications of our belief in limitless possibilities. Since the end of the nineteenth century, the Myth has been adapted to embrace expansive new frontiers in technology and space, as well as ironically inverted to suggest that small can be beautiful too, and that American Adam must learn the values of quality and economy as well as of quantity and consumption. And while the Myth structures debate about what social and political "progress" mean today, it also adapts the message of Thoreau and the Transcendentalists to a new age, urging us still to develop that "furthest Western Way" inside our own souls.

As a literary theme the dynamic adaptability of the Myth of America derives from the power of its central symbols and narrative structures, which evoke continuity with our heritage yet also generate visions of new possibilities, new frontiers. For the Frontier Archetype provides symbols that embrace the full range of human experience. The relationship between the Old World and the New World is indeed ambiguous and ambivalent. Traditionally the Old World primarily signifies the dead hand of the past, yet it can also represent civilization as grace and power. The New World can represent both unlimited promise and brutish deprivation, Nature in harmony or Nature red in tooth and claw. And the hero's rebirth can be stillborn or monstrous; the ideals pursued can be inspiring, unworthy, or unrealized; the urgency of the struggle to realize the Dream can be ennobling, absurd, or self-defeating. "Progress" often destroys what the frontier heroes most love, so that the visionary metamorphosis theme can also dramatize the ironic price of "success." From Mary Rowlandson's captivity in the wilderness to Bradbury's ironic Martian fables, the basic patterns of the Myth adapt and transform, yet they preserve their basic structure. As Eric Rabkin observes, explaining the mythical context of *The Martian Chronicles,* the ambiguous implications of the Frontier Archetype continue to structure visions of contemporary and future possibilities:

> As is well known, much of American literature can be viewed as a single myth in which much of human experience can be organized into two dichotomous sets. In the East are civilization, old age, intellect, the head, the cities; while in the West are the frontier, innocence, youth, emotion, the heart, and wilderness. In the American myth people from the Old World journey to the New World in the hope of rejuvenation and the regaining of innocence, trying to return to a time before the Fall, to become what R. W. B. Lewis has called "the American Adam." Life on the frontier or in the wilderness is supposed to be redemptive; Natty Bumppo is superior to the East Coast stay-at-homes. As we see in the transatlantic novels of Hawthorne and James, all Americans are morally superior to Old World Europeans. Suckling at what Fitzgerald called the "fresh, green breast of the new world" is supposed to make one innocent again–young and strong and sensitive. The wilderness experience, like the later melting pot, is supposed to convert Europeans into true Americans. But of course the myth has in many ways proved hollow: financial independence often leads to barbarism and wage slavery; the westward rolling tides of Americans have wiped out the indigenous "native Americans"; moral uprightness and religious freedom often petrify into self-righteousness and religious exclusivity. Finally,

racism has blighted the land, from the landing of the first slave ship in 1619 until and including the present. Those are the conditions Bradbury would have his fairyland book change.[8]

As Bradbury's strategy indicates, in American science fiction especially, the Frontier Archetype has mutated into exotic new forms, evoking our expansive nineteenth-century heritage, often ironically, as it structures visions of more drastic metamorphoses and ironies on wondrous New Worlds in space. But paradoxically such new transformations also revitalize and reinterpret fading traditions, creating new environments in which Manifest Destiny can ride again.[9] Thus our literature has always employed the Myth to generate new images of the Dream, to dramatize and resolve contradictions in our cultural heritage, to adapt our central symbols to express disillusionment or to interpret new opportunities and challenges. When Frederick Jackson Turner proclaimed that as of 1890 the historical American frontier was settled, he threatened the very spirit of the Dream, and thus provided an elegiac and ironic theme for much twentieth-century American writing. Yet for better or worse our frontier mentality did not vanish with the historical frontier. It adapted to the times. Itself an image of adaptation, the Frontier Archetype continues to generate new visions of the American Dream.

Yet the Dream itself remains, almost by definition, elusive. Frederic I. Carpenter recognized its importance to literature back in 1955 when he began his study, *American Literature and the Dream,* by noting that, vague as it seems, the Dream profoundly structures our imaginative creations:

> "The American Dream" has never been defined exactly, and probably never can be. It is both too various and too vague. . . .
>
> But "American Literature" has been defined more exactly, and has been outlined in courses and embodied in anthologies. Most men agree that it is something very different from English literature, and many have sought to describe the difference. . . . American literature has differed from English because of the constant and omnipresent influence of the American Dream upon it.
>
> This influence has usually been indirect and unconscious, because the dream has remained vague and undefined. . . . But the vague idea has influenced the plotting of our fiction and the imagining of our poetry. Almost by inadvertance our literature has accomplished a symbolic and experimental projection of it.
>
> Traditionally, American literature has been described under such categories as "romantic" and "realistic," "transcendental" and "genteel." But considered in relation to the dream, it falls into new patterns: the old words persist, but in new relations.[10]

Carpenter's study ironically illustrates the relationship between the Myth and the Dream. His formulation in many ways defines the approach which implicitly informs much of the best American scholarship of the last four decades. But he himself rejects the most fruitful line of inquiry, ignoring the Myth that embodies the Dream to pursue disembodied abstractions: "This interpretation will emphasize neither the technical forms of the old literature, nor the historical patterns, but the ideal attitudes of American writers toward the dream" (p. 3). But when he releases the Myth itself to grasp at its meanings the Dream simply vanishes, no longer merely protean but formless, leaving him empty-handed. Thus Carpenter himself was diverted by the search for an illusory Northwest Passage, while others forged inland to explore and settle the territory he sighted.

Following perhaps the older, more cryptic map provided by D. H. Lawrence's inspired incantations in *Studies in Classic American Literature,* critics began to chart the specific mythic patterns that give American writing its character: R. W. B. Lewis in *The American Adam,* Henry Nash Smith in *Virgin Land,* Leslie Fiedler in *Love and Death in the American Novel* and *The Return of the Vanishing American,* Leo Marx in *The Machine in the Garden*—all followed Lawrence's lead, interpreting the symbolic drama of American consciousness "shifting over from the old psyche to something new."[11] The methodology these scholars developed prepared the way for a more meaningful integration of American criticism with American studies, a fusion of historical knowledge with mythic sensibility that informs the work of contemporary scholars such as Richard Slotkin and Annette Kolodny.

Forty years of such investigation have clearly established the complex relationships between our frontier experience and our ongoing dialectic about the values represented in the American Dream, though we still have not revised our curriculum and our anthologies to reveal the dynamics of the debate. Perhaps we are at that stage of cultural self-awareness where we can begin to see an underlying unity in our diversity, the common patterns of discourse that structure our disagreements, the shape of the overriding cultural mythology that incorporates our historical, regional, and personal mythologies. For better or worse, America still pursues the Dream. Like a will-o'-the-wisp, or an insistently recurring mirage, the allure of the Dream remains, tantalizing, potentially destructive, yet undefined. The implicit subject both of our popular culture and of our most searching imaginative creations, it can never be reduced to a simple formulation. If the Dream is our mythical oracle, our artists are its voice, delivering messages which speak both of apotheosis and apocalypse, messages no less important for being ambiguous. And if the Dream itself remains indistinct, its presence nevertheless defines our national identity. America without the Dream would be something other than we know, either incomprehensibly more mature or incorporated at last into the Old World complacency it sought to leave behind. "So we beat on," Fitzgerald observes, "boats against the current, borne back ceaselessly into the past."[12]

NOTES

1. Howard Mumford Jones, *Theory of American Literature* (1948; Ithaca, N.Y.: Cornell Univ. Press, 1965), p. 168.

2. See Harold P. Simonson on "Frederick Jackson Turner: Frontier History as Symbol," in *The Closed Frontier: Studies in American Literary Tragedy* (New York: Holt, Rinehart and Winston, 1970). See also my own "The Frontier Metaphor in American Culture," in *Wilderness Visions: Science Fiction Westerns, Volume One* (San Bernardino, Calif.: Borgo Press, 1982).

3. Don D. Walker, "Who Is Going to Ride Point?" in *The Westering Experience in American Literature,* ed. Merrill Lewis and L. L. Lee (Bellingham, Wash.: Bureau for Faculty Research, Western Washington University, 1977), p. 27. Subsequent references in the text are to this edition.

4. See the chapter on Twain, Howells, and James in David W. Noble's *The Eternal Adam and the New World Garden* (New York: George Braziller, 1968), 51–98. Noble's study, subtitled "The Central Myth in the American Novel since 1830," describes how the nineteenth-century formulation of frontier mythology was adapted by twentieth-century writers.

5. Richard Slotkin, *Regeneration through Violence* (Middletown, Conn.: Wesleyan Univ. Press, 1973), p. 8.

6. The structure of my own paradigm was suggested partly by Edwin Fussell's suggestive definition of "frontier": "The frontier was a figure of speech, gradually but never entirely sloughing European implications as it assumed new functions in a new context, and thus incidentally a splendid illustration of the Americanizing process Turner used it to describe. The frontier was the imaginary line between civilization and nature, or the uncreated future." In *Frontier: American Literature and the American West* (Princeton, N.J.: Princeton Univ. Press, 1966), p. 17.

7. Leslie Silko, *Ceremony* (New York: New American Library, 1977), p. 273.

8. Eric Rabkin, "To Fairyland by Rocket," in *Ray Bradbury,* ed. Martin Harry Greenberg and Joseph D. Olander (New York: Taplinger Publishing Co., 1980), pp. 123–24.

9. My own *Wilderness Visions: Science Fiction Westerns, Volume One* (San Bernardino, Calif.: Borgo Press, 1982) and the forthcoming second volume, *New Frontiers, Old Horizons: Science Fiction Westerns, Volume Two,* examine in detail the use of the frontier archetype in science fiction.

10. Frederic I. Carpenter, *American Literature and the Dream* (New York: Philosophical Library, Inc., 1955), p. 3. Subsequent reference in the text is to this edition.

11. D. H. Lawrence, *Studies in American Literature* (1923; reprint, New York: Viking Press, 1966), p. 1.

12. F. Scott Fitzgerald, *The Great Gatsby* (1925; reprint, New York: Charles Scribner's Sons, 1953), p. 121 (the final line of the novel).

Our Pursuit of Loneliness: An Alternative to This Paradigm

LANGDON ELSBREE

One of the central myths, or paradigms, in American literature has been characterized in a number of ways–by Richard Poirier's *A World Elsewhere,* Wright Morris's *The Territory Ahead,* R. W. B. Lewis's *The American Adam,* and Henry Nash Smith's *The Virgin Land,* to mention but a few. Yet whatever the differences among their accounts, these critics (like many others) stress the related themes of movement, the hero as restless quester, the flight from traditional social and cultural definitions, the pursuit of a radically innocent or natural vision of self and society. *The Prairie,* "Walking," *The Adventures of Huckleberry Finn,* "Song of Myself," *The Adventures of Augie March, On the Road*–these will serve as well as any to exemplify the pattern.

This narrative paradigm has, of course, saturated other media as well. Until recently, the Western was dominated by it, and even now the reruns of Clint Eastwood's violent and dark versions of it remind audiences of its continuing power. Much of the popular culture in the 1960s enacted it: films like *Midnight Cowboy* and *Easy Rider,* the lyrics of Bob Dylan, the whole mystique of "splitting" and "dropping out." One of the more probing treatments of this paradigm was Tom Wolfe's *The Electric Kool-Aid Acid Test,* in which Wolfe followed Ken Kesey and the Merry Pranksters from San Francisco to New Orleans and Florida and back to California again, and Kesey into his Mexican refuge. During the 1960s and early 1970s, however, the paradigm included in the handling of this myth questions about the costs–the attempted transcendence through drugs of self and society that sometimes ended in despair and insanity, the dangers of solipsism and surreality when the imagination pursues freedom from all traditional restraints, the mayhem and carnage committed by men questing without clear purpose or direction, brutally rendered in *Why Are We in Vietnam?* and *Apocalypse Now.* It was as if Kurtz and *The Heart of Darkness* had become, for a time,

Americanized. But this myth was, of course, questioned as well in the nineteenth century by Hawthorne and Melville.

Concurrent with the media probing of this paradigm has been a scholarly and critical one. The reasons for the reassessment are complex, rooted partly in the ways that the social movements, political rebellions, and the violent politics of the 1960s and early 1970s confronted Americans with their own history, more than three hundred years in the making. D. H. Lawrence's pioneering *Studies in Classic American Literature* has been one major inspiration in this reassessment. For example, his understanding of the "true myth of America" as the "sloughing off of the old skin, towards a new youth"[1] is cited by David W. Noble in *The Eternal Adam and the New World Garden,* who is himself skeptical about "the central myth of our civilization–the transcendence of time" (p. xi). And Lawrence's definition of the American hero enacting this myth is not only cited by Richard Slotkin but present on almost every page of Slotkin's indictment of the destructive aspects of the myth, *Regeneration through Violence: The Mythology of the American Frontier, 1600–1860*. Lawrence writes:

True myth concerns itself centrally with the onward adventure of the integral soul. And this, for America, is Deerslayer. A man who turns his back on white society. A man who keeps his moral integrity hard and intact. An isolate, almost selfless, stoic, enduring man, who lives by death, by killing, but who is pure white.[2]

More recently, feminist studies have given us some of the most telling and incisive revisions of the myth and its costs, particularly the work of Nina Baym and Josephine Hendin. And, most recently, Annette Kolodny's *The Land before Her* has documented the existence of and pointed toward the possibilities of a radically contrasting myth, a far less acknowledged paradigm, which is the essential argument of this essay.

I propose that there is another body of texts which, though not always easily accommodated in conventional accounts of American literature, embodies a significantly different narrative paradigm. That paradigm is what I have called elsewhere (in *The Rituals of Life*) the archetypal action of establishing, consecrating a home.[3] This archetype enacts the making of the garden, the building of the home (town, city), the clearing of the land–the sustaining of the human community. Examples of the works and writers I have in mind include (though are not confined to) Willa Cather's *Death Comes for the Archbishop* and *My Ántonia,* Rolvaag's *Giants in the Earth*, Harriette Arnow's *The Dollmaker,* Steinbeck's *The Red Pony* and *The Grapes of Wrath,* Glenway Wescott's *The Grandmothers,* Wright Morris's *Ceremony in Lone Tree,* Joyce Carol Oates's *A Garden of Earthly Delights* and *them,* Malamud's *The Assistant,* and almost all of Anne Tyler's fiction.

My argument is not that these works are explicitly counter-myth by intent but rather that they may be read dialectically as a critique of the primary tradition of American myth and narrative paradigm. These and similar works derive their meaning in part from a larger context, the one that David Mogen calls the "Frontier Archetype." This context is the perennial American obsession with the questing male, the flight from stasis, the Poundian injunction to "Make It New," the transformation of Turner's frontiersman into science fiction's spaceman. These writers and works "rewrite" the myth. To them, self-renewal is daily, communal, concrete, and specific, not the radical individualism of the journey, the flight, or the adventure. Freedom is the acceptance of limits and the completion of self through suffering for and with others, not the rejection of roles and routine, nor a nostalgia for lost innocence. Above all, their garden is *not* the Eden of the New World or the Virgin Land, but a third term, one that mediates between those two poles of Self and Nature that dominate so much American literature. In these works and writers, the garden is the dialectical result of the human and the natural; it signifies the domestication of self and nature, the creation of home and an inhabitable world. It is the fantasy of so many women diarists and writers that Annette Kolodny has reclaimed for us, as "They dreamed, more modestly, of locating a home and a familiar human community within a cultivated garden."[4] Even when the garden becomes blighted, as it does in many of these works, the tragedy is not so much the result of sin or some species of metaphysical overreaching as it is the result of intelligible human failure in the face of intelligible human causes.

Central, frequently, to these works and writers is a second archetypal action: enduring suffering (*RL,* pp. 51–52). Sometimes, this action concludes triumphantly: Ántonia Cuzak, though a "battered woman, . . . had only to stand in the orchard, to place her hand on a little crab tree and look up at the apples, to make you feel the goodness of planting and tending and harvesting at last."[5] Father Latour, near the end of his life in the New World, "often quoted to his students that passage from their fellow Auvergnat, Pascal: that Man was lost and saved in a garden."[6] More often, however, this action concludes in failure, as in the case of Joyce Carol Oates's characters who suffer the memory of home lost or who can barely imagine or define the order and domesticity they crave. But, whether triumphant or tragic, the action of suffering in these works and writers is a form of witness. Amid the pain of the rupture of leaving the Old World or one's early roots, the harshness and strangeness of the New World or new life, the striving to achieve status or to make a place for family and self, or the dislocations of war and depression, the commitment to home endures. However confused the protagonists may sometimes be about the nature of home, more often than not they cling to the hope for roots, for connectedness, for a habitable garden.

These two archetypal actions – making the garden and enduring suffering – are usually closely related in these works and together help determine this alternative paradigm. They stand in decisive contrast to the archetypal action one finds in "Walking" or *On the Road* – the pursuit of consummation. Thoreau's declaration in *Walden* is one of the more disciplined rationales for pursuing consummation: "I went to the woods because I wanted to live deliberately, to front only the essential facts of life, and see if I could not learn what it had to teach, and not, when I came to die, discover that I had not lived."[7] Wright Morris's exasperation with "the love that has no appeasement, the quest that has no resolution, the hunger that has no gratification"[8] found in Thomas Wolfe's fiction is the more common experience one has of this archetype in works like *Winesburg, Ohio* or *The Adventures of Augie March*. For every Augie March who eludes definition by time and place and exults, "Look at me, going everywhere. . . . a sort of Columbus of those near-at-hand,"[9] the pursuit of consummation also results in the pathetic failures left behind: Anderson's "grotesques," Robinson's Miniver Cheevy and Old Eben Flood, or Carson McCullers' victims in *The Ballad of the Sad Cafe* and *The Heart Is a Lonely Hunter*. The pursuit of consummation is the ritual action that seeks the transcendence, the obliteration, or the abolition of the self. Sometimes it ends in triumph, more often in failure, but it is relentless in its denial of limits, its refusal of the ordinary, the quotidian, the golden mean. Its motto might be summarized as "Death *or* Transfiguration."

To summarize what I have argued elsewhere, the pursuit of consummation has been the dominant ritual action in American literature. In our classics, especially in Cooper, Hemingway, and Faulkner, this ritual has been the hunt. Their heroes share a family resemblance. Childless and womanless, each teaches the son he never had something of the code by which he has lived: Leatherstocking and Middleton, Sam Fathers and Isaac McCaslin, Santiago and Manolin. Each achieves purification by the wilderness, forest, lake, or sea and by identification with the prey, whether deer, bear, or marlin. Their world, the pristine world of the sacred, speaks silently and universally in the language of sky, water, land, and animals for those who patiently attend it. These heroes exist like Nimrod, "a mighty hunter before the Lord": theirs is the Creation before the city of man profaned it, Nimrod's kingdom of Babel where men were "of one speech" before the building of the tower (*RL,* p. 98).

But, whether hunt, flight, or quest, the pursuit of consummation and "the onward adventure of the integral soul" exact a high price. The rigidly "masculine" that fears dependence, craves separateness, and rejects the quotidian; the distrusted "feminine" that cherishes intimacy, accepts vulnerability, and finds meaning in daily custom and routine – these gender definitions become polarized, reified, and absolutized. At their most extreme, these polarized definitions produce something like the pure double bind that Bateson and others see as schizophrenic. Anderson dramatizes this terror of the divided self in "The Man Who Became a Woman." These polarized definitions are deeply rooted in our understanding of our history, particularly our myth of the frontier as influenced by Frederick Jackson Turner. In *Childhood and Society,* Erik Erikson, noting that "if you come down to it, Momism is only misplaced paternalism,"[10] implicitly modifies Turner's hypothesis as follows:

The frontier, of course, remained the decisive influence which served to establish in the American identity the extreme polarization which characterizes it. The original polarity was the cultivation of the sedentary and migratory poles. For the same families, the same mothers, were forced to prepare men and women who would take root in the community life and the gradual class stratification of the new villages and towns and at the same time to prepare these children for the possible physical hardships of homesteading on the frontiers. (P. 293)

Erikson's thesis about the contradictions in the American identity, especially his insight into the impossible demand that mothers teach both domesticity and self-reliance, should be read in the light of Turner's peroration about the frontier's influence:

The result is that to the frontier the American intellect owes its striking characteristics. That coarseness and strength combined with acuteness and inquisitiveness; that practical, inventive turn of mind, quick to find expedients; that masterful grasp of material things, lacking in the artistic but powerful to effect great ends; that restless, nervous energy; that dominant individualism, working for good and for evil, and withal that buoyancy and exuberance which comes with freedom – these are the traits of the frontier, or traits called out elsewhere because of the existence of the frontier.[11]

The energy that so often informs the pursuit of consummation in American letters and American life has usually been "that restless, nervous energy" and "that dominant individualism, working for good and for evil." And one of the central evils has surely been this polarization Erikson speaks of, the ultimate consequences of which can be felt in the deeply ambivalent treatment of women, in the meanings assigned to "masculine" and "feminine," and in men's hostility to, or avoidance of, the very relationships they need and crave. These relationships, to judge by their absence, include sexuality that is neither violent nor possessive but mutually gratifying; companionship that is neither competitive nor unequal but playfully serious; and parenthood that is neither authoritarian nor timid but lovingly disciplined.

Yet even during the pursuit of consummation these relationships seep through the fabric of the narrative, producing a curious tie-dye staining that hints at the presence of feelings, however spotty. One doesn't have to agree with all of Leslie Fiedler's readings in *Love and Death in the American Novel* to realize that he is essentially right about the refusal of adult sexuality in so many American novels and the nostalgia for a childlike innocence that licenses gentleness and friendship among boy-men. Because the powers of eros are ritualized, ostensibly tamed and contained by the demands of the journey and the marginality of the characters, Queequeg and Ishmael, Huck and Jim can love one another. If, however, one turns to works in which the archetypal action is the making of the garden (often accompanied by the enduring of suffering), one finds quite different meanings attached to the "masculine" and the "feminine" and to the attendant qualities assigned to each of them.

To put it summarily: the archetypal action of establishing, consecrating a home directs human energies and intelligence toward cooperative and corporate actions, not separation and self-assertion. Its aim is the creation of order, continuity, and permanence; its dominant rituals are those of planting, harvesting, gratitude, and thanksgiving. And even when the partners are forced by task or circumstances to be apart, they try to keep the fact of their mutual dependence in mind. Further, while there are often assigned roles and distinct spheres of authority, these distinctions are neither absolute nor unambiguous. Necessity frequently demands that men learn patience and caring, introspection and self-sacrifice; women solitude and independence, individuality and leadership. Such complementarity, whether of "masculine" and "feminine" qualities demanded of a single person or within the group, does not occur easily. Frequently enough, the archetypal action of enduring suffering defines the limits of growth a person or group is capable of. Loneliness, failure, paranoia, or even insanity–these are sometimes the consequences of ethnic or personal history, the period or place which inhibits change. Yet even in extreme cases the tragedy is the gap between specific aspiration and specific achievement, not the unqualified attempt to transcend time and the human condition. The ideal is the consecration of a particular home, the cultivation of a particular garden that is shared and sustaining. Most of these generalizations are dramatically clear in Willa Cather's *My Ántonia* and *Death Comes for the Archbishop.*

In differing ways, the garden image dominates both of Cather's novels. Near the beginning of *My Ántonia,* we experience through Jim Burden's eyes the empty Nebraska landscape in the darkness that precedes birth: "There seemed to be nothing to see; no fences, no creeks or trees, no hills or fields. . . . I had the feeling that the world was left behind, that we had got over the edge of it, and were outside man's jurisdiction"(*MA,* p. 7). From this opening, through the Shimerdas's suffering during the harsh months and life on their crude homestead, through the vicissitudes of Ántonia's adolescence and her isolation while pregnant, to her triumph at the end with her husband, family, and farm, the imagery of the garden marks the stages of birth, growth, and fruition. From the start, Ántonia is identified with the earth and life—her eyes "big and warm and full of light, like the sun shining on brown pools in the wood," her skin "brown" and her cheeks glowing with a "rich, dark colour" (*MA,* p. 23). She is apotheosized at the end by signs of the cost of her endurance and her fidelity to her commitment. A "stalwart, brown woman, flat-chested, her curly brown hair a little grizzled" (*MA,* p. 331), still she "had not lost the fire of life," and "her skin, so brown and hardened, had not that look of flabbiness, as if the sap beneath it had been secretly drawn away" (*MA,* p. 336). Centered in her garden, her "orchard full of sun like a cup" (*MA,* p. 341), her dark cellar-cave of preserves from which one emerges into the sunlight with a "veritable explosion of life" (*MA,* p. 339), and her parlor filled with her children who "were not afraid to touch each other" (*MA,* p. 349), she has become the vision of the frontier woman that Turner largely ignores and fails to mythologize.

While Ántonia is often rendered as the archetype of the great mother—her cellar-cave, her essence as "a rich mine of life" (*MA,* p. 353)—she has also when necessary put on her dead father's boots, done a man's work, and at the day's end "yawned often at the table," stretching "her arms over her head, as if they ached" (*MA,* p. 125). The fusion of these qualities is strikingly evident in her dancing. Each schottische with her is "a new adventure": "she had so much spring and variety, and was always putting in new steps and slides"; she teaches Jim to dance "against and around the hard-and-fast beat of the music" (*MA,* p. 223). Her vitality and resolve as a dancer are synecdochic of her destiny. Leading when she can and waiting when she must, Ántonia moves both against and around "the hard-and-fast beat" of convention and circumstance—from leaving the Harlings, through enduring desertion and bearing her child, to her marriage and fulfillment. In her partnership with Cuzak, Jim realizes, "she was the impulse, and he the corrective" (*MA,* p. 358). As in her dancing with Jim, so in her relationship with her husband: she has made him "the instrument" of her "special mission" (*MA,* p. 367). Although he is still a "city man," Ántonia has "managed to hold him here on a farm"; at first "crazy with lonesomeness," he now knows she "always make it as good for me as she could" (*MA,* pp. 366–67).

Ántonia proves to be the living refutation of the Virgilian melancholy that characterizes Jim Burden's adult life, his sadness "that, in the lives of mortals, the best days are the first to flee" (*MA,* p. 263). Horrified by the snake in the field, its "abominable muscularity" and "loathsome fluid motion," its "disgusting vitality" (*MA,* p. 45), he renounces all possibility of adult love with Ántonia or Lena Lingard and seals up the past like a flower in amber. For Jim, the garden becomes the asexual memories of childhood, of beginnings which must remain unchangeable and innocent. His "romantic disposition" may explain his success as a lawyer, but it finds no satisfaction in an empty marriage (*MA,* "Introduction"). Jim's way of life is essentially a passive and vicarious one, and his reunion with Ántonia after many years, while it occasions his joy over her fulfillment, defines his incompleteness. Childless and loveless, he has merely passed the years. Without irony, Ántonia says, "You wouldn't have known me, would you, Jim? You've kept so young, yourself. But it's easier for a man. I can't see how my Anton looks any older than the day I married him" (*MA,* p. 335). Anton's youth, however, seems at least partly due to his accepting Ántonia's vital leadership and what they have created together. Jim's youth has the pathos of the *puer eternatatis,* the Jungian Peter Pan.

Ántonia's story incorporates inseparably the archetypal actions of consecrating the garden and enduring suffering. The transcendent curve upward that her life has taken by the novel's conclusion is the graph against which the other characters are measured. Tiny Soderball's tough independence and risk-taking, while making her wealthy and free, leave her a "thin, hard-faced woman," interested in nothing "much but making money" (*MA,* p. 301). Lena Lingard, for whom the garden was only a place "where there are always too many children, a cross man and work piling up around a sick woman" (*MA,* p. 291), retains her sweetness and her freedom, her spontaneity and her gifts as a seamstress. Her choice, to give affection but to be "accountable to nobody," least of all husbands who "turn into cranky old fathers" (*MA,* p. 291), has been a clear-eyed one, which she abides by. Yet in one of her partings from Jim, she wistfully teases him about what might have been–not marriage, but perhaps an ongoing sexual relationship. She says, among other things, "What's on your mind, Jim? Are you afraid I'll want you to marry me some day?" (*MA,* p. 292); confesses "I've always been a little foolish about you" (*MA,* p. 293); and concludes "It seemed so natural. I used to think I'd like to be your first sweetheart" (*MA,* p. 293). Jim's gratitude at her allowing him the same freedom she claims for herself–"she never tried to hinder me or hold me back" (*MA,* p. 293)–is subtly tainted. His is the relief of the man who prefers separation to possible involvement and who pretends that choice is irrevocable rather than ambiguous and tentative. Here and elsewhere, his renunciations gain their full significance by their contrast to Ántonia's commitments, as she lends herself "to immemorial human attitudes which we recognize by instinct as universal and true" (*MA,* p. 353).

While *My Ántonia* juxtaposes the Bohemians, the Danish, the Norwegians, and various Americans of English ancestry, its primary antitheses are those between the energies and endurance of the young farm women and the repressed sexuality and enervating decorum of town gentility. In *Death Comes for the Archbishop,* Cather evokes a wider range of dramatic tensions and cultural values. The sacred and the profane; the Old World and the New; the ancient communities of Acoma and Taos and the newer ones of Durango and Santa Fe; the varied Catholicisms of the French priests, the rebellious Padre Martinez, the Mexicans and the Indians; the wealthy rancheros of Spanish descent, the peons and rough frontiersmen; the missionary vision of Father Vaillant and Father Latour and the slaughter of the Navajos by their friend Kit Carson–these are but some of the novel's materials. And, while the novel lacks the complexity of characterization found in *My Ántonia,* it achieves another type of density through its basic theme and image: the ways "that Man was lost and saved in a garden" (*DCA,* p. 3).

Essentially, the garden represents the possibility of fusing the customs, beliefs, and rituals of Europe and the Southwest, of creating in the Territory of New Mexico a shared culture, faith, and future. The novel begins with "three Cardinals and a missionary Bishop from America. . . . dining together in the gardens of a villa in the Sabine hills, overlooking Rome," their table surrounded by "potted orange and oleander trees, shaded by spreading ilex oaks that grew out of the rocks overhead" (*DCA,* p. 3). It ends with the Archbishop's dying memory of "standing in a tip-tilted green field among his native mountains," trying "to give consolation to a young man who was being torn in two . . . by the desire to go and the necessity to stay" (*DCA,* p. 299). Between what is commenced in a garden in Rome and concluded with the Archbishop lying "before the high altar in the church he had built" (*DCA,* p. 299), Father Latour never loses his faith, though it is often challenged. It is his trust that the "Faith planted by Spanish friars and watered with their blood was not dead; it awaited only the toil of the husbandman" (*DCA,* p. 32).

The garden takes varied forms. It may be the simple Mexican settlement of *Agua Secreta,* Hidden Water, where the young Father Latour is fed "frijoles cooked with meat, bread and goat's milk, fresh cheese and ripe apples" (*DCA,* p. 25) and where the settlers "spun and wove from the fleece of their flocks, raised their own corn and wheat and tobacco, dried their plums and apricots for winter" (*DCA,* p. 26). It may be the pueblo of Isleta where the church garden is "full of domesticated cactus plants, of many varieties and great size . . . and among these hung huge wicker cages made of willow twigs, full of parrots" (*DCA,* p. 85). It may be the pueblo of Acoma, where the legendary Friar Baltazar compelled the Indians to water and cultivate his garden on top of the rock and lost his life through greed and violence. It may be Los Ranchos de Taos, where the charismatic, gifted renegade Padre

Martinez defies Rome, saying "Our religion grew out of the soil, and has its own roots. . . . The Church the Franciscan Fathers planted here was cut off; this is the second growth, and it is indigenous" (*DCA,* p. 147). It may be the garden Latour plants for himself of "fruit trees (then dry switches) up from St. Lewis in wagons," the cuttings of which are "already yielding fruit in many Mexican gardens" (*DCA,* p. 201). Or it may be the way the landscape itself is understood, the Indians having "none of the European's desire to 'master' nature" but rather the belief that "the spirits of earth and air and water were things not to antagonize and arouse" (*DCA,* p. 234).

For Father Latour, the garden epitomizes many things. Most immediately, it must be planned, laid out, and cultivated, whether on top of the hard rock of Acoma, where it and the faith were once perverted by Baltazar's selfishness, or in the more fertile soil near Santa Fe, where Latour raises "cherries and apricots, apples, and quinces, and the peerless pears of France" (*DCA,* p. 267). Moreover, in Latour's view, the best gardens combine the roots of the Old and New Worlds, the "peerless pears of France" and the "native wild flowers" (DCA, p. 267), especially the purple verbena of New Mexico, whose shades "the dyers and weavers of Italy and France strove for through centuries," the "true Episcopal colour and countless variations of it" (*DCA,* p. 268).

Above all, in Latour's understanding, the garden makes no sharp distinction between the sacred and the profane. Rather, its tending, its produce, and its uses are the results of long traditions and patiently acquired skills and knowledge which gratify both the body and soul: in Latour's quite French view, the garden *is* civilization. On Christmas day in Sante Fe, the young Father Latour and Father Vaillant celebrate these meanings. While lamenting the absence of lettuce and green vegetables, they still find comfort in the olive oil brought from Durango, the light from the silver candlesticks brought from France, and a special pleasure in "a dark onion soup with croutons" (DCA, p. 39) that Father Vaillant has prepared. Speaking in French, Father Latour says, "I am not deprecating your individual talent, Joseph . . . but, when one thinks of it, a soup like this is not the work of one man. It is the result of a constantly refined tradition. There are nearly a thousand years of history in this soup" (*DCA,* p. 39). Their meal, like the novel itself, points toward a climax in which the past and present are commemorated by memories of the gardens that have sustained them. The trust is that such gardens, or their equivalents in the New World, will do so for others:

> Over the compote of dried prunes they fell to talking of the great yellow ones that grew in the old Latour garden at home. Their thoughts met in that tilted cobble street, winding down a hill, with the uneven garden walls and tall horse-

chestnuts on either side; a lonely street after nightfall, with soft street lamps shaped like lanterns at the darkest turnings. At the end of it was the church where the Bishop made his first Communion, with a grove of flat-cut plane trees in front, under which the market was held on Tuesdays and Fridays. (*DCA*, pp. 41–42)

In Cather's handling of it, the garden becomes an image of complementarity. It suggests the possible balancing, not the polarizing, of many things. The seeds, cuttings, and fruit of both Europe and New Mexico, the transplanting of Spanish zeal and French knowledge of Santa Fe and Taos, the Southwest's "light dry wind . . . with the fragrance of hot sun and sagebrush and sweet clover" that "made one a boy again" (*DCA*, p. 275)–these are a few such reconciliations. But there are others, at least as crucial to my argument, that I wish to get at through one of D. H. Lawrence's insights in *Classic American Literature:*

Men are free when they are in a living homeland, not when they are straying and breaking away. Men are free when they are obeying some deep, inward voice of religious belief. Obeying from within. Men are free when they belong to a living, organic, *believing* community, active in fulfilling some unfulfilled, perhaps unrealized purpose. Not when they are escaping to some wild west. The most unfree souls go west, and shout of freedom. (P. 6)

In Lawrence's terms, Father Vaillant and Father Latour are free men. In their different ways–Vaillant the enthusiatic proselytizer, Latour the natural and elegant aristocrat–both obey the inward voice of belief and belong to (are responsible for) the organic community of the Church, active in fulfilling its unfulfilled purpose. Yet the raw stuff of their lives, on the surface at least, is the substance of the primary American myth and narrative paradigm–the separation from home, the journey to and the exploration of the territory ahead, the various adventures, encounters, and brushes with death, the largely male world of questing, movement, and roughing it. Moreover, the affective bond between men as a substitute for wife and children is conspicuous in the relationship between the two priests. But in choosing two protagonists bound by vows of chastity, poverty, and obedience, Cather is able to celebrate the ways that willing submission liberates. Submission to one's vocation gives one a center, a psychic home, a locus for choosing. In the lives of her two priests, eros is sublimated into mutual concern and dependence; "maleness" and "femaleness" become possible roles for each man. Father Vaillant begs Latour to choose for him between family and calling at the beginning of their careers, and he cooks for and waits on Latour when they are together. Yet it is also Father Vaillant, the resourceful and adventuring missionary, who obeys his Bishop and returns because his Bishop is lonely. Father Latour is the diplomat, planner, and leader, yet it is he who is profoundly sensitive to the Virgin's unique presence and meaning. As he kneels with Sada, the devout Mexican who has been a slave of American Protestants, Latour feels "the pity that no man born of woman could ever utterly cut himself off from. . . . The beautiful concept of Mary pierced the priest's heart like a sword" (*DCA*, pp. 217–18).

Death Comes for the Archbishop is one of Cather's most luminous and compelling works. Much of the novel's authority, I believe, lies in her handling of the image of the garden and the action of enduring suffering. By allowing for the individuality of culture and personality, the garden is the source of the reconciliations which make civilization possible. Through the willing submission to the vows of one's calling, enduring suffering becomes discovery of freedom and purpose. Together, the garden and the enduring of suffering make possible the integration of the self through its relatedness to others; the exception of Baltazar merely proves the case. Thus, near the end of his days, Latour reflects, "More and more life seemed to him an experience of the Ego, in no sense the Ego itself" (*DCA*, pp. 289–90). For finally, "He sat in the middle of his own consciousness; none of his former states of mind were lost or outgrown. They were all in reach of his hand, and all comprehensible" (*DCA*, p. 290). Approaching death, Latour becomes wholly free, not from his past but through his past, of which the garden and enduring suffering have been so much a part.

To turn, more briefly, to other examples, I wish to consider Steinbeck's deceptively simple fable in *The Red Pony* and his more complex one in *The Grapes of Wrath*. In *The Red Pony,* the boy Jody must learn to accept the cycle of life and death–the old green water tub *and* the black cypress tree where pigs are slaughtered, the saving of his colt through the sacrifice of its mother. Carl Tiflin, his father, faces a more difficult set of challenges: to make a place for those weaker or less useful than himself, to unlearn his habitual sternness with his son, to forgive his father-in-law's tedious recalling of the heroic days of westering. Steinbeck's parable concerns the enduring of routine, the daily demands and occasional crises of farm life, the humdrum events and undramatic solaces of domesticity. For father and son, in different ways, the creation and the sustaining of home often involves suffering. As is often the case in Steinbeck's fiction, the men who understand the meaning of home most fully are single, solitary figures: the ranch hand Billy Buck and the old *paisano* Gitano. Billy, whose gentleness and know-how with horses and boys make him Jody's real teacher, tries to counter Carl's public stance that home is merely an economic unit of production, from which the unfit must be excluded. Rather like Mary answering Warren in Frost's "The Death of the Hired Man," he objects when Carl harshly suggests shooting an old horse (and by implication the likes of Gitano): "They got a right to rest after they worked all their life. Maybe they like to just walk around."[12] And Gitano, ancient, mysterious, proud, indigenous, rebukes all hints that he belongs elsewhere: "I was born here" (*RP,* p. 47).

The related themes of home and suffering reach a climax in the last pages in the tension between Carl and his father-in-law. Carl, often torn between kindness and the fear of letting up and not setting an example, has been reminded too many times that he lives after the great days of adventure, the collective saga of westering. He is only a husband, a parent, a rancher. Exploding with anger, he exclaims, "Why does he have to tell them over and over? He came across the plains. All right! Now it's finished. Nobody wants to hear about it over and over" (*RP,* pp. 88–89). In the face of his wife's silence, he finally manages an apology to the grandfather, who in turn tells Jody, "Westering isn't a hunger anymore. It's all done. Your father is right. It is finished" (*RP,* p. 91). It *is* finished: the West having been "won," there being no place to go now, the real challenge is different and perhaps harder. For Carl's generation and Jody's, heroism must entail living with the ordinary and finding satisfaction in the familiar. Domesticity, reconciliation, the acceptance of what is possible conclude the fable when Jody wants to make some lemonade for his grandfather and his mother gives him a lemon and a squeezer.

The related themes of home and enduring suffering permeate *The Grapes of Wrath* and have been amply written about.[13] Here, I wish only to make two connected points. The first is that the uprooting of the Joads and the other tenant farmers and their continued dispossession in the San Joaquin Valley are the results of intelligible causes, not of some species of metaphysical overreaching: inadequate crop rotation, erosion and bad weather, profit-taking by owners and foreclosures by banks; a surplus of labor, Ricardo's Iron Law of Wages, and the hostility of the growers. Exodus and the economic exclusion from the land of milk and honey are human tragedies, at least ameliorable by planning and cooperation, as the government camp suggests. The biological, social, and economic forces of human ecology may be complex, but they are not incomprehensible: the tragedy is that home for the Joads should have been possible. My second point is that the ending, far from being unmotivated or forced symbolism, is Steinbeck's primal image of the enduring meanings of home: continuity, the furthering of life, giving what one has to give, whatever affirmation one can make in the face of death. Critics, mainly male, may have been embarrassed by Rose of Sharon's nursing a man dying of starvation, but Steinbeck's ending is wholly consistent with the rest of the novel. It underlines the Joads' and the reader's instruction of a fundamental perspective—that home entails the interdependence of all humans. As Ma Joad says, "Use' ta be the fambly was fust. It ain't so now. It's anybody. Worse off we get, the more we got to do."[14]

To turn from Steinbeck to Joyce Carol Oates means juxtaposing two quite different fictional worlds. Yet the migrant workers of *A Garden of Earthly Delights* are also often haunted by the vague recollection of home, of "going back," of finding Kentucky: "Each remembered his own farm and a few other farms and that was it."[15] The struggle for status, the effort to possess and not be dispossessed, is central to Clara's life, as it is to the lives of Loretta and Maureen in *them*. And, like Steinbeck, Oates is acutely conscious of the ways that twentieth-century American history victimizes. This is especially true in *them*. The social and economic dislocations of the Depression, World War II, and the 1960s infiltrate the lives of her characters, and the violence, pain and confusion they experience are numbly borne by these "Children of Silence," who have so few words for either their suffering or their hopes of a better life. Oates's vision of a society racked by class divisions, the frustrated passion and pent-up anger of the losers in the rat race after the American dream is not a pretty one, but it gains much of its power because of its unsparing concentration on these divisions and the human waste. The small-town hostility to migrant workers; the fear and condescension on the part of church women scavenging for converts among the children in work camps; the empty purity of the wealthy in Grosse Pointe and the stink of oil and plastic money in Beaumont, Texas; the young Maureen's prostituting herself with strangers for the dollars which become her fetish; the riots and fires in Detroit—these and dozens of other scenes dramatize the consequences of these divisions and the resulting pathology of dispossession. And, while both novels share in the spirit of Bosch's painting, the torments of the *Garden of Earthly Delights,* they also give voice to the deepest cry of the tormented, especially the women. It is Maureen Wendall's "Everything in me aches for a husband. A house."[16] However confused they may be about the differences between apparent status and real security, middle-class privacy and actual intimacy, their anguish is real and their need is deep. For them, a husband and a house mean control, order, and a shape in lives that otherwise lack coherence.[17]

Oates tests these meanings of home through the life and vision of Jules Wendall, in whom dwells "the spirit of the Lord" (*them,* p. 461). On first glance, Jules would seem closer to the traditional male hero of the traditional American narrative. He is a loner, sometimes violent, a picaro who moves among the strata of American society with ease, a restless wanderer who finally heads west to California. Yet his is the most comprehensive understanding of "them" in *them*. As a child, he reads a story in *Time* about Vinoba Bhave, and Bhave's words become a part of him: "I have come to loot you with love. . . . We are all members of a single human family. . . . My object is to transform the whole of society. Fire merely burns. . . . Fire burns and does its duty. It is for others to do theirs" (*them,* p. 95). Thanks to the freedom and the solitude of his childhood in the country, the proud love of his mother, and the fierce love of his grandmother, he is integral and unafraid, "the only real man in this tomb of a house of silent men" (*them,* p. 61). Gentle with all women, still loving the woman who tried to kill him, Jules learns there is no retreat, no such thing as safety, only that "Everyone must live through it again and again, there's no end to it, no land to go to" (*them,* p. 474). When Maureen rejects her family and her past for a house, husband, and child, and dismisses all her relatives with "I guess I'm not going to see them anymore," Jules answers, "But, honey, aren't you one of *them* yourself?" (*them,* p. 478).

Jules's question summarizes the novel's fundamental conflict: the desperation in the lives of men and women, the rich and poor, white and black, the law-abiders and the lawbreakers, the possessors and the dispossessed, the rioters and the victims–all of them divided by economic, social, and historical forces they hardly understand, all determined not to be "one of *them,*" none ready to see their only real home as a member of "a single human family." Through Jules Wendall, Oates transmutes many symbolic values of a certain type of American hero. While he is in recognizable ways an "American Adam," his quests are undertaken to find love and a place for himself, not to deny connection and flee society; his violence is self-protection, not a proof of manhood; his affection for his family proves abiding and liberating, not an impediment to his masculinity. Even during his darkest, most nihilistic period after Nadine has tried to murder him, he can answer the bloodthirsty rhetoric of the radicals with "Why? Why kill anybody? . . . It won't change anything" (*them,* p. 434). Jules belongs, in fact, to a group of recent male protagonists who, though diverse in other ways, call into question certain assumptions about the primary American narrative paradigm and myth.

Space permits discussion of only two other such figures–Frank Alpine of Bernard Malamud's *The Assistant* and Robert Pirsig's Phaedrus in *Zen and the Art of Motorcycle Maintenance.* Malamud's novel is a rich, sustained enactment of founding the home and enduring suffering. His hero, the classic American drifter, an orphan and marginal man, finally learns to obey Lawrence's "inward voice of religious belief" and to become free through "fulfilling some unfulfilled, perhaps unrealized purpose." Reconciling a latitudinarian Catholicism with a latitudinarian Judaism–the holiness of St. Francis with Morris Buber's "I suffer for you. . . . You suffer for me"[18]–Frank becomes a new man. His ultimate choices–Morris's store-tomb, circumcision, the burden and the joy of loving Helen without promise of return–are hard-won, haltingly arrived at, and costly to himself and others. But they are, by the novel's conclusion, free choices. In *Zen* Pirsig's narrator must journey westward, into the fragments of his past, and through the debris of Western philosophy, only to discover that after all the Chautauquas, all the movement, all the disquisitions, that "the biggest duality of all, the duality between me and him, remains unfaced. A mind divided against itself."[19] Dead-ended on the California coast, father and son finally achieve "Quality, . . . the event at which awareness of both subjects and objects is made possible" (*Zen*, p. 233). Their quest has been both necessary and ironic: necessary because they need the isolation to become subjects to each other, ironic because freedom lies not in an awareness of the territory ahead but the *terra incognita* of the present. Until Phaedrus embraces his breakdown and madness, fuses then and now, neither he nor Chris can be healed. Once he ceases flight and repression, both he and Chris can "[be] one person again" (*Zen*, p. 404).

The destinies of these two protagonists challenge not only the usual assumption about escaping the past and asserting a radical independence but also a whole series of other assumptions. In their different ways, both works imply that self-renewal is the acceptance of limits and a completion through suffering for and with others. Further, neither work relies on the usual poles of Self and Nature. In *The Assistant,* Frank finds *his* home in Morris's wretched city store, a far remove from his wandering as a carnie from one county fair to another. In *Zen,* Pirsig's narrator, looking back on the trip through Montana, recalls the words of an old Christian hymn: "You've got to cross that lonesome valley. . . . You've got to cross it by yourself" (*Zen*, p. 390). Precisely: as long as the mind is divided against itself, all valleys will be lonesome, whether they are in Montana, the streets of Chicago Phaedrus drove through while going over the edge, or the hospital where he was incarcerated and cut off from his son. Finally, in both works the father-who-is-absent of so many American novels is found. Taking on the store that Morris's dead son might have inherited, Frank becomes the family provider and discovers that his earlier lust for Helen has become almost a brotherly love. He imagines himself, like St. Francis, saying, "Little Sister, here is your little sister the rose" (*TA*, p. 438). And Phaedrus realizes that Chris has been burdened by mourning the father he lost. In accepting his former self, he frees both of them: the "Quality" missing between them emerges when they become related as father and son.

Other writers come to mind whose fiction is rooted in the archetypes of consecrating the home and enduring suffering, not in the pursuit of consummation. One is Glenway Wescott, especially for his *The Grandmothers: A Family Portrait,* a wide-ranging account of the men and women who have influenced Alwyn Tower's life. Another is Anne Tyler, whose fiction has a special feel for the family, both extended and nuclear, and for the eccentricity of the ordinary, which can redeem us from boredom and fantasy. Still another is Tillie Olsen, whose short stories in *Tell Me a Riddle* are among the finest treatment of these themes by any American writer. This is a minimal list. Alice Walker, Wright Morris, Toni Morrison, J. F. Powers—some of our most gifted novelists since World War II would need to be added for even a partial account. But rather than multiply examples, I will conclude with several of the broader implications of this analysis for our understanding of American fiction and culture.

First and foremost, we need to read the kinds of works I have discussed as a critique of the primary myth and paradigm, not in order to repudiate it but in order to see what has been left out and at what price. The primary American myth is in no danger: it is rooted in our history, culture, and popular arts. It has staying power and continued resonance because it is part of our national character. But, as feminists and other critics have been pointing out with increasing frequency, this myth (like all myths) gains its hold as much from what it excludes or denies as from what it includes and sanctifies. The complex networks of family, ethnic and national affiliations, and local and regional ties may be both as real *and* as fulfilling as solitary personhood, but these realities remain largely unsanctioned in the dominant American myth. If anything, they tend to be envisioned as wastelands, menacing gothic presences, or the nets and traps that fetter us. What Robert Bellah and his collaborators in *Habits of the Heart* call our "ontological individualism, the idea that the individual is the only firm reality," has become too exclusive, too simplifying and distorting as the primary story we tell about ourselves, our history, and our culture.[20] The result, to borrow Philip Slater's apt title, is a dominant narrative paradigm that enshrines "The Pursuit of Loneliness."

Second, we need to rethink the assumptions underlying our understanding and writing of American literary history. Granted that the writing of any literary history these days is problematic, most of the writers I have cited tend, in one way or another, to be pigeonholed, regionalized, or marginalized—Cather the memorialist of the Midwest and Southwest, Steinbeck the *soi-disant* proletarian, Oates the too-frequent author of Gothic romances, and the like. To the extent that they do not conform to the primary American narrative paradigm and myth, they have become writers of secondary or minor interest, at best treated defensively, at worst condescended to or largely ignored. There are signs this needed reassessment may already have begun. I am not claiming all these writers have equal merit or should supersede the worthies of the standard American literature survey, but I do strongly suspect that they have not, until quite recently, been given their due, in part because our assumptions have limited our choosing. We have narrowed our understanding of tradition at the expense of individual talent.

Finally, we need to reexamine certain works of our major writers which have questioned this paradigm. Faulkner's *The Bear,* Bellow's *Herzog* and

Mr. Sammler's Planet, Percy's *The Moviegoer,* and O'Connor's "The Displaced Person" come to mind as immediate examples. While the garden is not equally central in all of these works, the themes of home and suffering most certainly are. In their diverse ways, these works call into question certain American beliefs about the self that acknowledge no limits and/or our manifest destiny of possessing the natural world. These beliefs destroy the very possibility of home. What differentiates these works and writers from the ones I have discussed earlier is that their critique is essentially a religious one. All secular notions of home are seen as essentially profane; without the sacred, humans remain in exile. This critique has, certainly, been frequently discussed in relation to Faulkner and O'Connor, but I think it should also be treated in the larger context of the primary American myth and paradigm. The grounds for deconstructing this paradigm may already be at hand in the subversive works of these who have been canonized.

NOTES

1. David W. Noble, *The Eternal Adam and the New World Garden* (New York: Grosset & Dunlap, Universal Library Paperback, 1968), p. 24. Subsequent references in the text are to this edition.

2. D. H. Lawrence, *Studies in Classic American Literature* (New York: Viking Press, Compass Book, 1964), pp. 62–63.

3. Langdon Elsbree, *The Rituals of Life: Patterns in Narratives* (Port Washington, N.Y.: Kennikat Press, 1982), pp. 16–17. Subsequent references in the text refer to this edition and are abbreviated *RL*.

4. Annette Kolodny, *The Land before Her: Fantasy and Experience of the American Frontier* (Chapel Hill and London: Univ. of North Carolina Press, Paperback, 1984), p. xiii.

5. Willa Cather, *My Ántonia* (Boston: Houghton Mifflin, Sentry Edition, 1954), p. 353. Subsequent references in the text refer to this edition and are abbreviated *MA*.

6. Willa Cather, *Death Comes for the Archbishop* (New York: Random House, Vintage Book, 1981), p. 267. Subsequent references in the text are to this edition and are abbreviated *DCA*.

7. Henry David Thoreau, *Walden* and *Civil Disobedience,* ed. Owen Thomas (New York: Norton, Norton Critical Edition, 1966), p. 61.

8. Wright Morris, *The Territory Ahead* (New York: Atheneum Paperback, 1963), p. 31.

9. Saul Bellow, *The Adventures of Augie March* (New York: Viking Press, Compass Book, 1960), p. 536.

10. Erik Erikson, "Reflections on the American Identity," *Childhood and Society,* 2nd ed., enl. (New York: Norton, Paperback, 1963), p. 295. Subsequent references in the text are to this edition.

11. Frederick Jackson Turner, *The Significance of the Frontier in American History,* ed. Harold P. Simonson (New York: Frederick Ungar, Paperback, 1963), p. 57.

12. John Steinbeck, *The Red Pony* (New York: Bantam Books, Pathfinder Ed., 1963), p. 45. All subsequent references in the text are to this edition and are abbreviated *RP.*

13. For a lucid recent summary and discussion of these themes, see Louis Owen's *John Steinbeck's Re-Vision of America* (Athens: Univ. of Georgia Press, 1985).

14. John Steinbeck, *The Grapes of Wrath* (New York: Viking, 1939), p. 606.

15. Joyce Carol Oates, *A Garden of Earthly Delights* (Greenwich, Conn.: Fawcett, Crest Paperback, 1967), p. 14.

16. Joyce Carol Oates, *them* (Greenwich, Conn.: Fawcett, Crest Paperback, 1969), p. 317. All subsequent references are to this edition.

17. For an excellent discussion of this theme, see Robert H. Fossum, "Only Control: The Novels of Joyce Carol Oates," *Studies in the Novel* 7 (Summer, 1975): 285–97. I am indebted not only to his analysis but also to our conversations and his reading of this essay.

18. Bernard Malamud, *Two Novels:* The Natural *and* The Assistant (1952 and 1957; reprint, New York: Random House, Modern Library, n.d.), p. 325. All subsequent references in the text to *The Assistant* are to this edition and are abbreviated *TA*.

19. Robert M. Pirsig, *Zen and the Art of Motorcycle Maintenance* (New York and London: Bantam Books, 1975), p. 395. All subsequent references in the text are to this edition.

20. Robert N. Bellah et al., *Habits of the Heart: Individualism and Commitment in American Life* (Berkeley and Los Angeles: Univ. of California Press, 1985), p. 276.

Forging an American Style: The Romance-Novel and Magical Realism as Response to the Frontier and Wilderness Experiences

WAYNE UDE

A nation's literature cannot be studied only through the examination of content; a history of literature is also a history of technique. That is especially true of the United States, where our literary history has been bound up, perhaps more than in most cultures, with a search for both the techniques and the conceptual framework which might be capable of containing and presenting the full range of realities within which Americans have lived. Understandably, those realities begin with, and often return to, the experiences of wilderness and frontier. That search led our writers early on to what Northrop Frye called the American romance-novel,[1] which Richard Chase suggested underwent a "definitive adaptation to America,"[2] producing what we may as well call the American romance-novel. More recently, the traditional American romance-novel has developed into what we will call North American Magical Realism.[3]

But there was no American literary tradition available to the first European settlers (the flourishing American Indian literary traditions did not become known to Europeans until much later). Those settlers seem to have experienced this new–to them–continent less as frontier (a borderline, a buffer protecting, if not extending, what they knew as civilization) than as pure wilderness: a place not only where the familiar rules and laws of the European past did not apply but where it often seemed that no laws of any sort had ever existed. At any rate, any rules encountered in this wilderness would not be those of English literature; and yet, English literature provided the forms, the styles, most immediately available to settlers attempting to write about the new land. It was not likely that those first European newcomers would invent dramatic new techniques for prose and poetry–that sort of invention has generally developed in more settled and secure lands–though new techniques were what they most needed.

Because the sixteenth century was a great age of poetry, we can look first at the techniques and attitudes offered by poetry; attitudes, at least, were available to prose writers, and often techniques as well. Certainly the English Metaphysical poetry which influenced Anne Bradstreet's early career, and all of Edward Taylor's, offered little help. For all their elaborate conceits, the Metaphysicals had devised a style based on the elaboration of familiar imagery, not the presentation of the new and unfamiliar; their work finally centered not on emotion but on thought. They began with thought, attempted to embody thought in *familiar* images which they then turned and turned, elaborating to an extent not found in earlier poetry, to produce finally an emotional apprehension of thought. In form they were rational and controlled, with complex meter, rhyme, sound, syntax and diction.

Such poetry was designed to take writers and their readers more deeply into the familiar in hopes of reaching new understandings, but only of familiar things; the Metaphysicals operated within a conceptual framework which asserted that the world was both rational and rationally understandable. Techniques developed for such purposes are not of much help when one is surrounded by what appears to be a howling wilderness unlike anything one has ever imagined, much less seen, and finds oneself confronting emotions which are equally unfamiliar.

The results are startlingly inappropriate to their surroundings in the work of Bradstreet and Taylor, easily the best of colonial poets. But prose writers such as William Bradford or Mary Rowlandson did not fare much better. Because the Puritan typology which dominated their work insisted that the meaning of any event existed prior to the event and needed only to be discovered by comparing the event to its biblical model (a technique still used by contemporary American fundamentalists on the so-called religious right, of course), they did not search for ways of describing which would force the reader–or the writer–to discover meaning. Thus, even Rowlandson often seems to stand outside her own experience, cataloguing it. By the end of her captivity narrative, she can say of events only that the Lord answered her prayer and tested her. The structures within which she wrote did not provide her techniques that might have led to new understandings; for the Puritans, there were no new understandings, only reaffirmations of old ones.

The earliest Puritans had followed a general European practice of the age,[4] by thinking in terms of an opposition between civilization–the religious community, the city on a hill–and wilderness, with little notion of an extended frontier as a buffer between the two. (Frontier for them meant the town borders; thus, each community had its own little circular frontier, unconnected to the frontiers of other communities around them.) As the area claimed by civilization grew, and wilderness began to recede, the concept of an extended frontier began to develop, but the techniques which might have allowed a full description of both frontier and wilderness did not.

The age of Franklin, with its rational and Deist philosophies, was dominated by the techniques of a neoclassicism which supplanted the Metaphysicals and was not itself supplanted until the very end of the eighteenth century. Franklin and his contemporaries found the frontier itself of less importance than the attempt to create a secular American civilization away from–and protected by–the frontier. Neoclassical technique, with its insistence on the dominance of reason; its valuing of emotional restraint, restricted scope, moderation, and self-control, in prose style as well as content; its strong sense of form, decorum, and proportion, expressed in elegantly elaborate prose; and its intellectualism, its love of concepts rather than images, its seeking after clarity and simplicity based on the discovery of order within order, provided nearly the ideal conceptual framework and techniques for writing about Franklin's version of American civilization. Little in neoclassicism allowed for discerning–much less describing–a separate order on the frontier or beyond, in the wilderness, an order which needed first to be described and only later to be conceptualized. Instead, the wilderness was simply an extension of God's rational world. Even Crevecoeur, who attempted to write about life on the frontier, on the edge of the wilderness, was not able to see either frontier or wilderness separately from his ideas of what an ordered civilization should be.

Colonial and Revolutionary writers turned their attention away not only from frontier and wilderness but also from both poetry and fiction; certainly the greatest American writers of the age are not remembered for their work in those genres but for what we would now call their "prose nonfiction"–the personal and political essay, of course, but also the polemic, the philosophical and/or political meditation, and so on. Each of those modes tends toward the intellectual, rational, conceptual, and abstract. Both their concerns and their lack of appropriate technique led eighteenth-century American writers away from the emotional, individual, experiential, and concrete presentations of poetry and fiction.

Ironically, by the close of the American Revolutionary period–and partly in response both to that revolution and to the experience of wilderness–English and European literature had begun to develop those attitudes and techniques which would be reshaped by American writers to produce Richard Chase's American romance-novel, of which Magical Realism is the most recent development. When American writers again turned their attention to the frontier, a new set of techniques was waiting.

The European Romantic movement provided the most thorough rebellion against the restraints of neoclassicism in both poetry and prose. Of great importance to Americans were the Romantics' idealization of rural life (which became frontier life in American Romantic development); their love, not of formal gardens but of the wild, irregular, strange, or even grotesque in nature (and in prose and verse); and their idealization of the primitive. These three elements freed the American imagination (the more so as they came, in part at least, in response to the American wilderness experience) to see the frontier and wilderness in ways which, while idealized, at least came closer to the actual experience. When combined with Romantic interest in the past (including the noncivilized past); the Romantics' abandonment of conventional elevated diction in favor of freer and more informal language, of conventional rhythms for the bolder and more irregular; their emphasis on imagination over literal fact; and their mysticism, or emphasis on metaphysical as well as physical experience, American writers were finally provided both an attitude and a set of techniques that could allow them to report on frontier and wilderness and on human reactions to both. Again, it is important to keep in mind that American prose writers did read both the creative work and the theorizing of European Romantic poets as well as of prose writers. The tendency in western American criticism to separate poetry from prose ignores the actual reading habits of, and therefore influences on, writers.

Earlier in the eighteenth century, the Gothic novel had introduced other elements of what became the American romance-novel. Gothic admitted what realists would call the supernormal, events not possible to treat within the confines of the English or Continental realistic novel. It also allowed for the continued existence of the historical or legendary in the present, not only as ghosts and other demonic beings but even through its settings, the ruined castles and wild landscapes that are visible examples of a persistently continuing past, and that, as in the work of the Romantics, often seem to possess a life of their own. Further, the Gothic reached beyond rationality and presented images directly from the subconscious and unconscious mind (as we call them now), not all of which were simply nightmare images, and affirmed the value of intuition and emotion over reason.

Finally, as part of its attempt to speak to emotions through rhythm and sound rather than to the rational mind, Gothic tended to use both an emotionally heightened yet informal diction and a stronger, darker prose rhythm and sound than had been favored by either neoclassicism or the Age of Reason. It placed less emphasis on surface coherence, using juxtaposition of images or events in place of carefully ordered plot development. Imagery tended less toward the literal and even favored metaphor, in which something becomes something else, over simile, which can compare without transforming. These elements combined with looser syntax, which itself lessened the impression of surface coherence in Gothic works.

A third influence developed early in the nineteenth century: a growing interest in folktales, especially as those tales seemed to illustrate what we now recognize as human psychological archetypes; to embody both the dark and the light sides of the nonrational (not irrational) subconscious; to contain imaginative rather than literal truth; and to forge connections between humans and the past, between humans and the natural world. Again, the influence was not merely on or through writers of prose: the Grimm Brothers' *Household Tales,* published early in the nineteenth century, were to be the source for some thirty-five choral works in Germany alone before the century ended; more than fifty operas have been based on the Grimms' work.[5] The style of folktale also reinforced the tendency of Romantic poets and prose writers to use a more commonplace language and a syntax both less formal and less controlled than that prevailing in Europe and America in the eighteenth century.

Provided with these techniques and attitudes, American writers again turned their attention to the frontier and wilderness. Cooper's Leatherstocking romance-novels and Irving's *A Tour of the Prairies, Astoria,* and *The Adventures of Captain Bonneville,* testified to the strength of that impulse to report on the then-contemporary frontier. But both writers also turned back to re-create the earlier American past, recognizing that it had not yet been revealed in what they now saw as its true character. The prerevolutionary parts of the Leatherstocking series are evidence of this impulse, as are Irving's *History of New York* and *Sketchbook,* and, for that matter, Hawthorne's *The Scarlet Letter* and *House of the Seven Gables.*

Cooper's fiction was still what Richard Chase has called adventure-romance, which Chase distinguished from the more profound psychological romance[6] to be found in Hawthorne, Melville, and, at its most extreme and gothic, but also its most individually centered, in Poe. As Chase has said, it seems clear that in the work of these three writers the romance-novel moved beyond its European history, not least in its ability to create fully developed characters in place of the stock and idealized performers found not only in the English romance-novel, but also in Puritan prose typology-narrative. Thus, the most convincing re-creations of Colonial American minds seem to come not from colonial writers, but from Hawthorne, writing at a time when he had the full technique of the romance-novel upon which to draw.

Further, Hawthorne was able to re-create in his tales and short stories the experience of confrontation with wilderness at a time when there was not yet a clearly marked extended frontier behind which civilization might shelter (as in "Young Goodman Brown," for example). Romance was able to recognize, and techniques learned from romance, the Gothic novel, and the folktale were able to present, the possibility that wilderness existed not only as an external set of conditions but within characters as well, and so could not entirely be banished beyond a frontier. Melville's use of the sea as a setting allowed him to demonstrate the same possibility by removing entirely any protection which a frontier on land might have offered his characters, whether from the outer or their own inner wildernesses. His ships are, like those early New England towns, little individual civilizations surrounded by wilderness. Poe took the exploration of inner wildernesses further than did any other nineteenth-century American prose writer; his characters exist as isolated individuals, with only their own inner resources to protect them from their own inner wildernesses; civilization is no help to Poe's characters. Understandably, his style is also the most extreme, and most obviously influenced by Gothic.

By midcentury, the romance-novel seemed permanently established as the dominant prose style and most important fictional form in North America. That quickly changed, and after the Civil War prose romance was displaced by the flatter, more controlled styles of naturalism and realism.

During the latter part of the nineteenth and on into the early twentieth century, with the supposed closing of the American frontier and the belief that wilderness had ceased to exist, came a focus on urban and industrial America. The end of external wilderness seemed to mean, for such writers as Dreiser, Norris, and Farrell, the end also of inner wilderness, indeed of inner complexity. Such writers had little belief in the individuality of human character in a machine age; they saw their minimal characters in a world where the conditions of life were mechanistic, predictable, and deeply unfavorable to humans. (And they were basically correct about the urban world they chose to write about, as are their minimalist/naturalist successors today, who select a similarly narrow subject matter and treatment.) That the techniques of the romance-novel might have allowed them to explore more fully an emerging urban wilderness[7] does not seem to have occurred to the American Naturalist writers. Similarly, their style harkened back to the less adventurous diction of the eighteenth century–though with none of that century's elegance; and their syntax became predictable, their prose rhythms dull and unadventurous, their imagery literal to the point of boredom, the surface coherence of their work monotonous to an extreme.

The spirit of the romance-novel persisted to a very limited extent in the work of popular writers whose work dealt with a largely imaginary frontier of cowboys-and-Indians, cattle drives–and–fast draws. Thus, the romance-novel, a very serious literary form, was replaced by the romanticized-adventure-novel, an awkward term for an awkward simplification in which inner wildernesses were denatured and replaced by an "inner fire" or "inner power" which the hero might channel and control at need, and which would somehow lead him (always him) to do in the end what was (according to the limited and shallow moral conventions of the romanticized-adventure-novel) morally correct. Thus, the romanticized-adventure-novel preserved only a pale shadow of the romance-novel's attempts to intuitively understand deeper regions of the human psyche. Its manly prose read like sarsaparilla Gothic.

Among more serious writers, only Mark Twain and to a limited extent Stephen Crane seem to have recognized the existence of an inner wilderness that could not be banished to or beyond an artificial frontier, recognizing the frontier as a meeting place for inner and outer wildernesses. But Twain (like Steinbeck later) attempted to express that vision within the techniques of realism, which were not sufficient, and Twain (also like Steinbeck) left an uneven and flawed body of work. This era was not a prosperous one for the American romance-novel.

Probably the best American fiction writers to emerge from the early twentieth century's realist and naturalist influences were Hemingway, Faulkner, and Steinbeck, all three of whom turned away from urban settings in their best work, and all of whom were able, with varying success, to make use of the tradition of the American romance-novel. The greatest of these, William Faulkner, made the fullest use of the techniques, including style, of the romance-novel in the five books which are his best work: *The Sound and the Fury, Absalom, Absalom, Light in August, As I Lay Dying,* and *Go Down, Moses.* Of all his work, these five novels also show the greatest concern with wilderness, both inner and outer.

Faulkner was not content only to work within the tradition of the romance-novel as he received it; instead, he took that tradition a step further into what became the Magical Realism that has become so influential among Spanish-American writers and, more recently, among North American writers as well–including those who have produced the most interesting fiction about the American West.

We can see the six common elements of Magical Realism most clearly in *Go Down, Moses.* First, Faulkner firmly rejects the confines of traditional realism; in its place we find a multidimensional metaphysical as well as physical reality, in which a young deer in the woods may be transformed, if Sam Fathers shows us how to see it, into a sort of Platonic Ideal Deer. Second, the mythical or legendary as well as the historic past becomes an actual presence in contemporary life, as Faulkner mixes southern-white, native-American, and black legends, making them immediately present in his characters' lives. In the process, Faulkner seeks to fabricate poetic recreations, a third characteristic of Magical Realism, rather than mere imitations of reality. Fourth, he seeks to distort time, space, and identity as those elements are understood in conventional realism. Fifth, though his version of human psychology now seems Jungian and archetypal to us (as is the case with most Magical Realist fiction), it also represents the later and more complex development of what Richard Chase called the psychological romance of Poe, Melville, and Hawthorne. Sixth and finally, Faulkner mixes mystical or magical elements with the everyday details of commonplace reality in an attempt to generate in the reader a firm belief in the validity and genuineness–the reality–of his fictions. These are also the traits we recognize in both South and North American Magical Realism.

We also recognize the style Faulkner inherited from Hawthorne, Melville, and Poe, the style of prose romance, with its heightened yet commonplace diction; its loose, informal syntax; its strong, dark rhythms and sounds; its use of juxtaposition and metaphor; its lack of concern for surface coherence in the presence of deeper coherences. Significantly, Faulkner uses this style for all parts of his work; he does not have one style for "magic" and another for "reality," and thus the style itself asks us to take all elements of the work equally seriously.

Faulkner was not a writer who experimented for the sake of experimentation; he returned to and developed the techniques of the romance-novel (as did other modern novelists such as James Joyce and Virginia Woolf) because they were necessary for the full exploration of both outer and inner wildernesses. *Go Down, Moses* manages, among other themes, to follow the retreat of the southern forest's wilderness remnant in the years after the Civil War; *Absalom, Absalom* treats, among other issues, Sutpen's attempt to carve a small empire out of the pre-war southern wilderness, in addition to exploring the wilderness within Sutpen and his attempt to carve out a place for himself within the legend of the South. In other books the wilderness is moved more fully into individual characters–into Jewel and Anse in *As I Lay Dying* (in differing ways), Benjy and Caddy in *The Sound and the Fury,* Joe Christmas in *Light in August,* and into the entire Snopes clan in several books and stories.

Faulkner also does away with the idea of an extended, shared frontier: if there is no clearly delimited time or space in the conventional sense, if the past is also the present, then the frontier, no matter how far distant, is at the same time always here and always now, and the wilderness is always within us as well as all around us. If we clear the land, wilderness grows up through our own feet.

Americans do not much care for that idea; we prefer our wilderness "out there" somewhere, with a frontier to serve as our buffer, our protection from the wilderness: if there is an Alaskan frontier, if outer space is the final frontier, perhaps even if an Iron Curtain exists as a political frontier, then we will be safe from wilderness, inner or outer.

At this point we could discuss any number of twentieth-century writers: Gabriel García Marquez, Jorge Luis Borges, Nobel Prize–winner Yasunari Kawabata, Isak Dinesen, I. B. Singer, early Jerzy Kosinski, Margaret Atwood, John Gardner, William Kennedy, Toni Morrison, Ishmael Reed, Bernard Malamud, and Maxine Hong Kingston, all of whom use the techniques of the Magical Realist romance-novel (Kingston uses those techniques in her non-fiction!). Instead, we will limit our discussion to those writers who have written about the American West, both as frontier and after.

Western writers earlier in this century (about the same time as writers in other parts of the country) adopted realism, with all of its limitations, and most did not seriously challenge those limitations: one finds realist style employed almost exclusively in the work of Owen Wister, Willa Cather, Harvey Fergusson, A. B. Guthrie, Conrad Richter, Dorothy Johnson, Jack Schaefer, Paul Horgan, Wallace Stegner, Tom McGuane, Jim Harrison, and so on. Other writers have occasionally used the techniques of the romance-novel while remaining committed to realism in the bulk of their work. A smaller–but, to our taste, far more interesting–group has chosen to work almost exclusively within the tradition of the American romance-novel.

In twentieth-century western fiction, the Romantic attitude sometimes has to struggle to get past the author, as in the work of John Steinbeck, who seems to have tried to impose the realist straitjacket over the romantic impulses which break out in such novels as *The Grapes of Wrath* or *Cannery Row;* Steinbeck's case has been too well documented and is too well demonstrated by his stylistic inconsistencies to need further discussion here.

Frederick Manfred is another Western writer whose work never quite commits itself to the romance-novel tradition. *King of Spades,* with its parallel to the legend of Oedipus, and *Riders of Judgement,* with its attempt to raise its central character to the status of epic hero in the closing pages, hint at the existence of deeper levels within the characters and toy with the notion that time might not be linear, that the legendary past might still exist in the contemporary world; but they draw back from the techniques which might allow deeper and fuller exploration of those elements. Even *Lord Grizzly,* in which the moment-by-moment account of the crawl becomes something of a romance-novel epic in itself through the accumulation of detail and the use of a style which is clearly influenced by the romance-novel, nonetheless returns in its final section to a comfortable realism and a flatter prose. The shift in technique in that final section flattens and dulls the narrative, and as Hugh Glass returns from the wilderness his kinship (through a merging of his own inner wilderness with the external wilderness) disappears and he becomes another mildly confused pioneer.

A more startling example occurs in Vardis Fisher's *Mountain Man:* a basically realistic novel is interrupted by passages of the most effective prose

Fisher ever created. In those sections, we are allowed to perceive the world through the eyes of a woman deranged by the slaughter of her family by Indians. She lives in a shack built for her by the mountain men and tends her family's graves. On moonlit nights she sits out by those graves, nodding to the moonlit sagebrush, which she believes to be her children nodding back at her. In these passages, Fisher's prose sings; it creates the nonrational side of this woman's mind not only convincingly but with a beauty too often lacking in Fisher's more usual serviceable realist prose–and it does so in rhythms and images which seem to come from the romantic, not the realist, tradition. Nothing of the title character's grief for his family seems as convincing as does this madwoman's. Nor does his love for the mountains convince us, even when Fisher asks us to imagine him imagining that he is hearing Beethoven's symphonies as he looks out over the landscape. Instead, we imagine ourselves playing records of those Romantic symphonies as we try to gain from those passages what Fisher's prose by itself can create in the madwoman sections.

The madwoman sections are not integrated into the novel, and though they are the best thing in the book, they are not of a piece with the rest: Fisher uses one style for madness and another for ordinary reality, so the two cannot meet. A similar problem occurs in Don Berry's *Trask,* for more than half its length another mountain-man novel in the realist tradition. *Trask* changes to romance-novel–as–Magical Realism and finds real power when Trask, having gone into the mountains with an Indian shaman friend, kills that friend and then carries him back down the mountains while the two of them *continue* to carry on their conversation; all this is necessary to Trask's spiritual initiation. By the novel's end, Trask has moved back into the world of everyday reality, and the prose has moved back into the rhythms of everyday realism; but in between we have perhaps a hundred pages of powerful magic. Berry sustains the magic more fully than does Fisher, but neither writer can find a way to integrate the magic into the entire book–the visionary sections are separated from the rest of the book, they belong to some dimension other than reality, we do not take them quite so seriously as the rest of the book.

Other Western novelists seem more completely and comfortably to have assimilated romance-as-Magical Realism; one such is Frank Waters, whose *The Man Who Killed the Deer* was until very recently the best Western Magical Realism yet written and is still among the very best. *The Man Who Killed the Deer* appeared in 1941, a year before *Go Down, Moses.* Like Faulkner's novel, it deals in part with a young man's attempt to fit into, or at least come to an uneasy truce with, the world around him. Though in both books an Indian deer-vision is central, Waters's novel elaborates that vision far more than does Faulkner's and makes more use of Indian metaphysics throughout. In his other novels, Waters mixes white, Indian, Chicano, and even Asian versions of reality–of time, place, identity. Waters brings a less formidable sense of esthetics to his work than did Faulkner (there are few writers of whom that could not be said), but a more elaborate sense of metaphysical possibility, and his prose style, like Faulkner's, is definitely within the tradition of prose romance/magical realism.

More recently, John Nichols's New Mexico trilogy, with its walking ghosts and supernatural events, intermingles, with no apparent discomfort, elements of traditional realism and elements of romance in a genuinely Magical Realist fashion. And if one accepts that Ken Kesey's Chief Bromden has not given up his ideas about the Combine and its machine civilization by the time he escapes, then *One Flew Over the Cuckoo's Nest* is clearly a work of Magical Realism in the tradition of the romance-novel. Rudolfo Anaya's *Bless Me, Ultima* is even more clearly and completely a fully integrated work of Magical Realism in which transformational, magical reality is also ordinary reality. The two don't simply alternate or coexist; they are one. All three writers use a single style, derived from the romance-novel, for both "magical" and "realist" elements in their work.

But something has happened to the ideas of wilderness and of frontier in this last group of books, in the work of Waters, Nichols, Kesey, and Anaya. Their characters still find themselves on one side of a frontier, hoping that frontier can protect them against the wilderness beyond, but the terms have changed. For each of these writers, industrial and commercial civilization has become the savage wilderness, and their characters wish to retreat to a more natural world. Nature, once the wilderness, has become a place of peace, safety, and harmony, where intuition, perhaps guided and corrected by reason, is a human's most important sense. And civilization has become the untamed, savage, logical but not rational, dark side of life. The power of nature, which once seemed overwhelming and beyond understanding, is still strong, still beyond complete rational understanding, but not beyond intuition. It is not an alien force to be feared, but instead one with which an individual can hope to live in harmony.

We must turn, finally, with a sense both of irony and of appropriateness, to three contemporary American Indian novelists who belong among the best the West, and the nation, have yet offered: James Welch, N. Scott Momaday, and Leslie Marmon Silko. All three tend to work within the tradition of the American romance-novel, and yet all three also work, self-consciously and deliberately, from within an American Indian literary tradition, which was old when the first Europeans landed and began talking of a frontier, a boundary between their civilization and the supposed wilderness within which that Indian literary tradition flourished.

The novels of James Welch seem at first glance the least overtly romantic, the most completely rooted in realism, of the work of these three. Yet his prose is richer than that of most realism, and the characters in *Winter in the Blood* seek, desperately (even though they're often not aware of what they seek) for some connection with the land, with the past, with both the romantic and the traditional Indian vision even as they seem to deny those visions. Home for Welch's nameless narrator is always on the Reservation, uneasy as that home may be; away from home–especially out in the small urban wilderness of Havre, Montana–anything may happen, and usually does. In *The Death of Jim Loney* the title character hasn't got even an uneasy home–but he is offered, repeatedly, what seems to be a traditional Indian vision (of a large black bird, perhaps hawk, eagle, even Thunderbird; we don't know, because he doesn't). If Loney were able to understand that dream-vision, to accept it, he might find the connection he lacks. But Loney is so separate from his own Indian past that he has no notion of what the bird might be, what it might mean; he knows of no shaman who might guide him, perhaps doesn't even know what a shaman is. Finally he chooses to take a violent path–the only path he can imagine–back across the frontier, away from the wilderness of the twentieth century, back, perhaps, to harmony. (*The Death of Jim Loney* is usually read as a pessimistic book, since it promises us Loney's death in the title and gives us that death on the last page. I believe that's a misreading: despite Loney's inability to understand and make use of the dream-vision, the book seems to say quite clearly that old-time dream-visions still occur–and that means they can be offered to others, who can respond to them in ways Loney cannot. In that respect, the book is not about a failure of Indian culture but about Loney's personal tragedy. A way does exist for Loney to save himself; his alienation and ignorance keep him from doing so.)

For Momaday's characters in *House Made of Dawn,* and especially for Abel, some violence also seems necessary as preparation for the trip back across the frontier. Abel finds himself in Los Angeles, a larger and wilder urban wilderness than any of Welch's characters can find in Montana, and very nearly dies there. A friend begins Abel's healing process by performing a half-remembered Navajo healing chant, but not until Abel returns across the frontier to his home do genuine peace and harmony become possible for him. Momaday's novel is marred by his experiments with Post-Modernist technique, his forays away from either traditional tale-telling or the romance-novel's–and the best Magical Realism's–emphasis on narrative. His *The Way to Rainy Mountain* is the far more readable book (though by no means a simple book), with its triple structure of history, legend, and memoir. Importantly, it also represents a trip across that frontier, away from urban wilderness, but without present violence; violence exists in memory, but while not forgotten, it is also not continued. In technique, the book is at once traditionally Indian and yet within the tradition of the romance-novel, particularly in its use of juxtaposition, of metaphor, of sound and rhythm, of diction and syntax.

Leslie Silko's novel, *Ceremony,* most fully integrates these two American traditions and in fact does so completely enough to lead one to the conclusion that, in their essence, the framework and techniques of the romance-novel and of traditional Indian narrative may simply be separate branches of a single tradition. Silko integrates traditional Indian beliefs and traditional narratives (some of which she invents) into the body of a Magical Realist novel, which owes its conceptual framework and its technique equally to the Indian tradition; to such Modernist practitioners of the romance-novel as Faulkner, Joyce, and Woolf; and to the earlier romance-novel of Hawthorne, Melville, and Poe.

One theme in *Ceremony* revolves around the attempt by old Betonie and his various mixed-blood allies (mixtures of Indian, Mexican, and European ancestries) to restrain the twentieth-century wilderness created by technology gone amuck; but *Ceremony* suggests both that that wilderness began with the first European settlers, and that it has no boundaries–it exists not just "out there" in the cities but also in the countryside, in Indian communities as well as elsewhere. Importantly, Silko invents a legend which suggests that Indian evil may share responsibility for this twentieth-century wilderness. For Silko, as for Hawthorne, Melville, Poe, and Faulkner, wilderness is not merely physical (though it can have physical manifestations), but psychological and metaphysical, inner as well as outer, and inescapable. The victory achieved by the end of *Ceremony* is not permanent, as the last lines of the book remind us:

> It is dead for now,
> It is dead for now,
> It is dead for now,
> It is dead for now,
>
> Sunrise,
> Accept this offering,
> Sunrise.

As we look at the work of these three American Indian writers, two things become apparent: first, that all three work within the American tradition of serious romance as practiced by Hawthorne and Faulkner, in terms both of content and of style; and second, that they work within an even older Indian tradition–a *native-American* tradition–of tale and chant whose name for romance or for Magical Realism might go something like this: the world as it is, was, and shall be. Traditional native-American literature (like Greek and Norse mythology, among others) anticipated by centuries the conceptual framework, and the technique, of the romance-novel and the Magical Realist novel. And now, a bit suddenly, twentieth-century technological Anglos must certainly feel like terribly slow learners.

The frontier has indeed been an important concept in American culture, and therefore in American literature. It has allowed Americans to deny their own inner wildernesses, to project wilderness always "out there" somewhere, safely beyond a frontier. Further, it has allowed us to imagine that only on that frontier can wilderness and the "civilized" meet and mingle. Behind the frontier, we have regarded our lives as so safe, so tame, so minimally but rigidly rational as to be fully comprehensible within the limited conceptual and technical framework of realism, even of naturalism—in the 1980s, the neonaturalism of Raymond Carver and Tom McGuane.

But the richest, and riskiest, American literary tradition has not believed in frontier so much as it has believed in wilderness and has sought the techniques which might allow the depiction of that wilderness, both external and internal. Certainly one important result has been a characteristic American prose style, with its emotional heightening of everyday diction; its loose and informal yet often complex syntax; its strong, dark rhythms and sounds; its preference for metaphor over simile and certainly over literal imagery; its lack of concern for surface coherence in the presence of deeper coherences; its juxtaposition of images and events rather than carefully, logically linked linear plot development.

The romance-novel and its contemporary incarnation, the Magical Realist novel, contain a perception of reality so different from the perceptions allowed by realism as to be a separate, an altered, a fuller version of reality. To convey that reality, such writers as Hawthorne, Faulkner, and today Waters, Silko, William Kennedy, and Toni Morrison have had to invent a style whose conceptual and technical resources were sufficient for the task: first that of the romance-novel, then that of the Magical Realist novel.

NOTES

1. Northrop Frye, *Anatomy of Criticism* (Princeton, N.J.: Princeton Univ. Press, 1957), pp. 303ff.

2. Richard Chase, *The American Novel and Its Tradition* (New York: Doubleday, 1957), p. 19.

3. For a fuller discussion of Magical Realism, see George McMurray's "Magical Realism in Spanish American Fiction" and my own "North American Magical Realism," in *Colorado State Review* 8, no. 2 (1981): 7–20, 21–30, respectively; David Young and Keith Hollaman's introduction to *Magical Realist Fiction: An Anthology* (White Plains, N.Y.: Longman, 1984).

4. For a fuller discussion of European attitudes toward wilderness, see Marjorie Nicholson's *Mountain Gloom and Mountain Glory* (Ithaca, N.Y.: Cornell Univ. Press, 1959).

5. Stith Thompson, *The Folktale* (New York: Holt, Rinehart and Winston, 1946).
6. Chase, *American Novel,* p. 19.
7. For an interesting discussion of this notion of any emerging urban wilderness, see Benton MacKaye's *The New Exploration,* published in 1928 and republished by the University of Illinois Press in 1962. MacKaye wrote as a conservationist and regional planner rather than as a literary critic.

PART TWO

Period Studies

Expanding the Canon of American Renaissance Frontier Writers: Emily Dickinson's "Glimmering Frontier"

CHARLOTTE S. McCLURE

The impact of the frontier experience on the imagination of mid-nineteenth-century Americans appears in a wide range of expressions besides those in the writings of the five American Renaissance authors discussed by F. O. Matthiessen (1941). The works of Ralph Waldo Emerson, Henry David Thoreau, Nathaniel Hawthorne, Herman Melville, and Walt Whitman impart a vision of a new city on the hill carved out of the wilderness, a spiritual American Dream. At the same time these works reveal in their frontier metaphor an imaginary line between American civilization and the wilderness which they discover can reverse the expectations of that Dream.[1] Writers of the popular or domestic romance, Romantic historians Prescott and Parkman, artists like George Catlin, autobiographers of Western frontiersmen–all reflected their consciousness and awe of the vast new land stretching beyond the settlements, and all strove to make sense of it. Emily Dickinson, one of the six major writers of the American Renaissance, has been perceived as a white-robed recluse in Amherst, hence as someone unacquainted with the frontier. However, although Dickinson has never been considered a frontier writer, she nevertheless adapted frontier metaphors and images for her purposes of poetic expression. Like the other major American writers of this period, she too imaginatively recorded a vision of self-identity in the New World by adapting a frontier mythology that shapes and criticizes images of the American Dream.

Although this pattern was obscured because Dickinson's work was not fully published until 1955, from the 1850s to 1884 she wrote poetry on themes associated with the frontier myth. Though her poetry possesses a unique lyrical sensibility, it has clear affinities with Emerson's and Hawthorne's treatment of frontier metaphor. She uses the image of the hunt ("This Consciousness that is aware," 822:1864) to describe the soul's adventure to identify itself; the image of captivity to register her struggle to accommodate her own wilderness, her divided consciousness ("It ceased to hurt me," 584:1862); and the image of a "glimmering frontier" ("Their Height in Heaven comforts not," 696:1863) beyond the settlement to represent immortality that lies on the other side of earthly life ("I am afraid to own a Body," 1090: 1866).[2] Her image of a "glimmering frontier" subsumes her lifelong poetic attempt to express her own discovered self in relation to, and opposition to, her received Puritan beliefs. She deritualized the Puritan ideas of life and death, eternity and immortality, to create a source for her poetically ambiguous and oxymoronic phrasings on the human inability to know everything. By her re-vision of the settlement's beliefs, she placed her poetic persona–a "pagan"–on a frontier where glimmerings of new relationships between the individual and God, nature and humanity, seemed possible, though still ambiguous and uncertain. As she struggled on this "glimmering frontier," she created a new vision of the human world–a "magic prison" in which the individual can fuse apparent opposites of settlement and frontier and, through playful language, seriously create a reality that goes beyond biblical explanation by accepting one's inability to understand nature and death, immortality and eternity.[3]

In her letters as well as in her poetry, interpreting a domestic and mental landscape–a somewhat different frontier from that of the other major Renaissance writers–Dickinson adapts the images of frontier myth to explore the "undiscovered continent" of the mind. In oxymoronic language, she transforms the images of the historic frontier and Puritan heritage to complement simultaneously the world created by her imaginative exploration of the "undiscovered continent." She makes her imaginative life coincide with her actual existence. As Wendy Martin observes, Dickinson was a pioneer who chose the domestic as her frontier because it provided the space and freedom to write in a Victorian milieu that did not support such creative activity for a woman.[4] Hence choosing the conditions under which she would live her life as a poet, Dickinson expresses her perceptions of nature and daily activities, the pleasures of female and male friendship, the scrutiny of her mind as it forges a personal cosmology focused on earthly life, and the superiority of sensory and emotional experience over the utilitarian, commercial concerns of the public world. Her "glimmering frontier" criticizes the visible manifestations of the American Dream while it shapes a private domestic fulfillment of poetic ambition within that Dream.

As a major poet who is a woman, Dickinson contributes to the dialectic among her literary peers about the meaning of the frontier experience and Puritan heritage, but she also explores the resonance and ambiguity of the opposition of frontier archetypes such as those of "civilization" and "wilderness." Dickinson's use of frontier imagery is consistent with the practice of major writers who were her contemporaries, as described by scholars such as Edwin Fussell in *Frontier: American Literature and the American West* (1965) and Richard Slotkin in *Regeneration through Violence: The Mythology of the American Frontier, 1600–1860* (1973) and *The Fatal Environment: The Myth of the Frontier in the Age of Industrialization, 1800–1890* (1985), which discuss the importance of frontier myth in the works of Emerson, Thoreau, Melville, Hawthorne, and Whitman. Dickinson's affinities with them as well as her differences from them in her handling of setting, hero, and narrative–the basic concepts of the frontier myth–reveal her organic transformation of the vocabulary of the myth. This comparison, supported by studies of Dickinson by Margaret Homan's *Women Writers and Poetic Identity: Dorothy Wordsworth, Emily Brontë, and Emily Dickinson* (1980), Karl Keller's *The Only Kangaroo among the Beauty: Emily Dickinson and America* (1979), and Wendy Martin's *An American Triptych: Anne Bradstreet, Emily Dickinson, Adrienne Rich* (1984),[5] illuminates how Dickinson discovers the resonance and ambiguity embedded in the opposition of an Old World ("civilization") and a New World ("nature" and "wilderness"), which also contains a transition area ("frontier").

Dickinson's use of frontier imagery illustrates how she adapted cultural mythology to express a personal vision. For the typical frontier hero moving between the civilized and wilderness areas, Dickinson substitutes an imagined persona-hero who perceives the wilderness not as a primeval forest but as the unknown territory of the psyche, who expresses her explorations as a way of poetically lighting her way through that wilderness (Martin, p. 135). As lyric poets, both Dickinson and Whitman create a persona who dramatizes the hero's destined conflict between the Old World and the New World, and who may be perceived as a new Adam and a new Eve, respectively.[6] This approach also demonstrates Dickinson's artistic rendering of the resonance and ambiguity of opposition, as she oxymoronically pairs the opposing images contained in the frontier metaphor.[7] Her poems abound with paradoxical phrases such as "Captivity is . . . liberty," "bondage as Play," "fond ambush," and "Homeless as home." She joins these opposites in order to focus on the joys of earthly life, which the "glimmering frontier" promises, even if uncertainly, rather than on the narrow after-life expectations prescribed by the Puritan settlement. The imaginative impact of the frontier myth on Dickinson's poetry comes from her pairings of oxymoronic images contained in the opposing themes of the frontier myth: civilization/nature, East/West, garden/wilderness, settler/explorer (pioneer), earth/space, and continent/country. Through these pairings, Dickinson not only reveals the fictiveness of language that produces a "magic prison" in which one cannot with certainty know or understand what nature, life, death, and eternity mean, but she also shows how the exploration of the "undiscovered continent" of the mind integrates the inherited ideas of her Puritan settlement with her own vision of the American Dream.

Like Emerson, Thoreau, Hawthorne, Melville and Whitman, Dickinson also interprets the frontier myth in terms of the basic archetypes of the frontier as David Mogen describes them elsewhere in this volume: the conflict between an Old World (civilization) and a New World (nature, wilderness, frontier); the ironic drama of the frontier hero or figure of the hunter negotiating between old and new worlds; and the narrative theme of wilderness metamorphosis – the emergence of Emerson's and Whitman's American Adam and of Hawthorne's Eve (Hester and Pearl), of Melville's Ishmael and confidence-man, of Whitman's "I" and of Dickinson's own persona-hero, who, Margaret Homans finds in her deconstructive approach to Dickinson's poetry and letters, resembles Eve.[8]

Emerson's life and writings in part suggest how the frontier, the idea of both its opening and closing, was a metaphor for his philosophic speculations on the hoped-for transcendence of human limitations, which he named the "lords of life." In his early work, especially *The American Scholar,* Emerson optimistically called for writers to work up atmosphere and to develop a distinctly American idiom to express the special energies and eloquence of an expansive frontier culture. After the death of his son Waldo in 1842, Emerson began to struggle with the ideas of freedom and fate and the contradictory lessons of experience about which he wrote in 1843 and in which he acknowledged that wisdom consists in one's living in "the middle region," what Cooper and Hawthorne would name "neutral ground," a reconciling temperate zone where the limits on the human spirit find analogy in a closing down of the frontier. Hence Emerson's writings show less torment in facing the limiting "lords of life" than did those of Hawthorne and Melville (Simonson, p. 7). While this dualism of "me and the not-me" as analogous to the soul and nature seems always to have haunted Emerson's representative mind, as Fussell points out, Emerson still envisions in his essay, "Experience" (1844), that one could die "out of nature" and be born again into the new yet unapproachable America he found in the West (p. 21). For him, the dualistic mental attitude, expressed in artful epigrams and common language and diction, was a wilderness to be apprehended. When in 1850 Dickinson received a copy of Emerson's poems and later a copy of *Representative Men,* she felt pulled or pushed, Keller (p. 154ff) and Martin (pp. 118–122) suggest, by Emerson's call for a Renaissance poet.

Like Emerson, Henry David Thoreau stayed home on "neutral ground" rather than go west and face the larger questions the figurative frontier raised (Fussell, p. 238). Thoreau internalizes the idea of the wilderness, the West, so deeply that he uses the idea both literally and figuratively. As a result, he blends realistic native materials with social criticism, moral commentary, and philosophical speculations. He makes the West a metaphor for his turning inward and becoming the "chaste hunter of the mind," while in his essay "Walking," he calls for an American mythology, claiming that "The West is preparing to add its fable to those of the East."[9] Dickinson shows some similarity to Thoreau as a loner and in his image of the hunter-poet. Staying home in Amherst, she portrays with the image of the hunt a "soul" (self), "attended by a single Hound," condemned to seek understanding of death without being able to experience and discover death's meaning simultaneously ("This Consciousness that is aware," 822:1864). Sharing with Thoreau the Puritan inward-looking self, Dickinson evokes the "undiscovered continent" of the mind (832) and the "landscape of the spirit" (*Letters* II, 315, p. 450) to explore and speculate on an alternative world to that of the Puritan cosmos.

In "Walking" (c. 1851–52) and *Walden, or Life in the Woods* (1854), Thoreau's thematic opposition between society and wild solitude (the West) appears. Slotkin explains Thoreau's role as pioneer and hunter-poet and his conception of the meaning of his experience in the woods in *Walden* as

> a systematic attempt to live by the methods and in the manner of the hunter-poet, to place himself on the frontier between society and solitude, art and nature, civilized and primitive, written record and live observation, and to submit himself absolutely to the natural necessities imposed on man by unmediated nature. (P. 526)

In the less frequently read essay, "Walking," however, Thoreau does not advocate moderation and mediation between Walden and the village but appeals to nature as the goal of his request for release and liberation of the imagination (Slotkin, p. 535). In this essay, "the longest, sustained meditation on the West in American literature," as Fussell remarks (p. 181), Thoreau uses the West as metaphor more loosely and unreasonably; he gives lip service to prevailing platitudes–e.g., that the West would some day, somehow, reconcile North and South–and he objects to the tendency of his countrymen to walk eastward while he desires to walk toward Oregon before returning home.[10] In twenty-seven poems, Dickinson uses the word "West" in its traditional connotations of death, immortality, and compass direction; playfully she makes "West" exchange places with "East" (meaning life and sovereignty), which then becomes death, immortality, or passion. In her ambiguous connotations for these common images of direction, place, and conditions of life or death, Dickinson avoids the clichés of expression that Thoreau, awakened to the ironic reversals in the frontier metaphor, succumbed to in his essay on the West.

While probing the inward Puritan soul, Nathaniel Hawthorne conceived of himself as a Western writer, emphatically believing, Fussell observes, that in the West was the meaning of America which had to be imagined (pp. 78, 93). In *The Scarlet Letter,* Hawthorne uses the frontier as the meeting place, the neutral ground, of the East (the Old World, the past) and the West (the New World, the future). Exploring this dualistic view of reality, which also influenced Dickinson's imagination, Hawthorne sensed, as Fussell further explains, that the frontier metaphor could resolve the inescapable American dualism of society and self, of "Manifest Destiny versus inferiority complex" (pp. 125–26). In other words, on Hawthorne's frontier, the neutral ground between the Puritan settlement and the wilderness, the American mind could test whether it was creating its own destiny with nature or was being formed by its experience with the older civilization's idea of a Puritan city on the hill that destroyed nature. An early instance of the possible resolution of the dualism occurs in Hawthorne's repudiation of Cotton Mather's version of the story of Hannah Dustin in *Western Magazine,* which he edited from March to August 1836. In his own version of Dustin's captivity by and escape from the Indians, Hawthorne took a pro-Indian view (nature) in a setting that was more west than northeast because, as both Slotkin and Leslie Fiedler in *The Return of Vanishing American* (1968) claim, he saw violence and cruelty in the older New England society (civilization) (Slotkin, pp. 89–90, 514). Again, Hawthorne criticizes the idea of the city that destroys nature. In a more familiar metaphor of resolution, the forest, with which Hester Prynne is frequently identified, represents Hawthorne's neutral territory, the meeting point between the facts of American history, particularly of the Puritan seventeenth century, and the American mind newly conscious of other sources of authority. In this meeting of past and present in Hawthorne's narrative, the forest, or frontier, is an inward and outward place, dark and light, for attempted reconciliation of opposites; it is a place which Dickinson transforms lyrically into an equally ambiguous "glimmering frontier" and "undiscovered continent" of the mind. Because both Hawthorne and Dickinson explore ambiguity, Keller says (pp. 127–31), both utilize the oxymoron as the rhetorical form in their writings to "realize in their art an ineffable complexity–[nothing is certain, everything is possible]–and in written form [to represent] a struggle with materials without victory" (p. 129).

Hawthorne apparently arrived at this metaphor of neutral territory through his 1830s tales in which he both criticized and participated in the Puritan myth of the wilderness (Slotkin, p. 477). In "Young Goodman Brown," the wilderness plays the role that Cotton Mather feared it would play–the place where the devil would disclose to Brown the dark impulses and suspicions he had suppressed and thus teach him the hollowness of civilization. In the early 1850s, after Hawthorne's twenty-year literary treatment of the frontier metaphor, the frontier physically vanished, and Hawthorne, still uncertain about the darkness in the wilderness and in the hearts of men (Fussell, p. 131), withdrew from his fictional consideration of the West as a reconciliation of opposites.

In his 1850 review of Hawthorne's *Mosses from an Old Manse* in *Literary World,* Herman Melville identified a quality of the Americanness of American literature when he called on his countrymen to acknowledge Hawthorne as "the American, who up to the present day has evinced, in literature, the largest brain with the largest heart" and "a power of blackness" derived from the appeal of the Puritan sense of depravity and original sin. As a writer himself, Melville was also concerned with truth that had the "power of blackness." How was Melville to narrate the possibilities in the West of a new democratic cosmopolitan order that would overcome the inherent flaws that men bring to society? Melville tried several literary inspirations, based on metaphors of the frontier myth: a contrast between civilization and savagery, a hunting story, and an attempted comic masquerade that was close to apocalyptic satire and that contained the unique American "metamorphic" hero (the hero with multiple roles). A sea traveler in his early years and a writer influenced by Richard H. Dana, Jr.'s *Two Years before the Mast* (1840), Melville early identified the Western ocean he traveled with the American West and life in the wilderness (containing unspoiled landscape, Indians, settlers, and hunters) with truth. His first three novels, *Typee, Omoo,* and *Mardi,* contrast savage life and civilization, the first two looking at savage life from a highly civilized point of view, the third looking at a civilization from a presumed native point of view. This shifting point of view reveals his uncertainty about the meaning of his Puritan heritage, but it also provides a device for narrative viewing from the circumference rather than from the center, a position that Dickinson also poetically practices as she examines her fading Calvinistic-derived beliefs. *Moby-Dick, or The Whale* (1851) basically is a hunting story, and regardless of its ostensible locale, as Fussell acknowledges, a story about the West (pp. 258–59). The myth of the hunter, as it developed in America, has centered on the theme of initiation into a new life, a new world, imagined variously as unifying the spirit of the white man with that of the Indian wilderness or as a boy's initiation into the mysteries and skills of natural powers (Slotkin, pp. 152, 538). Ishmael takes a Daniel Boone approach to adventure, while Captain Ahab is both Calvinistic hunter and Quaker as they pursue Moby-Dick, whose appearance resembles that of the buffalo and the prairie. Dickinson's persona also is a quester on the "undiscovered continent" of the mind, inviting the mysteries of a sensory and emotional experience in nature hitherto masked by the Puritan civilization's precepts.

Although in *Moby-Dick* Melville seemed to understand America's westward destiny, thereafter, like Hawthorne, he lost confidence in his vision. *The Confidence-Man* (1857), in which he employs the metaphor of the Mississippi River and the image of the Indian hater, displays his loss of confidence in the nation and, in Fussell's estimate, signals the moment in American literary history when the values optimistically attributed to the Western frontier were suddenly inverted and harmony and reconciliation were revealed to be chaos and nightmare (Fussell, p. 287). Melville presents the consciousness of the nation just before the Civil War by analyzing the most accomplished mask of the confidence man–Herman Melville himself–who narrates at every turn a shrewd attack upon American intellectual laziness, habits of thought, and inclinations. Hawthorne's and Melville's re-examination of their Puritan heritage led them to discover, as did Dickinson, the inaccuracy of the Puritan structure of earthly and heavenly life and of its attempted secular replacement, Transcendentalism. Their frontier metaphor failing them also, they preferred uncertainty, a position of finiteness, which in Dickinson's lyric becomes "I'm finite, I cant see."

In "The Poet" (*Essays: Second Series,* 1844), Emerson described the poet as a democratic, representative man who taps hidden spiritual and imaginative resources that lead to great change in the perception of things and who can bring about the revolution in consciousness he called for in *Nature.* A little over a decade after "The Poet" was published, Walt Whitman was inspired by this Emersonian hope, drew on its language in writing the preface to the first edition of *Leaves of Grass,* and offered poetry which Emerson immediately recognized as the American revelation of the new "unapproachable West" he had awaited. Of course, Whitman differs from Thoreau, Hawthorne, and Melville as well as Dickinson. He espouses a harmony with nature in free verse that answers Crevecoeur's question–"What, then, is the American, this new man?"–in ways that the earlier writers' occasional estrangement from their environment could not allow them to envision. Unlike Thoreau's epic *Walden* or Melville's epic *Moby-Dick,* Whitman's modern and personal, yet traditionally romantic, epic, "Song of Myself," introduces a hero, or heroic spirit, that fits the present into the future, an Adamic hero, who, according to Roy H. Pearce in *The Continuity of American Poetry* (1961), will be the poet who can shape the way things are and will become. In "The Sleepers," Whitman moves to the deeper, more troubled levels that bothered Hawthorne and Melville. By using the genre of the "inward journey" that goes back to the Puritan habit of self-inquiry, Whitman suggests an exploration of the frontier that is both a descent into the unconscious (where in modern terms the ego or conscious self confronts the wild energies of the id) and a resulting psychic recovery and self-assurance that can lead to reconciliation of the parts of the broken world at large. However, just as Hawthorne's and Melville's optimistic visions of man and the frontier disappeared, so also did Whitman's. In subsequent editions of *Leaves of Grass,* Whitman sees the inward "journey ever continued"[11] ("Poem of the Road," 1856), but he also expresses failure, disillusion, and despair because he and his America had never been educated to difficult perceptions. In "Son of the Open Road" (1856, 1881), he wrote, "I do not offer the old smooth prizes, but offer rough new prizes."[12] Like Melville, he brooded on the mystery and futility of it all, as in "Facing West from California Shores" (1860, 1867), where he is "inquiring, tireless, seeking what is yet unfound" and ponders "(But where is what I started for so long ago? / And why is it yet unfound?)."[13] In this poem, continuing to look west to India where the idea of the birth of civilization lies, Whitman along with Thoreau, demonstrates that the idea of the West is more important than the Western expanse itself.

Whitman extricated himself somewhat from this frustration by seeing the vision of the age-old westward movement of humanity as only an episode in the essential journey toward self-definition, self-knowledge, and confrontation with actual horrors and discontinuities of life in the so-called New World. In *Democratic Vistas* (1870), Whitman returned to a kind of journalism, becoming the pioneer again, exploring critically as well as any later writer the connections among American literature, American civilization, and their background realities. Examining how with platitudes and repetition the aging Whitman oscillated between the image of the West as a reconciler of opposites and his scorn of American materialistic, hence soulless, expansion after the Civil War, readers recognize the ironic reversal of the values in the American Dream, the American not knowing for sure whether he can shape his destiny and nation or is being shaped by an irrevocable past.

Like Hawthorne and Melville, Emily Dickinson tried to make sense of her Puritan heritage. Paradoxically, she used this heritage, which encouraged individual salvation and turning inward for a private life, to create a radical, liberating, and authoritative life as a woman and a poet along the side of the traditional life of a woman residing at home; this was a western-type of transformation of the expected role of an American woman in the American Dream. While in the 1860s Whitman refined the romantic poetic ritual that transformed man into a new personality, a new Adam, hoping he was taking part in a cosmic design and helping to shape and fulfill it, Dickinson, only eleven years younger, took Eve's position in the use of language to create a reality different from that of Adam (Homans, pp. 167–71). Dickinson declared she had never read Whitman's book "but was told he was disgraceful" (Dickinson in Keller, p. 252). She realistically sided with Melville in forecasting the closing of the frontier and the irrelevance of the moral, social, and historic ideas associated with it (Simonson, p. 13). Though like Thoreau and Emerson she stayed at home in New England, through her Amherst windows she observed and explored distances as expansive as those Melville covered. She expressed her sense of the closed frontier in ambiguous, oxymoronic language–"I'm finite–I cant see" (696)–as a recognition that language is fictive and that understanding the human inability to grasp everything to be known puts humanity in a "magic prison" (*Letters,* III, 976, pp. 866–67). Although her poems and letters contain images of security found in home, garden, friendship, and spiritual comfort as well as images of awesome power in the Puritan definition of security, like Hawthorne she discovered the uncertainty principle in the ironic contradictions of the frontier myth. To express her understanding of reality as an ambiguous "glimmering frontier" where simultaneous opposites fuse, she creates images and a symbolic vocabulary that articulates, examines and criticizes American beliefs and values.

To convey her consciousness of this "glimmering frontier" that keeps her from knowing anything with certainty, Dickinson imagines contrapuntal worlds and oxymoronic language to fit them. She uses the frontier as a metaphor for the historical fact of America ("Trust in the Unexpected," 555), for a world beyond this world ("This World is not Conclusion," 501), and for exploration of the "undiscovered continent" of the mind ("Soto! Explore Thyself!" 832). She clusters familiar images around the metaphoric frontier–settler, wilderness, west, land (landscape), earth, and country–in order to transform the words of the Puritan settlement for security–God, heaven, hell, sin, redemption, immortality. Using her own images, she creates contrapuntal worlds that exist simultaneously. She pairs explorer with settler, east with west, garden with wilderness, sea with land (landscape), heaven or space with earth, and continent with country.[14] To watch what Dickinson does with these images of her "glimmering frontier" is to observe how a "New Englandly" (285:1861) spiritualized poet re-imagines her settlement's beliefs. She sets up a dialectical medium for debate from her unique perspective, but she also neutralizes the debate by offering a world of earthly sensation and feeling simultaneously with the Puritan after-world that she criticizes.

In "Their Hight in Heaven comforts not" (696:1863) and "Soto! Explore Thyself!" (832:1864), Emily Dickinson describes her frontier.

Their Hight in Heaven comforts not–
Their Glory–nought to me–
'Twas best imperfect–as it was–
I'm finite–I cant see–

The House of Supposition–
The Glimmering Frontier that
Skirts the Acres of Perhaps–
To Me–shows insecure–

The Wealth I had—contented me—
If 'twas a meaner size—
Then I had counted it until
It pleased my narrow Eyes—

Better than larger values—
That show however true—
This timid life of Evidence
Keeps pleading—"I dont know." (696)

Her frontier lies between settlement, with its inherited suppositions about life, death, and eternity, and unsettled and even unknown lands and states of mind beyond ("The Acres of Perhaps") toward which her speaker's self journeys. "I'm finite—I cant see," she exclaims when considering, on the basis of "timid Evidence," whether the Puritan belief—the public doctrine of heaven and immortality—is true. Yet as she is eager to know (to argue for personal experience as a test of the received suppositions), she speculates that she must compare the "Wealth" of her settlement life with a "glimmering" or faintly seen frontier that only "perhaps" offers heaven or eternity, the spiritual American Dream. She considers that she does not know the truth in either of the simultaneously existing worlds, that neither the Old World of Puritan precepts nor her imagined possible New World shows her security.

In "Soto! Explore Thyself!" Dickinson names the place, the frontier, to be explored.

Soto! Explore Thyself!
Therein thyself shalt find
The "Undiscovered Continent"—
No Settler had the Mind. (832)

She calls the place the "Undiscovered Continent," the mind, which the comfortable settler, accepting a self identified by other's supposition, did not have the mind or the desire to explore. The poem's exhortation to Hernando de Soto, the Spanish discoverer of the Mississippi River in 1541, emphasizes the necessity to leave the familiar, the settlement, in order to explore unknown space, both inner and outer (*Letters* II, 456, p. 515).[15] Here she adds a new dimension to the dichotomy between the Old World and the New World, joining an Outer World prescribed by inherited beliefs with an Inner World that is capable of defining itself. This exhortation to explore is echoed in a later poem—"The Heart Is the Capital of the Mind" (1354)—a centennial poem of 1876, in which she calls upon this "ecstatic Nation" to "Seek—it is Yourself."

The Heart is the Capital of the Mind—
The Mind is a Single State—

The Heart and the Mind together make
A single Continent–

One–is the Population–
Numerous enough–
This ecstatic Nation
Seek–it is Yourself. (1354)

It is possible to read the poem as exhortation to the nation as well as to the "ecstatic" individual self to examine the issues of power, struggle, or unity within the territory of the self, as Suzanne Juhasz suggests.[16] In contrast, Keller observes Dickinson's refusal to identify the self with America as millenarian, noting that she follows early Emerson in putting a self in place of the nation (Keller, p. 101). Perceiving new dimensions, or "glimmerings," in the inner–outer frontier she explores, Dickinson calls forth multiple meanings and demonstrates, as Juhasz believes, that her inward exploration is poetic strategy, not a retreat from reality or experience (Juhasz, p. 4).

All five of F. O. Matthiessen's American Renaissance writers used "West" as a literal place as well as a figurative frontier or wilderness that opposes civilization. Emily Dickinson employs "West" not only as the place and its opposite but also as the west associated with the color red or purple, with sunset, night, and direction. However, she also gives "west" connotations of death (550:1862) and eternity (336) and contrasts it with "east," the source of the sun and life, identified with the color yellow (783:1863). To keep this scheme from seeming too neat as evidence of spiritual or cosmic things, she equates east with west (871:1864) or reverses these attitudes (1032:1865) just frequently enough to keep the explorer's mind and discoveries, not the settler's, under scrutiny.[17]

In the following poem, the effect of her mental exercise, probing for evidence of the truth of the received suppositions, places the speaker in a new position to examine and question them.

Behind Me–dips Eternity–
Before Me–Immortality–
Myself–the Term between–
Death but the Drift of Eastern Gray,
Dissolving into Dawn away,
Before the West begin–

'Tis Kingdoms–afterwards–they say
In perfect–pauseless Monarchy–
Whose Prince–is Son of None–
Himself–His Dateless Dynasty–
Himself–Himself diversify–
In Duplicate divine–

'Tis miracle before Me–then–
'Tis Miracle behind–between–
A Crescent in the Sea–
With Midnight to the North of Her–
And Midnight to the South of Her–
And Maelstrom–in the Sky– (721)

Here the poet confronts the enormous themes of death, immortality, and eternity, preached from Puritan pulpits, and tries unsuccessfully to understand them through a consciousness that she imagines stands between a heavenly vision (settlement, Old World) and earthly experience (wilderness, New World) of them. Here her creation of simultaneous worlds does not remove her uncertainty about what to believe. The second stanza reports, not on the precise nature of Christ's princely rule in the heavenly kingdom, but on what the settlement's rumor and tradition have said about it. The force of the poem's emotional impact comes from the almost violent shift in the third stanza from the twice-repeated "Miracle" to the twice-repeated "Midnight." As the heavenly vision recedes, consciousness (her frontier in this poem) edges back to earthly experience. Seen from within, the earthly experience seems a chaos, a maelstrom, that exists between two domains that are now dark as midnight, hence not understood.

For Emily Dickinson, wilderness is an image indicating an internal rather than an external place of chaos ("It would never be common," 430:1862; "The Auctioneer of Parting," 1612:1884); confusion ("Like eyes that looked on," 458:1862); "Had I not seen the sun," 1233:1872); and the unknown ("From us she wandered now," 890:1864; "There is a finished feeling," 856:1864). Her wilderness, Martin remarks (p. 135), is not a primeval forest but her own psyche. The chaotic, confusing, and unknown conditions of wilderness, often expressed with intense emotion, result from the loss of loved ones or from conflict within herself and between others and herself. She uses "wilderness" most frequently in poems written in 1862, the year of personal crisis but also one of great poetic productivity. The image "wilderness" in "It ceased to hurt me" (584) connotes a past state of anguish that slowly ceases to cause pain; in "It would never be common" (430), she replaces her brocade gown that earlier she wore to dower with her "gold attentions" with a sackcloth that expresses her humility; and in "Like Eyes that looked on Wastes" (458), a night is a "steady wilderness diversified." She offers escapes from the wilderness, caused by human failure, in her library of "Kinsmen of the Shelf" (604) and in the "Stimulus of an Hermetic Mind" (711:1863).[18] In these poems as well as in later ones with wilderness images (1233, 1612), Dickinson recognizes that her desire to accept death and eternity and her simultaneous skepticism concerning the received suppositions about them require each other in order to exist. As the evidence of this mode of thinking makes her conclude "Therefore–We perish–tho' We Reign" (458), she rejects the either-or thinking of the suppositions of the settlement for the awe of paradoxical understanding derived from intertwining suppositions and imagining the unknown.

Offsetting the painful confusion of a wilderness, she often imagines a garden where she may gain some control over the contradictions of life and death. In this image Emily Dickinson unwittingly expresses the behavior of pioneer women who dealt with the strangeness of the frontier by planting gardens that reminded them of the places they had left.[19] In "For this–accepted breath" (195:1860), Dickinson views her life as a crown given by God that competes with death ("frost"). As long as she has this bestowed crown, she believes

> No Wilderness can be where this attendeth me–
> No Desert noon–No fear of frost to come–
> Haunt the perennial bloom–

In other garden poems of the critical years 1862–1864 (339, 484, 500, 631, 944), nature comforts, but still the garden suffers separation from life by frost. Hence wilderness and garden are intertwined but only faintly controlled.

The frontier, imagined as the land (line) beyond the settlement and as the sea stretching beyond the horizon, beckons literary adventurers like Thoreau, the "chaste hunter of the mind,"[20] and Dickinson, explorer of the "Undiscovered Continent," who also names her inward journey the "Landscape of the Spirit" (*Letters* II, 315, p. 450). She makes the land and sea, surfaces over which journeys are taken, stand for eternity and causes each to examine the other's perspective on eternity. Out of this juxtaposition of perspectives, she achieves a kind of delight or ecstasy. In "Once More, my now bewildered Dove" (48:1858), the poem's speaker, like Noah and Columbus, both of whom sent out a questing dove to find land, discovers in their success the courage to believe in the possibility of eternity. Though in Dickinson's poems the sea stands for eternity more often than does land, here the speaker stands on the sea of eternity questing for land as eternity. In contrast, in "Exultation is the going" (76:1859), she is the exultant "inland soul" going "Past the houses–past the headlands– / Into deep Eternity–." Continuing to play with simultaneous opposites in "It might be lonelier" (405:1862), the speaker, musing that her crowded little room could be lonelier if she did not know loneliness, imagines herself aboard a ship, feeling it might be easier to fail "with land in sight" than to gain it and "To perish–of Delight." Frequently Dickinson sees loss–gain and delight–pain as coexisting oppositions whenever she quests for clearer understanding.

Other paired images of the quest for experience, by which to understand the Old World suppositions and the potential though the "glimmering" New World frontier, are those of earth seen as a "traffic frontier" compared with the Puritan heaven ("Not that he goes we love him more," 1435:1878) or Eden (211:1860; 1657, n.d.), and those of heaven seen as paradise (215:1860; 1069: 1866). In part this questioning reflects a theological testing of settlement words and a probing of the idea of America as an Edenic second chance for humankind. Dickinson speculates on these spiritual matters as a different way of knowing from experience what the Puritan spiritual position explains. Using these images, she repeats her ploy of looking at one image on the ground of another. She even introduces outer space for extraterrestrial journeying. In "It was a quiet way" (1053:c.1865), she mentally explores both earth and heaven (eternity) from different perspectives in a balloon. In "I saw no way" (378:1862), seeking ultimate experience in the mind, the explorer stands on earth, shut out or trapped by a conventionally "stitched" heaven; to compensate for her alienation, her fluid, expanding brain turns her inside out. In this position the speaker touches the universe and then the "Circumference," Dickinson's preferred viewing point, which Albert Gelpi interprets as "the farthest boundary of human experience."[21] More concretely, Dickinson describes another imagined extraterrestrial experience. She magnifies her self, big as the universe; the stars are about her head and the sea about her feet. From this exaggeration, she learns the precarious "Gait / Some call Experience" ("I Stepped from Plank to Plank," 875:1864). In spite of her experimentation with varied viewpoints and oxymoronic pairings, the poet's speaker never reaches certainty about anything.

In a further pairing of oxymoronic images of space, Emily Dickinson joins country and continent with her inner self. To show that she was conscious of her country–its politics, the westward movement, and similar events,[22] though she refers to America only three times in her poetry–she prefers to see her inner self as country (nation) and continent to be explored by herself and then identified. In *The Puritan Origins of the American Self* (1975), Sacvan Bercovitch explains that Dickinson rejects Cotton Mather's Puritan identity of an American as a saint-in-service-of-national destiny.[23] She scoffs at public duty ("My Country calleth me," 3:1852); at patriotic attention to parades and flags ("To fight aloud," 126:1859); and at America, which to her is a figment of the imagination that, like a circus tent, dissolves and retreats ("I've known a Heaven, like a tent," 243:1861). In another mood, in her "letter to the World / That never wrote" to her (441:1862), she addresses the recipients as "Sweet–countrymen" because, she claims, she loves them. In a poem of 1881 that could have been written for a patriotic occasion, she accepts the American past in order to save it.

My country need not change her gown,
Her triple suit as sweet
As when 'twas cut at Lexington,
And first pronounced "a fit." (1511)

On the individual level, she prefers to make her non-Puritan self stand for the nation, a self somewhat like Emerson's imperial self. In "The Heart is the Capital of the Mind," Dickinson's language is political; she treats the issue of power, the struggle for unity within herself, her own frontier. Juhasz describes the "single Continent" as made up of various landscapes and climates, all of which are Dickinson, even as she is all of its inhabitants (p. 25). In this image, Dickinson portrays her most paradoxical persona–the pagan believer–and displays the richness that comes from her poetic exploration of the inner life. Margaret Homans points out that because lyric poetry lacks the novel's representational framework of character and plot, Emily Dickinson had to imaginatively invent and use language to depict a new type of inquiring self and manner of living that was shaped by, but also shaped, the frontier myth within the American Dream (p. 6).

Only the complete publication of Emily Dickinson's poetry in 1955, one hundred years after the American Renaissance described by Matthiessen,[24] and of the facsimile edited by R. W. Franklin (1981) fully reveals her "glimmering" transformation of several aspects of frontier myth. Though her wilderness is less a primeval forest than the unknown landscape of her psyche, she reveals the effect of the Puritan heritage on herself and, by extrapolation, on others. She experienced captivity when as artist she tried to create a world apart from God and when as woman she asserted herself against nineteenth-century proscriptions of womanhood.[25] Like Ralph Waldo Emerson and Margaret Fuller, who called for a Eurydice to sing of the female half of "the idea of man,"[26] Dickinson in effect looked toward future poets to discover important truths, a higher consciousness, and a new perception of things as well as of woman. As Karl Keller points out, Stephen Crane, Amy Lowell, Carl Sandburg, Hart Crane, William Carlos Williams, and Robert Frost have recognized Dickinson's achievement (pp. 294–326); and Adrienne Rich[27] and Denise Levertov acknowledge her influence.[28]

Emily Dickinson's "glimmering frontier" serves as her way of clarifying and integrating the Puritan experience into the present and future. Her frontier image simultaneously measures her inherited faith and the poetic inventions of her own "pagan" mind on the same questions of life and death, eternity and immortality. Wendy Martin believes that her poems reshape the Puritan ideal of the city on the hill into a vision of Earth (not Heaven) as Paradise, and on this paradisal earth she was a pioneer because she refused to dilute the intensity of her emotions and sensory responses by accepting the Old World plan (p. 81). Yet Dickinson was well aware of the uncertainties expressed by her "glimmering frontier" and "magic prison."[29] This poetic admonition on the fictiveness of language–on thinking that one can understand everything by organizing spiritual beliefs or by creating literary and historical figures of speech to explain the quest for self and national identity, nature and civilization–lies at the heart of her "letter to the World" that in her lifetime no one heard, but which predicted that ambiguity and uncertainty would prevail in the modern world.

NOTES

1. Edwin Fussell, *Frontier: American Literature and the American West* (Princeton, N.J.: Princeton Univ. Press, 1965), pp. 16–17.

Abundant critical evaluation of the impact of the frontier experience on mid-nineteenth century American thought and literature exists: Michael H. Cowan, *City of the West: Emerson, America and Urban Metaphor* (New Haven, Conn.: Yale Univ. Press, 1967); Christopher Durer et al., eds., *American Renaissance and American West* (Laramie: Univ. of Wyoming, 1982); Leslie A. Fiedler, *Love and Death in the American Novel* (New York: Criterion Books, 1961); Fiedler, *The Return of the Vanishing American* (New York: Stein and Day, 1968); Edward Halsey Foster, *The Civilized Wilderness: Backgrounds to American Romantic Literature, 1817–1860* (New York: Free Press, 1975); Sam B. Girgus, *The American Self: Myth, Ideology, and Popular Culture* (Albuquerque: Univ. of New Mexico Press, 1981); Kristin Herzog, *Women, Ethics, and Exotics: Images of Power in Mid-Nineteenth-Century American Fiction* (Knoxville: Univ. of Tennessee Press, 1983); F. O. Matthiessen, *American Renaissance: Art and Expression in the Age of Emerson and Whitman* (New York: Oxford Univ. Press, 1941); Roderick Nash, *Wilderness and the American Mind,* 3rd ed. (New Haven, Conn.: Yale Univ. Press, 1967); Museum of Fine Arts Boston, *Frontier America: The Far West* (Boston: Museum of Fine Arts, 1975); James Robertson, *American Myth, American Reality* (New York: Hill and Wang, 1980); Harold P. Simonson, *The Closed Frontier: Studies in American Literary Tragedy* (New York: Holt, Rinehart and Winston, 1970); Richard Slotkin, *The Fatal Environment: The Myth of the Frontier in the Age of Industrialization, 1800–1890* (New York: Atheneum, 1985); Slotkin, *Regeneration through Violence: The Mythology of the American Frontier, 1600–1800* (Middletown, Conn.: Wesleyan Univ. Press, 1973); Larzer Ziff, *Literary Democracy: The Declaration of Cultural Independence in America* (New York: Viking Press, 1981). Subsequent references in the text are to these editions.

2. Texts of the poems cited are from *The Complete Poems of Emily Dickinson,* ed. Thomas H. Johnson (Boston: Little, Brown, 1960). The number of the poem and the year of its writing follow the reference or citation. Although *The Manuscript Books of Emily Dickinson,* edited by R. W. Franklin (2 vols., Cambridge, Mass.: Belknap Press, Harvard Univ. Press, 1981) restore the original order through facsimile reproduction, altering the sequence and dating of some poems in Johnson's 1955 chronology, the facsimiles do not change the date or cause a different interpretation of the poems referred to in the essay. References to Dickinson's letters are from *The Letters of Emily Dickinson,* 3 vols., ed. Thomas H. Johnson and Theodora Ward (Cambridge, Mass.: Belknap Press, Harvard Univ. Press, 1958). The volume, the number of the letter, and the page will follow the reference or citation to the letters.

3. Karl Keller, *The Only Kangaroo among the Beauty: Emily Dickinson and America* (Baltimore: Johns Hopkins Univ. Press, 1979), 131–32.

4. Wendy Martin, *An American Triptych: Anne Bradstreet, Emily Dickinson, Adrienne Rich* (Chapel Hill: Univ. of North Carolina Press, 1984), pp. 80–81.

5. Margaret Homans, *Women Writers and Poetic Identity: Dorothy Wordsworth, Emily Brontë, and Emily Dickinson* (Princeton, N.J.: Princeton Univ. Press, 1980).

6. See ibid., pp. 167–73. Homans deconstructs Dickinson's poetry and letters to identify the poet's taking the role of Eve, who according to the Bible did not die.

7. Keller's list, referred to by Martin (p. 82) includes "sumptuous solitude," "reward of anguish," and "Safe despair" (pp. 133–34) as well as those mentioned in this text.

8. See Homans, pp. 29–33, 167–77.

9. Quoted in Robert D. Richardson, *Myth and Literature in the American Renaissance* (Bloomington: Indiana Univ. Press, 1978), p. 33.

10. Thoreau, "Walking," in *Thoreau: The Major Essays,* ed. Jeffrey Duncan (New York: E. P. Dutton, 1972), p. 204.

11. Walt Whitman, *Leaves of Grass,* ed. Sculley Bradley and Harold W. Blodgett (New York: W. W. Norton, 1973), pp. 149–59.

12. Ibid., p. 155.

13. Ibid., p. 110–11.

14. In *A Concordance to the Poems of Emily Dickinson,* ed. S. P. Rosenbaum (Ithaca, N.Y.: Cornell Univ. Press, 1964), the following words and varied forms of them are cited as occurring in her poems: frontier, 4; settler, 3; explorer, 4; wilderness, 14; garden, 19; west, 27; east, 33; land, 30 (landscape, 11); sea(s), 133; earth, 57; heaven, 177, or space, 11; country, 14; continent, 8.

15. Compare Dickinson's letter 456 to Susan Gilbert Dickinson, about March 1876 in *The Letters of Emily Dickinson* (II, p. 551), in which Emily thanks Susan for a copy of a book by George Eliot, of whom she writes: "She is the Lane to the Indes, Columbus was looking for." In *Walden* Thoreau exhorts his readers to "Explore thyself. Herein are demanded the eye and nerve" (quoted in Fussell, p. 229).

16. Suzanne Juhasz, *The Undiscovered Continent: Emily Dickinson and the Space of the Mind* (Bloomington: Indiana Univ. Press, 1983), p. 24. All subsequent references in the text are to this edition.

17. Dickinson's letters connect incidents in her life with attitudes toward the West. Writing to a school friend teaching in Willoughby, Ohio, on March 23, 1852, Emily Dickinson exhorted the "folks at the West to be kind to her friend for Emily's sake" (*Letters,* I, 81, p. 189). When her family moved to a different house in Amherst, Emily Dickinson wrote to Mrs. J. G. Holland about January 20, 1856, concerning the effect of moving. "It is a kind of gone-to-Kansas feeling, and if I sat in a long wagon, with my family tied behind, I should suppose without doubt I was a part of immigrants" (*Letters,* II, 182, p. 324). In a letter in early 1862, recipient unknown, Emily Dickinson apologized for offending someone, perhaps because "her odd-Backwoodsman . . . ways . . . teased his finer nature" (*Letters,* II, 248, p. 391).

18. In a letter to her sister Lavinia from Cambridge, July 1864, Emily Dickinson described being in Cambridge for eye treatment under the care of a physician as being in a prison and a wilderness, yet she found "friends in the wilderness" (*Letters,* II, 293, 432–33).

19. See Annette Kolodny, *The Lay of the Land: Metaphor as Experience and History in American Life and Letters, 1630–1860* (Chapel Hill: Univ. of North Carolina Press, 1975).

20. See Fussell, pp. 191, 211, 229, and Slotkin, *Regeneration through Violence,* pp. 520–21, 524.

21. Albert Gelpi, *Emily Dickinson: The Mind of the Poet* (New York: W. W. Norton, 1965), p. 122.

22. In poem 3, "St. Valentine–'52," Dickinson facetiously says her country bids her go to the legislature, while in a letter (94) to Susan Gilbert, June 11, 1852, she complains: "Why cant I be a Delegate to the great Whig Convention in Baltimore, June 16, 1852–dont I know all about Daniel Webster, and the Tariff, and the Law?" (*Letters,* I, p. 212). Her father, Edward Dickinson, was a delegate to the convention.

23. Sacvan Bercovitch, *The Puritan Origins of the American Self* (New Haven, Conn.: Yale Univ. Press, 1975).

24. F. O. Matthiessen, *American Renaissance: Art and Experience in the Age of Emerson and Whitman* (London and New York: Oxford Univ. Press, 1941) deals with the frontier as Emerson, Thoreau, and Melville related it to the common man (pp. 631–36). Matthiessen's belles-lettres aesthetic had to omit the "other" American Renaissance, which suggests a similar kind of America's coming to first maturity and which is portrayed by women, blacks, and artists of the West. Three times Matthiessen compares Dickinson's poetry with the writings of Emerson and Melville. He favorably related Dickinson's "Our private theater is ourselves" to Emerson's journal passages that praised an individual's turning upon his own inner life as a matter for exuberance, not for resignation (p. 8). Later he claims Emerson's poetry lacks the tension of the struggle between good and evil of the metaphysical poets, a tension which Dickinson's poems possess, but then adds that "she does not have any of [Emerson's] range as a social critic" (p. 115). Matthiessen makes a similar claim of Dickinson's narrowness when he compares Melville's redefining of American ideas of madness and sanity ("man's insanity is heaven's sense") to Dickinson's "Much madness is divinest sense / To a discerning eye." While Melville and Dickinson present almost the same idea, Matthiessen interprets Dickinson's treatment of madness as less persuasive because "her own drama, however intense, remained personal and lyric." Matthiessen wrote: "Melville's greater horizon of experience, the vigorous thrust of his mind, and the strength of his passion carried him . . . into wider and more dangerous waters" (p. 434). While here Matthiessen interprets Melville's experience as wider and more penetrating than Dickinson's, he overlooks the different ways that Dickinson explored a "glimmering frontier" beyond her Amherst settlement.

25. Sandra Gilbert, "The Wayward Nun beneath the Hill: Emily Dickinson and the Mysteries of Womanhood," *Feminist Critics Read Emily Dickinson,* ed. Suzanne Juhasz (Bloomington: Indiana Univ. Press, 1983), p. 23.

26. Margaret Fuller, *Woman in the Nineteenth Century* (New York: W. W. Norton, 1971), pp. 23–24.

27. Adrienne Rich, *On Lies, Secrets, and Silences* (New York: W. W. Norton, 1979), p. 158.

28. Although Hyatt H. Waggoner, *American Poets from the Puritans to the Present,* 3rd ed. (Boston: Houghton Mifflin, 1968), p. 621, does not directly compare Denise Levertov and Emily Dickinson as poets, his report of Levertov's description of the state of the poet when writing strongly echoes Dickinson's "ecstasy": "The 'state in which poems get written . . . may be called' a heightened consciousness, but it's not a heightening of the intellect. It's a heightening of the emotions and of sensuous perception."

29. Dickinson uses the phrase, "a magic prison," in a letter to Helen Hunt Jackson in which she tries to define her "paganism," a description of herself as one who wants to believe in a supreme being but who cannot accept the received tenets of that being. In this letter (*Letters,* III, 976, pp. 866–67), Dickinson tells her friend Helen Hunt Jackson that though she wants to pray for her recovery from a broken foot, "I am but a Pagan"; not knowing how to pray, Dickinson encloses the following poem:

O God we ask one favor,
That we may be forgiven—
For what, he is presumed to know—
The crime, from us, is hidden—
Immured the whole of Life
Within a Magic Prison
We reprimand the Happiness
That too competes with Heaven.

Imaginative Safety Valves: Frontier Themes in the Literature of the Gilded Age

JAMES K. FOLSOM

On the face of things, Americans' preoccupation with the frontier and literature about it during the Gilded Age (I use the term "Gilded Age" to refer to that period in American history between the Civil War and World War I) is evident. Popular writing forsakes its roots in the Crockett almanacs and the humorists of the Old Southwest to develop into the dime novel, set preponderantly in the West; the locale of Western fiction follows the successive stages of the American frontier;[1] Mark Twain, the author usually viewed as the greatest single voice Western American literature has produced, is a product of the period, as well as the author of the sobriquet "Gilded Age" for it;[2] and the Western, in its modern form, is defined toward the end of the Gilded Age, most importantly by Owen Wister in *The Virginian,* but also by Zane Grey, especially in *Riders of the Purple Sage.* At the same time, the unromantic West of the farm and small town appears as symbol of the often harsh reality rather than the romance of Western American life following the Civil War.

During this period as well American social historians develop the idea, based originally on the so-called Teutonic theory of democratic origins and culminating in the famed frontier hypothesis of Frederick Jackson Turner, that the presence of the frontier is the single most important fact distinguishing America from its European progenitors. Long before Turner, a relatively unsophisticated statement of his basic idea—that the frontier served as a safety valve for removing dangerous pressures from the society behind it—seemed so self-evident to late nineteenth-century Americans as scarcely to require proof. This notion also explains many literary developments during the Gilded Age and is by no means limited to writings which we have traditionally termed Western.

The Gilded Age also marks the emergence of the United States as an industrial giant, a world economic power rather than a provincial backwater.

Brother Jonathan, as the infant United States had demeaningly been referred to, is transformed into Uncle Sam, a figure to be reckoned with, if not always approved of. If, as one plausible etymology suggests, the name Uncle Sam is based on the dollar sign, we are back again to the frontier myth, the long way around: for the omnipotence of the almighty dollar, which as much as any single factor created American cultural unease during the period, was often interpreted as the result of an ill-defined Eastern conspiracy to crush the noblemen of nature living in the West. Just as American political dissent in the period was primarily a Western phenomenon – it is no accident that the most famous dissident voice of the Gilded Age belonged to a Nebraskan – so artistic dissent often expressed itself in terms of Western values, even when not specifically Western in subject-matter.

The gradual redefinition of the nature of the conflict in the American Civil War, culminating in the so-called "moonlight and magnolia" school of writing, offers a convenient example. The myth of the antebellum South, like most myths of a Golden Age, does not purport to present sober historical truth: in this myth the romantic South, rather than being visualized as a particular place in a specific historic era, is conceived primarily as representative of a complex of values standing in opposition to those often shoddy values of finance capitalism which dominate the reader's real-life world. Simon Legree disappears: in his place stands the benevolent figure of Ole Massa, beloved of all, including his black slaves. Life on the old plantation becomes a bucolic idyll, destroyed by the Yankees for no good reason. In this fiction the South normally loses the Civil War not because of moral delinquency, let alone military ineptitude or political incompetence, but simply because it is overwhelmed by a gigantic and ruthless enemy armed with greenbacks rather than swords and pistols.

Several years ago David B. Davis indicated the resemblances between the myth of the antebellum South and the myth of the West, which "purified and regenerated" the original myth "by the casting off of apologies for slavery."[3] In terms of the present discussion, both the South and the West represented ideals opposed to "the peculiar social and economic philosophy of the Northeast," values "beyond the utilitarian and material" (p. 18). If we expand Davis's line of reasoning, we may suggest that American fascination with both imaginative locales is essentially a fascination with the myth of the frontier: somewhere must be a land of heart's desire, untainted by the commercial values of the present. The regional West itself is not particularly important to Horace Greeley's oft-quoted maxim, "Go West, young man, go West." More basic is the idea that an unbearable present may be redeemed by changing one's situation and starting over.

Perhaps this explains as well as any single thing the American fascination with the frontier in the Gilded Age. For the Gilded Age was nothing if not a restless one. As the disparity between the promises of America and the realities of late nineteenth-century American life grew more obvious, American writers often opted for a world of ideals rather than of unpromising realities. "Frequently sold," as a familiar contemporary song had it, the American nonetheless continued the search for the good life, wherever it might lead.

It did not always lead west, as Henry James, the literary giant of the period who stands at first glance most directly opposed to Twain, shows. In James's world the land of opportunity, the "last frontier," if one will, is generally Europe. The American abroad, although by no means a novel figure at the beginning of the Gilded Age, develops new complexity in the work of this fictional master of the "international subject." James's questing characters, although they may not know specifically what they hope to find abroad, know that in a general way they are searching for life, something they seem unable to find in the comfortable down-home existence that surrounds them. The possibilities of their lives at home seem suddenly too limited, and they seek the challenge of a new environment where opportunities are less confined. When occasionally James turns his international subject around, the Europeans visiting America–as in the short novel *The Europeans*–also feel, more in accord with our own historic expectations, the need for a New World in which they may find more opportunities than they had had in the Old.

Yet no matter which way James's characters cross the Atlantic, they do so for essentially the same reasons: to find a new frontier in which their potential can be realized. What they find is a land remarkably like the one they have left behind. As the Baroness remarks at the end of *The Europeans,* "Europe seems to me much larger than America."[4]

The ironies which reside in the notion of the "new start" fill James's fiction from the beginning until the end of his career. One irony, of course, is that in one sense beginning anew is impossible, since one always brings one's own self along. More basic to James's world, however, is that the people one meets abroad are virtually indistinguishable from those one has, presumably forever, left behind. In *The Portrait of a Lady* Isabel Archer finds one titled Englishman as a possible suitor, but finally marries–unhappily, it is true–a denationalized American. Her circle of friends in Europe contains relatively few Europeans. This may well be a Jamesian barb at the propensity of Americans abroad to associate almost entirely with their own countrymen and -women, but Isabel Archer's fruitless quest indicates as well James's immersion in American frontier mythology–the search for a better land somewhere beyond the limits of the known, and the disillusionment this search must entail.

It is no accident that James's questing Americans are so often female. The frontier myth in its typically Wild Western format is almost entirely a male myth. Although one may not totally agree with Davis's statement that the Eastern belle in the typical Western is "a glorified horse" (p. 22) his general point that female characters are almost always stereotypical in one way or another is well taken. Kansas, or Oklahoma, or wherever, was, according to the old wheeze, tough on women and horses, and the comparison, unflattering as it may be, contains a grain of truth. Horace Greeley knew what he was doing when he suggested that young men go west, for the West, unless one were brawny and physically robust, was not a land of opportunity. Young women would have been better advised to follow Isabel Archer to Europe or Dreiser's Carrie Meeber to Chicago. No matter what one might find in the fleshpots of Chicago, let alone Europe, it would be better than what one got by remaining at home. Mary E. Wilkins Freeman's New England nun, living out her days in a moribund New England village, is in a worse plight than any of her more venturesome sisters.

Just as James's frontiers are not specifically Western ones, so other American writers often chronicle what are essentially the concerns of frontier mythology in works which are not, when considered strictly in terms of subject matter, directly concerned with the American West. Hank Morgan, the Yankee of Twain's consistently under-praised *A Connecticut Yankee in King Arthur's Court,* is a case in point. Among its other concerns this novel records what is almost an allegorical demonstration of the negative effects of American westward expansion: the Yankee, armed with all the technological prowess of nineteenth-century America, brings the benefits of civilization to a frontier populated by a group of amiable savages. The benefits he brings turn out not only to be prophetic of America's new role as a world power but also agents in the destruction of the natives to whom he brings them. This novel, as well as any literary work of the period, shows the double-edged quality of the American's frontier vision: the quest for a new start, what Oswald Spengler would later name the Faustian vision of Western man, is hailed as a virtue, while the results of this Faustian quest are seen as disastrous.

Edward Bellamy's *Looking Backward,* the most widely read utopian novel ever penned, affords another convenient example. Although the primary concern of this work is to demonstrate the present ills of late nineteenth-century society and to suggest a future cure for them, the vehicle of Bellamy's parable is saturated with frontier ideals. Bellamy's utopia is conceived as a place free of the disagreeable qualities of nineteenth-century industrial life, yet located geographically in the same area. What more graphic illustration of the promise of the frontier—and by extension of America—could be imagined than Bellamy's city of the future sited on the remains of the past, where the evils of the present have been eradicated and where mankind's restless spirit is at last satisfied.

Frontier writing has of necessity always contained a strong utopian component, but in the Gilded Age the predominant utopias are negative ones, dystopias, as they have come to be known, more on the model of Twain than of Bellamy. The optimistic vision which redeems them, as at the end of *Looking Backward,* normally seems unreal, a product more of wishful thinking than of careful examination of the evidence. Ignatius Donnelly's *Caesar's Column,* more typical of the mass of utopian novels than *Looking Backward,* is memorable primarily for its pictures of the frustration and despair of society's members rather than for the rays of hope with which Donnelly, himself a prominent political figure, attempts to paint it. Indeed, even in *Looking Backward* the multiple shifts in time with which Bellamy brings about his happy ending have struck many readers as absurd. In any event, the idea of a frontier is of primary importance to this novel and, Turner to the contrary, the last frontier can never, literally at least, be reached.

It is also in the Gilded Age that our modern view of Western and Eastern values as diametrically opposed becomes clearly articulated. Earlier fiction had denied a basic conflict between them or, if the conflict was theoretically admitted, had done its best to gloss over it. Who in the Gilded Age would write an epic of the West on the model of Washington Irving's *Astoria,* in which the hero is John Jacob Astor, truly an empire builder, whose vision brought the success of the Western fur trade despite the ineptitude of his sometimes disloyal, almost always incompetent Western employees? Who also, from the perspective of the 1800s, would even speculate with Timothy Flint's perception that Daniel Boone's primary significance lay in the fact that he demonstrated the validity of a universal historic truth: that providence provides the undesirable elements of society as shock troops for westward expansion, thus minimizing the chance that more worthwhile members of the social order might be slain.[5] Not so. For the Gilded Age the Westerner is a valuable member of society in his own right, and it is his values which will redeem that society. For the first time in the Gilded Age the modern imaginative theme clearly emerges that the West will redeem the East, instead of the more traditional idea that the East will reform the West in its own image. The change is, of course, not absolute and the tension between the older vision of the West as East manque and the newer that the two are essentially opposed is felt throughout Western writing of the period, not always with the most fortunate results. Many readers have felt that the change in Owen Wister's Virginian from reckless cowboy to budding entrepreneur is one of the weakest features of *The Virginian;* and Hamlin Garland, to use a very different example, never seems to be quite sure whether the misfortune in his tales is primarily the fault of some representative of Eastern values or simply due to the hardships of Western life. In "Under the Lion's Paw" he argues the former case; in "Up the Coule" the latter; in *A Spoil of Office* and *The Moccasin Ranch* he is not quite sure.

The primary significance of the emergence of this modern notion that Western and Eastern values are essentially opposed again reflects the vast changes in American life following the Civil War and, more important for this discussion, the feeling that the East had abandoned that questing spirit which Westerners still possessed. If in Western writing Eastern and Western values are visualized in conflict, this is primarily, to Western eyes at least, a result of the East's having lost the idea of the West that the West itself still retains. This being the case, abandonment of frontier values is tantamount to renunciation of one's American identity.

This, it seems to me, is a major thrust of the Turner hypothesis, and it is unfortunate that Western Americanists, with their eyes fixed upon the presence of the physical frontier, have by and large overlooked it. For to Turner the frontier in itself is not an especially desirable place. In his view, the first wave of settlers has a hard enough time living at all even to think of living well. The primary significance of the frontier for him lies in its effect upon the society behind it, which is constantly revitalized by its impact. Going native is not Turner's idea of the good life. Instead, the presence of the frontier represents a force which constantly rejuvenates an American society that, left to itself, would become constantly more over-refined and decadent.

To borrow a phrase from the Old Testament prophet Amos, those who are at ease in Zion are the primary villains to the Western writers of the Gilded Age. Perhaps this, as well as any single factor, explains the cultural miasma which hangs over the writing of the period dealing not directly with the frontier but with the "agricultural paradise" succeeding it. From E. W. Howe's *The Story of a Country Town* through the works of Hamlin Garland and Sinclair Lewis to the present, the basic enemy in writing about rural America has been complacency, and the ultimate literary sin, unwillingness to change a bad present situation for an unknown future which, although it may not turn out better, will at least be different. This itself indicates, if only inversely, the general cultural importance of the idea of the frontier.

As a case in point let us briefly glance at how often in Hamlin Garland's *Main-Travelled Roads* the ideal of successful fulfillment in life is coupled with some image of escape from a stagnant rural society in which existence has turned sour. Howard McClane of "Up the Coule" is the most familiar example, but other less well-known characters also emphasize the idea that rural life, unmixed with any ideal of westering, is closer to hell on earth than to the heaven its proponents claim. In "Among the Corn Rows" a representative of the frontier, or at least of a society closer to it, rescues an almost legendary damsel in distress from the toils of a life not only of grinding poverty but of smug self-satisfaction. When Bob carries Julia off farther

West, his action signifies not so much a change of geographical locale as a moral rebirth. Similarly, in "A Branch Road" Will is also able to rescue his bride only after some time spent working on the railroad, a clear image for the notion that going somewhere is what is important. Even Mrs. Ripley must leave, if only temporarily, the familiar routine she has endured all her life. In all these examples the idea of the frontier plays an important metaphorical role.

E. W. Howe's country town, left behind when the frontier passed it by and hence a stagnant backwater rather than a vibrant community, offers another striking image for essentially the same concern. The beginning line of Howe's tale, "Ours was the prairie district, out West, where we had gone to grow up with the country," is immediately qualified by the notation that "our section was not a favorite" and that other settlers went farther West.[6] It is not beside the point to note as well that the town is named Fairview, another hint that the going may be better if one moves on.

When William Dean Howells, in consonance with Horace Greeley's practice rather than his precept, left Ohio for the East, he was in his own person expressing the validity of frontier mythology, even though his removal to Boston and later to New York is often interpreted as a denial of his Western heritage. The opposite point, that Howells by his move East and subsequent admission to the Eastern literary establishment was affirming rather than denying frontier values, seems more valid. Howells is a good figure with whom to close this discussion because his career as a man of letters sums up, better than any of his contemporaries', the ideals of the new start symbolized by the presence of the frontier. Born a poor Ohio boy, at his death Howells was the preeminent man of letters in the United States, and his career indicated to many of his fellow Americans the nearly limitless opportunities available to one who, primarily by hard work, was willing to wrest success from the unpromising intellectual landscape of the United States just as his more muscular countrymen had wrested it from the often unpromising physical environment of the West.

Howells was, his contemporaries would instantly have noted, a writer of utopias. *A Traveller from Altruria,* although by no means so popular as *Looking Backward,* was still one of the best sellers of the late nineteenth century. Like the latter, it too is interpretable as a statement of the primacy of frontier values, insofar as Howells's Traveller castigates Gilded Age society on the basis of values to be found in another country, albeit one which is not specifically located across the wide Missouri. The promises of Altruria are basically those offered by the frontier and are attainable by those willing to seek them out.

A Hazard of New Fortunes is similar, although here the story is much more directly related to Howells's own biography. In this novel Howells took the chance to show his public that he would practice what he preached. It becomes clear during the course of the novel that the gain was worth the risk involved. Life in New York rejuvenates March, just as it had revitalized Howells. March has accepted the challenge of the frontier, realizing that refusal to adapt is only another term for moral cowardice.

In closing let us mention an oft-noted point about Howells—his championing of new American literary talent, much of it Western. A close friend of Mark Twain (his essay "My Mark Twain" remains one of the best appreciations of that author), he also championed Hamlin Garland when that very different young Western author was trying to get a start. The fictional worlds of both authors are vastly different from Howells's own as well as from each other's; but to deny either one would have been to deny a major premise on which Howells had built his life and around which he organized his fiction: the premise of that constant renewal necessary for literature, symbolized by the frontier.

NOTES

1. This is by no means a self-evident point. European fiction dealing with the American frontier, far more directly primitivist in concern, tends to remain in the woodland areas east of the Mississippi.

2. Twain's Huckleberry Finn, refusing to return to civilization at the end of *Huckleberry Finn* and opting instead to go off to the Indian territory, is probably the single best-known image in American writing of the lure of the frontier.

3. David B. Davis, "Ten-Gallon Hero," in *The Western,* ed. James K. Folsom (Englewood Cliffs, N.J.: Prentice-Hall, 1979), p. 18. Subsequent references in the text are to this edition.

4. Henry James, *The Europeans* (Harmonsworth, England: Penguin Books, 1964), p. 173.

5. These are in my opinion underlying general morals to *Astoria* and the *Biographical Memoir of Daniel Boone,* respectively.

6. E. W. Howe, *The Story of a Country Town* (Cambridge, Mass.: Harvard Univ. Press, 1961), p. 7.

The Significance of the Frontier in Contemporary American Fiction

MARK BUSBY

Although Frederick Jackson Turner's frontier thesis has been widely attacked by historians over the years, it is clear that images of the frontier continue to be important to American writers. Certainly the frontier remains central to writers of formula Westerns, for they set their stories during the golden days of the American West. But the frontier is significant in works by "mainstream" American writers too. Saul Bellow, Ralph Ellison, Ken Kesey, Joseph Heller, Kurt Vonnegut, John Barth, Alice Walker, Joan Didion, Edward Abbey, Larry McMurtry, Ray Bradbury, Philip Caputo, even a "nonfiction" novelist such as Michael Herr–all continue to use frontier imagery as significant elements of their works. Most of these writers express a deep ambivalence toward the frontier. On one hand, they nod longingly toward some frontier American values and recognize positive traits associated with the pastoral frontier. On the other hand, they acknowledge the limitations that a nostalgic, rearward-looking frontier emphasis produces, and they recognize the problems spawned by playing what McMurtry calls "symbolic frontiersman." Many of these writers, therefore, feel a greater affinity for the gothic frontier of the Puritans and American Renaissance writers such as Poe, Hawthorne, and Melville.

Let me specify what I mean by "frontier" before turning to specific contemporary writers who use images associated with the frontier. Although we usually associate the frontier with the American West of the 1800s, I do not refer to a specific place but to a cluster of images and values that grew out of the confrontation between the uncivilized and the civilized world, what Turner called the "meeting point between savagery and civilization."[1] Civilization has generally been associated with the past and with Europe, which for early American thinkers was withering and moribund, the "dead hand" of the past. Civilization, then, is associated with society–its institutions, laws, and restrictions, its demands for compromise and restriction, its cultural refinement and emphasis on manners, its industrial development, and its class distinctions.

The wilderness that civilization confronts suggests many opposite ideas. Rather than the restrictive demands of society, the wilderness offers the possibility of individual freedom, where individuals can test their sense of self against nature without the demand for social responsibility and the compromise of being part of a community. Cultural refinement and emphasis on manners give way to pragmatic empiricism. Rather than industrialism, agrarianism is the major force. Class distinctions disappear. In the wilderness breathes the all-enfolding spirit, a deity worshiped alike by Indians, Transcendentalists, and Naturalists.

These positive images are associated with the pastoral frontier, made familiar through Cooper and Thoreau. But another image cluster has grown out of the gothic frontier, the product of the Puritans' confrontation with the dark forces represented to them by the Indians. Violence, captivity, and metamorphosis are the major aspects of this strain of frontier imagery.

The literary importance of these image clusters appears in many works of literature through archetypal patterns such as those identified by D. H. Lawrence in *Studies in Classic American Literature,* Henry Nash Smith in *Virgin Land,* R. W. B. Lewis in *The American Adam,* Leo Marx in *The Machine in the Garden,* Roderick Nash in *Wilderness and the American Mind,* and Richard Slotkin in *Regeneration through Violence* and *The Fatal Environment.* Let me try to simplify this archetypal pattern. Over and over, American literature concerns itself with innocent American individuals who find themselves in conflict with the oppositions suggested by the east/west, civilization/wilderness grid I described earlier. The archetypal American figure, attempting to free himself from the constrictions of civilization, has moved into the wilderness where, as R. W. B. Lewis has demonstrated, he has become a new Adam in the Garden. The process, though, according to Richard Slotkin, often involves a ritualistic hunt in which the American hunter regenerates himself through violence so that he can return to the familial bonds of civilization with a renewed awareness of his own individuality. The change, Leslie Fiedler and D. H. Lawrence have pointed out, often involves a coming to terms with the nonrational forces that the native American has come to represent.

With the end of the frontier, how can the contemporary American novelist present any of these same concerns, since the primary field of action–the Wilderness, and its principal representative, the native American–have almost vanished from the physical world?

In fact, many important critics specializing in post–World War II fiction deny or ignore the significance of frontier images for contemporary American writers. Raymond Olderman, for example, in *Beyond the Waste Land: The American Novel in the Nineteen-Sixties,* goes so far as to assert categorically that some of the important frontier images have disappeared. Olderman states:

> Eden, Utopia, and the New Adam have no major significance in the novel of the sixties. If the memory of Eden and a related sense of loss continue to appear, they appear only as the universal remembrance of the eden of childhood. . . . As images haunting our imagination, these memories no longer connect to a sense of a lost America. If the promise of Utopia should continue to appear in the novel of the sixties, it exists as the universal hope for self-discovery. The old theme of the American Adam aspiring to move ever forward in time and space unencumbered by guilt or reflection on human limitation is certainly unavailable to the guilt-ridden psyche of modern man.[2]

And Josephine Hendin, in *Vulnerable People: A View of American Fiction since 1945,* finds that American writers react to the changes in contemporary life by moving in one of two directions–through "holistic" or "anarchic" fiction: "Fiction divides over the methods that will reduce emotional vulnerability and alternates between two extremes. One is holistic, stressing the virtues of management, wholeness and reason. The other is anarchic, stressing the mystical values of self-effacement and disintegration."[3] These impulses grow from contemporary American life, particularly from the successes of American capitalism. Both appear "memoryless," with little concern for the ideas produced by the frontier past.

Jerry Bryant in *The Open Decision* finds European philosophy, particularly Existentialism, to be the nurturing agent for contemporary fiction.[4] Jack Hicks in *In the Singer's Temple* concludes that diversity prevails in contemporary American fiction, that contemporary writing reveals the diversity and fragmentation of American life, and that little coherence exists.[5] Warner Berthoff, in *A Literature without Qualities: American Writing since 1945,* seems to despair when he examines contemporary writing, for, as his title suggests, he sees little of quality, and he finds a retreat from distinguishing qualities as well.[6]

If one were to read the last few years' entries by Jerome Klinkowitz on "Fiction: 1950 to the Present" in *American Literary Scholarship,* the inevitable conclusion would be that the only significant concerns among contemporary novelists revolve around innovation or reaction. For Klinkowitz, the only legitimate choice is for them to throw their lots in with the postmodernists, who embrace experimentation and plow the fields of self-reflexive fiction. God forbid that writers–or critics–cast their buckets down with the reactionaries like John Gardner or Gerald Graff, who call for referential and moral fiction. Klinkowitz discusses literature of the American West as a "subgenre" that he includes with "Native American, Chicano Writers and Oriental-American Literature."

How then can one approach contemporary American fiction in any coherent way? The standard approach is exemplified by the organization of the *Harvard Guide to Contemporary American Writing,* edited by Daniel Hoffman, and that is to categorize writers by region, ethnic background, style, or sex. Thus, the chapters are titled "Southern Fiction," "Jewish Writers," "Experimental Fiction," "Women's Literature," and so forth.[7] But among the diverse groups of mainstream American writers are discernible ideas that grow out of these American writers' concerns with "frontier" images, and these concerns cut across these standard categories.

Contemporary novelists embed elements of the frontier mythos into their novels in various ways. In some cases they use some remaining natural wilderness: Saul Bellow removes the title character in *Herzog* to the Berkshires, where he contemplates his existence; James Dickey sets *Deliverance* in the southern backwoods; and Flannery O'Connor does the same in *The Violent Bear It Away;* John Barth uses the early Maryland frontier in *The Sot Weed Factor;* William Styron in *The Confessions of Nat Turner* explores the diminishing wilderness of Virginia in 1831; and Thomas Berger examines the historical west in *Little Big Man;* Edward Abbey used the post-war West in *The Brave Cowboy* and *The Monkey Wrench Gang.* Philip Caputo employs Hemingway country up in Michigan in *Indian Country.* Some introduce elements of the natural world to suggest the power of the mythical West. Ken Kesey, for example, used the flight of the geese in *One Flew Over the Cuckoo's Nest* to remind Chief Bromden of this connection to the healing power of nature.

In other cases these wilderness concerns take place on a new field of action rather than in the West itself. Bellow has Henderson travel to Africa in *Henderson the Rain King.* The war becomes the focus of action in *Catch-22, Slaughterhouse-Five,* Tim O'Brien's *Going After Cacciato,* and Michael Herr's *Dispatches.* For Ralph Ellison's *Invisible Man* it is the city. For John Irving it is the old world of Vienna, and for Garp it is a young girl's rape in Central Park. Larry McMurtry's new frontiersman in *Cadillac Jack* is a junk dealer who finds the world of possibility in the flea markets of the world. Ray Bradbury replicates these concerns on the Martian frontier. Kurt Vonnegut in *Galapagos* and Bernard Malamud in *God's Grace* create post-apocalyptic frontier islands.

At the center of many of these novels we find the frontier paradigm. An innocent figure (or more likely an ignorant one) undergoes an initiatory experience that grows out of the elements he confronts in the transformed wilderness he faces. Ironically, the difficulties he faces often result from elements of the pastoral frontier myth, which emphasizes the primary need for unfettered individual freedom of action. Bellow's Henderson must escape the submerged voice crying "I want" before he can dissolve the sense of having a separate self when he confronts Dahfu's lion. Kesey's gambler, rounder, cartoon-cowboy hero in *One Flew Over the Cuckoo's Nest* must give up his selfish concerns before he can regenerate himself and the inhabitants of the asylum. John Irving's Garp must learn how to sympathize with the oppressed and recognize the human potential for violence so that he can become a redemptive figure. Styron's Nat Turner must turn from the "Old Testament God of Hate" and embrace the "New Testament God of Love" before he can sense the morning star. Heller's Yossarian, inspired by the innocent Orr of the apple cheeks who hails from the undefined border territory outside New York City, must give up his singular desire for survival and strive to save the kid sister of Nately's whore. Michael Herr's persona in *Dispatches* must confront the dislocations he discovers in the Vietnam wilderness before he can use language to attempt to come to terms with that disquieting experience.

One major element in the character's metamorphosis–and another theme inherited from frontier mythology–concerns captivity. From Mary Rowlandson and other Puritan captivity narratives to Cooper's tales about Leatherstocking's quests to recapture white maidens, captivity has been an important element of the narrative. Likewise, captivity of various sorts enters the contemporary American novel. For many writers, the captivity comes from the military: Yossarian cannot escape flying in *Catch-22*, and Billy Pilgrim is first captured by the military and later by the Germans in *Slaughterhouse-Five*. Vietnam novels like *Going After Cacciato* or Herr's new-journalism *Dispatches* also concentrate on the military, but the military during Vietnam takes on a more sinister nature than in the other two books mentioned. In *Cuckoo's Nest* it is the asylum that encaptures; in *Nat Turner* it is slavery; in *Deliverance* the hillbilly capturers are dispatched ironically by the hero's bow and arrow; in John Cheever's *Falconer* and Vonnegut's *Jailbird* it is prison. Captivity is important to Flannery O'Connor too; in *Wise Blood* Haze Motes is uprooted from home by the army, and Old Tarwater captures both Rayber and young Tarwater. For some contemporary women writers, such as Alice Walker and Joan Didion, marriage is captivity.

Another element important to older American literature that reappears in contemporary fiction concerns the confrontation between the Old and the New World presented through the American's journey to the Old World. Twain and James traveled with the innocent abroad to point to these differences. Likewise, the motif appears in contemporary American fiction. Saul Bellow has Charlie Citrine travel to Europe in *Humboldt's Gift*. In *The Dean's December* Bellow narrows the focus: Chicago represents the anarchic American world where death and captivity permeate the texture of life:

Bucharest is the old, entropic world of restriction. John Irving uses Vienna in several of his novels to represent the Old World, especially in *The Hotel New Hampshire,* where the escape-and-return pattern familiar to American literature appears when the characters move from a hotel in America to one in Vienna and then return to one in America.

Another aspect of the frontier emphasis in contemporary fiction concerns the continuing appearance of the innocent figure identified by R. W. B. Lewis as the American Adam. In the nineteenth century, when the pastoral vision of the wilderness took predominance over the Puritan one of evil, the figure that often personified the new American was the New Adam, innocent, full of possibility and potential. Contemporary American novelists do not use the Adam figure as a realistically possible heroic figure, but many of them do present the innocent Adam in the process of becoming Adam's counterpointing figure in religious typology: Christ. The tension between the innocent Adam and the aware Christ is a sustaining part of the narrative pattern in *Invisible Man, Henderson the Rain King, One Flew Over the Cuckoo's Nest, Catch-22, The Confessions of Nat Turner, Slaughterhouse-Five, Going After Cacciato,* and *The World According to Garp.* In these works the main character begins as an American Adam who believes some of the illusions spawned by the vision of the American wilderness as Eden and the American as innocent (characterized by self-centered individuality, desire for simplicity and harmony, recoil from death, materialism, anarchic freedom, and self-righteousness). The character is established as Adamic through his grappling with these problems; often, too, clusters of images are associated with the American as Adam (nakedness, blindness or sleep, garden, tree, snake, open air). Occasionally the main character is also associated with the various transformations of the American Adam as he moved west across the American frontier–frontiersman, riverboatman, tinker, trickster, logger, cowboy. Events challenge the reality of the character's illusions, and often some form of captivity or attempted escape from captivity causes the transformation. As a result the character's illusions are challenged, and he is forced toward experience or knowledge. Usually the main character must face the reality of death; either his own life is threatened or he witnesses the death of another character. The resulting awareness dawns slowly in most cases, suggesting a gap between seeing and understanding and the difficulty in overcoming illusions.

When the main character finally achieves knowledge, he attempts to become a conscious Messiah who sees clearly that his purpose is to transform the world into one of hope, community, and love, or at least one in which it is easier to live. The character usually comes to understand the illusory nature of his world, and he knows that for destructive illusions to be overthrown they must be clearly articulated. Contemporary writers emphasize the importance of language that creates illusions and that conversely can be used to strip away inhumane beliefs and create humane ones. Usually when the character becomes Christlike, he also becomes a writer (*logos*). Besides an awareness of language, the Christlike traits are an awareness of discord, complexity, human limitation, the problems of the past, and the need for community and love. Various images are associated with Christ—cross, tree, burdens, suffering, crown of thorns, rebirth, baptism, light, sight, and seed, among other aspects of Jesus' life.

The metamorphosis from Adam to Christ owes much to the Puritan emphasis on biblical typology, where, as Ursula Brumm has demonstrated, "characters and events of the Old Testament are prefigurations and prophecies of future events, mainly of Christ and His works."[8] What gives the transformation its particular connection with elements of the frontier myth is the corresponding movement in native-American culture. Joseph Campbell in *The Masks of God* points out the significance of two opposing figures—the "hunter" or "warrior," and the "shaman." Slotkin examines the similarity between the "warrior" and the Adam figure and the "shaman" and Christ:

> Both the hunter and the shaman had their counterparts in white mythology. Indians were generally quick to notice the similarity between the laws of shamans like Quetzalcoatl and Deganawidah and the tenets of Christianity (especially those of Quaker Christianity). The spirit of the hunter likewise corresponded to the entrepreneurial spirit of the colonist-adventurers; the traders in furs and hides and land.[9]

Another similarity to native-American culture concerns the pattern the characters follow toward spiritual redemption. Joseph Epes Brown in *The Spiritual Legacy of the American Indian* identifies a three-stage pattern common to native-American cultures:

> All true spiritual progress involves three stages, which are not successfully experienced and left behind, but rather each in turn is realized and then integrated within the next stage, so that ultimately they become one in the individual who attains the ultimate goal. Different terms may be used for these stages, but essentially they constitute purification, perfection or expansion, and union.[10]

So it is not unexpected to find variations of this pattern in native-American literature, where the main character must transform from warrior or hunter to shaman who, like the Christ-logos figure, values the power of language. N. Scott Momaday's *House Made of Dawn* is the prototype of the native-American novel, and Leslie Silko in *Ceremony* and James Welch in *Winter in the Blood* present similar patterns. In these novels the hunter/warrior must be initiated into a shamanistic view of the world and must strip away the demands of the warrior ideal. Some form of captivity (the military for Momaday's and Silko's main characters, the past for Welch's) must be overcome. In each case a shamanistic mentor aids in the process of returning to some fundamental ideas about native-American culture. These native-American writers have made a major impact on contemporary American fiction, so much so that they have moved into the mainstream of American literature, and it is important to note how the frontier elements provide the basis for the narrative structure of various works.

Hispanic writers have also moved into the mainstream, as is illustrated by Rudolfo Anaya's *Bless Me, Ultima,* which adapts the pattern for a Hispanic novel. His youthful character, Tony, witnesses death in various forms before he escapes from the potential captivity of a life as a Catholic priest. He will become a shaman for the Christlike teachings of the Golden Carp as he is reintegrated into a primitivistic approach to the world, and he becomes the writer who tells his own story.

Although the Adamic figure seems inherently masculine, some contemporary women writers present women main characters who undergo an initiatory experience similar to the one I have described. In Alice Walker's critically acclaimed *The Color Purple* Celie must break out of her captivity and establish a singular identity outside of her forced marriage to Albert. Her journey is a tenuous one, but aided by the model that Shug Avery provides and guided by the letters her sister Nettie writes about her confrontation with the African frontier, Celie uses her own writing first to become independent and then to establish her own community. Her letter-writing is compared to her sewing, first with Sofia in making a quilt and later by making pants and becoming independent through her own work. Along the way she learns from Shug (a shaman in her own right) the native-American emphasis on the spirit that exists in all things.

To summarize how these various elements of frontier mythos inform contemporary American fiction, let me concentrate on a single novel, *One Flew Over the Cuckoo's Nest.* McMurphy in Ken Kesey's novel initially represents the Western figure, a cowboy, gambler, logger–a composite of stereotyped Western heroes. McMurphy's captivity is in an insane asylum, where his principal antagonist is Big Nurse, a figure of control and restriction associated with the East and civilization in the frontier paradigm. McMurphy's Adamic innocence involves first his ignorance of the system in which he finds himself and later his childlike self-interest, which he ultimately relinquishes to become a Christlike martyr. His metamorphosis–symbolized by a violent confrontation with Big Nurse–is effected partially by his association with the native-American shaman, Chief Bromden, who follows a path to redemption similar to McMurphy's. In fact, McMurphy's death has a profound effect on all the men in the insane asylum, but especially on Chief Bromden, who also moves from innocence to knowledge, from withdrawal to participation. Chief Bromden becomes the conscious writer who tells McMurphy's story.

This loop I toss is wide, encompassing much, but I think it is important to round up as much as possible to prove my point–that, contrary to what many critics have stated about contemporary American literature, significant elements of frontier mythology continue to appear in American fiction. And those elements cut across the categories popularly used to classify contemporary American fiction: Eastern–Bellow, Irving, Heller, Cheever; Southern–Styron, O'Connor; Western–McMurtry, Abbey, Kesey; Women –O'Connor, Silko, Walker; black–Ellison; native American–Momaday, Silko, Welch; Hispanic–Anaya; Experimental–Vonnegut, Barth, Irving. I do not mean to suggest that the frontier has arisen Phoenix-like in these novels. Rather, like Proteus or Coyote, it has simply taken new shapes to adapt to new circumstances.

NOTES

1. Frederick Jackson Turner, "The Significance of the Frontier in American History," in *Selected Essays of Frederick Jackson Turner: Frontier and Section,* ed. Ray Allen Billington (Englewood Cliffs, N.J.: Prentice-Hall, 1961), p. 38.
2. Raymond Olderman, *Beyond the Waste Land: The American Novel in the Nineteen-Sixties* (New Haven, Conn.: Yale Univ. Press, 1972), p. 9.
3. Josephine Hendin, *Vulnerable People: A View of American Fiction since 1945* (New York: Oxford Univ. Press, 1978), p. 6.
4. Jerry Bryant, *The Open Decision: The Contemporary American Novel and Its Intellectual Background* (Detroit: The Free Press, 1970).
5. Jack Hicks, *In the Singer's Temple* (Chapel Hill: Univ. of North Carolina Press, 1981).
6. Warner Berthoff, *A Literature without Qualities: American Writing since 1945* (Berkeley: Univ. of California Press, 1979).
7. Daniel Hoffman, ed., *The Harvard Guide to Contemporary American Writing* (Cambridge, Mass.: Harvard Univ. Press, 1979).
8. Ursula Brumm, *American Thought and Religious Typology* (New Brunswick, N.J.: Rutgers Univ. Press, 1970), p. 23.
9. Richard Slotkin, *Regeneration through Violence* (Middletown, Conn.: Wesleyan Univ. Press, 1973), p. 49.
10. Joseph Epes Brown, *The Spiritual Legacy of the American Indian* (New York: Crossroad, 1982), p. 45.

PART THREE
Regional Adaptations

Frontier Yeoman versus Cavalier: The Dilemma of Antebellum Southern Fiction

RITCHIE D. WATSON

In the summer of 1845, Fauquier White Sulphur Springs, a popular Virginia spa, hosted a "Tournament of Knights." The object of competing cavaliers was to spear from the back of a galloping horse a small ring which dangled from a cord eight feet above the ground. The knight who successfully speared the ring presented it to his lady and crowned her "The Queen of Love and Beauty." Competitors included gentlemen with the assumed names of Brian de Bois-Guilbert, Wilfred of Ivanhoe, and the Knight of La Mancha. They were urged on by a crowd of genteel spectators, who shouted: "Love of ladies–glory to the brave!"[1]

The tournament at Fauquier White Sulphur Springs was typical of a host of such equestrian competitions which were being held throughout the South at that time, merely one symptom in antebellum Dixie of what might best be described as the Walter Scott cultural syndrome. Goaded by attacks from the North, accused of maintaining an inhuman and immoral social institution, Southerners turned to Scott's romantic rendering, in ballad and novel, of medieval Scottish and English society. In these colorful period pieces the South found not only an escape from increasingly bitter sectional tensions but also a justification of its way of life. For in Southern eyes Scott's courageous and honorable feudal lords and Scottish chiefs had been reborn in the nineteenth century in the person of the Southern planter. The planter's slaves, like the feudal lord's medieval serfs, reasoned Southerners, were necessary to nurture the flowering of the South's aristocratic society.

It is not surprising that such phenomena as the "Tournament of Knights" imbued the culture of the older Southern states of the Atlantic seaboard. By the time of the Revolution the coastal regions of Virginia, the Carolinas, and Georgia had developed a prosperous plantation economy whose *raison d'être* was essentially the Old World aristocratic ideal, an ideal which this part of the South would evoke more frequently as the nation moved through the bitter debate over slavery toward the Civil War. Neither is it surprising that this aristocratic code was adopted in certain regions of the newly settled South, such as the Mississippi delta–areas which sought to reproduce as nearly as possible the social patterns of the plantation Tidewater. But it is astonishing that this aristocratic ethos came to permeate all of Dixie, including semifrontier sections so distant from the leavening influences of the Tidewater tradition that one would have thought their inhabitants impervious to notions of aristocracy. As Wilbur J. Cash has astutely observed, the South–that vast and varied territory that extends below the Mason-Dixon line from the Chesapeake Bay and the Atlantic capes across mountains and hills to the Texas plains–arbitrarily appropriated and adopted as its own the figure of the courtly planter.[2]

During the early nineteenth century the aristocratic ideal was transplanted and nurtured in the remotest parts of Dixie. Thus Henry Stanley, the famous African explorer, was surprised to discover antebellum farmers of the Arkansas hills and even crossroads store clerks strictly upholding the code of personal honor. He noted, for example, that a Jew of German extraction, who was the proprietor of a country store in the village of Cypress Bend, owned a fine pair of dueling pistols.[3]

By the time the Civil War began, residents of the interior South had so thoroughly identified themselves with the aristocratic myth that they would probably have been shocked had they been reminded that the frontiersman, not the planter, had been the dominant mythical figure in the settlement of their region fifty years earlier. Henry Nash Smith points out that in the early decades of the nineteenth century Jefferson's noble yeoman was a social concept embraced with equal fervor by pioneer farmers from Indiana and Illinois to Tennessee and Mississippi. Yet by the 1850s, Smith observes, the states south of the Ohio River had become "actively hostile to the yeoman ideal which had been developed as a rationale of agricultural settlement in the Mississippi Valley."[4]

The South's abandonment of its yeoman heritage is not as puzzling as it may at first appear. Charles Sydnor points out that because the region did not develop an industrial base comparable to that which was being established in the North, the South began to perceive itself as part of a nation increasingly dominated by Northern interests. The cultural and political isolation of the Southern states was exacerbated by the eventual merging of midwestern with Northern economic interests, a union ordained by such technological triumphs as the completion of the Erie Canal, tying the Great Lakes region with New York, and by the subsequent forging of numerous east-west rail links between the Midwest and the Northeast. As Sydnor notes, the South had begun to view itself as both a distinct and a beleaguered region by the 1830s. "Perhaps the chief product of the troublesome early 1830's" he writes, "was the strong charge of emotion added to matters that had hitherto been on the level of thought and calculation. In the previous decade, something of a Southern platform on national issues had evolved. Clashes over that platform convinced many Southerners that their interests were seldom respected by the rest of the nation and that the fabric of their way of life was being destroyed. A feeling of oppression, of defeat, and even of desperation was engendered."[5]

This feeling of oppression was heightened by the increasingly acrimonious debate over slavery. Although we now know that the great majority of Southern farmers did not own slaves,[6] Southerners nonetheless sought to present a united front to the North by embracing the aristocratic plantation ideal which ran so obviously counter to the yeoman ideal. As Richard Gray points out in *The Literature of Memory,* they embraced both the yeoman and the planter, blinding themselves to the antinomic relation between the two types.[7] But as the nation moved toward the Civil War Southerners tended to appeal less and less to their yeoman heritage. Responding after 1830 to increasingly bitter attacks from the North on Dixie's social institutions, Southerners from all areas, from James River plantations to Arkansas shanties, used the aristocratic ideal more and more frequently to justify their way of life, no matter how removed this ideal was from their daily existence.

The commanding presence of the planter-aristocrat in antebellum Southern literature can thus be understood as the fabrication of a culture which felt its very foundations being undermined. Yet a closer look at the literature of the period reveals that this Cavalier figure was not as absolutely dominating as one might initially assume and that even the South's most romantic writers found it impossible to ignore completely the figure of the frontier yeoman that had played such a critical part in the settlement of their region. In novels rooted firmly in the plantation genre one often encounters among predictable and clichéd characterizations of southern gentlemen more vibrant and original characterizations of yeomen. As an examination of John Pendleton Kennedy's *Horse-Shoe Robinson* and William Alexander Caruthers' *The Knights of the Golden Horse-shoe* will demonstrate, Southern writers were strongly drawn to the potent figure of the frontier yeoman, despite the fact that his presence in their novels implicitly repudiated the very aristocratic values their fiction sought to validate. This fictional paradox reflected the South's antebellum cultural dilemma, a dilemma which, as William R. Taylor discerns, forced Southerners to choose between living with the values of the nation at large or inventing alternative ideals "which had even less relevance to the Southern situation."[8]

Horse-Shoe Robinson (1835), published three years after John Pendleton Kennedy's more famous *Swallow Barn,* gives intriguing expression to the unreconciled tension between aristocratic and yeoman values with which the

South's antebellum writers found themselves persistently grappling. The main plot line of *Horse-Shoe Robinson* concerns the misadventures of Arthur Butler, a Revolutionary War officer from the low country of South Carolina. During most of the novel Butler is a captive of the British and their American Tory allies. Not until the climactic Battle of King's Mountain is he freed, whereupon he is reunited with Mildred Lindsay, a Virginia belle who hails from Dove Cote Plantation. Mildred is the daughter of a Tory gentleman, whose convenient death at King's Mountain allows Butler to reveal that he and Mildred have been secretly married for a year. One may well wonder why, in a novel that focuses on the fate of Arthur Butler, Kennedy titled his narrative *Horse-Shoe Robinson*. The answer is that Robinson, who is Butler's military guide and companion, is responsible for efforts to free the officer and dominates the action, while Butler languishes as a prisoner during the major portion of the novel. The title represents Kennedy's own understanding that the yeoman frontiersman, and not the aristocratic young officer, is the *de facto* protagonist of his narrative.

In his seminal *Cavalier and Yankee* William R. Taylor contends that Horse-Shoe represents a successful amalgam of yeoman with Cavalier traditions. His character is, Taylor writes,

> the Southern Yeoman become Chevalier Bayard; he is the wild Scot become gentleman warrior. Horse-Shoe Robinson is to the South what Harvey Birch of James Fenimore Cooper's *The Spy* was to the North: a defensive fiction. Harvey was a triumph over predatory greed. Horse-Shoe was a triumph over back-country brutality. Each in his own way held the American wildness at bay. Horse-Shoe's superiority to Butler lay in the fact that he belonged to the American present and future, while Butler took his gentlemanly social values from the European chivalric past. Horse-Shoe was a Scotch-Irishman's symbol of hope; Arthur Butler was a part Englishman's idea of a conventional gentleman. Horse-Shoe accommodated to the American present those qualities which Kennedy admired in his Pendleton ancestors; he promised to carry these qualities into the future. He was a mounted knight with his feet on native ground, a Cavalier who could shoe, as well as ride, a horse. (P. 197)

There is ample evidence in Kennedy's novel to support Taylor's view of Horse-Shoe Robinson as representative of a kind of compromise between the extremes of aristocratic chivalry, on the one hand, and uncivilized frontier brutality, on the other. Representing the chivalric attitude, of course, is Arthur Butler. Although Butler is not subjected to the kind of gentle satire which Kennedy directs toward his aristocrats in *Swallow Barn,* it is not difficult to identify the quixotic aspects of his character that make him—conventional hero though he may be—a less effective soldier than Robinson. Butler is brave and honorable. As he warns his Tory captors, "If aught be said against me that shall be intended to attaint my honor as a gentleman, I will, in the same presence and before God, throw the lie in the teeth of my accuser."[9] Butler's chivalric bravado, however, cannot deliver him from the British. In fact it is the timely intercession of Horse-Shoe Robinson, who is one of the leaders of a raid on the Tory camp, that saves Butler moments before he is to be executed as a traitor.

Butler's sense of honor and of noblesse oblige, though perhaps worthy of a certain admiration, can also be judged as ill-adapted to the kind of irregular guerrilla warfare that rages across the interior of South Carolina. For example, Butler is rescued at one point in the novel by John Ramsay, a yeoman farmer who sacrifices his life in the rescue attempt. Unfortunately, Butler is almost immediately recaptured because he insists on remaining in hostile territory to give John a proper military burial. This is a ritual that includes the firing of muskets over John's grave, firing that immediately brings British troops to the scene. One cannot help but feel that Butler's behavior is more stupid than noble and that his chivalric attitude in this instance is simply self-destructive.

If Butler represents the chivalric extreme, Wat Adair embodies the savagery of the uncivilized frontiersman. He is a man who sells his loyalties to the highest bidder and whose only concern is for himself. He represents a kind of lower-class brutality, the reverse or the shadow of Thomas Jefferson's noble yeoman figure. Cooper had recognized this darker element of American democracy and had given it fictional substance, most notably in the characterization of Ishmael Bush in *The Prairie*. Later Mark Twain brought the type violently to life in *Huckleberry Finn*. In the twentieth century William Faulkner would describe the same viciously solipsistic character in the Deep South and give him a name and a label–Snopes.

Wat Adair's identification with Snopesian characters who have both preceded and come after him in Ameircan fiction is dramatized in a scene of shocking savagery, one of only a few scenes in an otherwise pedestrian and formulaic romance that conveys the power of truly felt experience. Just before Adair betrays Butler and Horse-Shoe to the Tories, we see him reveling over the capture of a she-wolf who has long eluded his traps. Ignoring Horse-Shoe's admonition to kill the animal quickly, Adair proceeds slowly and methodically to skin the miserable creature alive. Kennedy describes the process with clinical precision:

> Adair proceeded with his operation with an alacrity that showed the innate cruelty of his temper. He made a cross incision through the skin, from the point of one shoulder to the other, the devoted subject of his torture remaining, all the time, motionless and silent. . . . He applied the point of his knife to separating the hide from the flesh on either side of the spine, and then, in his eagerness to accomplish this object, he placed his knife between his teeth and began to tug at the skin with his hands, accompanying the effort with muttered expres-

sions of delight at the involuntary and but ill-suppressed agonies of the brute. (P. 131)

In the face of such a disgusting and perverse scene, Butler can only "withdraw himself from a sight so revolting to his feelings" (p. 131).

Kennedy seems to understand that in a head-to-head confrontation between the Cavalier and a Snopes, the ferocity of the savage frontiersman would be more than a match for the chivalry of the gentleman warrior. Only a man like Horse-Shoe Robinson, who combines earthy strength and pragmatism with moral principle, can contend with the likes of Wat Adair. Horse-Shoe displays on occasion a hard resolve that borders on cruelty. He warns a British officer whom he has captured that if a hair of Arthur Butler's head is hurt, "I myself will drive a bullet through from one of your ears to the other" (p. 210). Later, in a raid on British forces, he urges his men to cut the enemy down without mercy. Kennedy tells us that "he accompanied his exhortation with the most vehement and decisive action, striking down, with a huge sabre, all who opposed his way" (p. 260).

In spite of a bloodthirsty quality that attaches to his yeoman hero in certain scenes, Kennedy would have his reader understand that there is a clear distinction between Horse-Shoe's ferocity and that of Wat Adair. Horse-Shoe's methods are dictated by the particularly savage nature of the conflict between Patriot and Tory in frontier South Carolina. He understands that the "game of war is a stiff game" and that he must play the game according to the rules currently in force. He does not simply kill for the joy of killing, and he does not derive unhealthy pleasure in inflicting pain. His severity of character is modified by a humane concern for others. In contrast to Arthur Butler's unbending principle, Robinson displays flexibility and pragmatic shrewdness at every turn. When the British officer who is his prisoner pledges upon his honor that he will make no attempt to escape, Horse-Shoe sensibly replies: "I can take no pledge in the dark; daylight mought make a difference. If we should happen to fall in with any of your gangs I'm thinking a pledge wouldn't come to much more than a cobweb when I ax you to gallop out of the way of your own people. Flesh is weak when the arm is strong or the foot swift. . . . No, no, Mr. Ensign, you may get away, if you can; we'll take care of you whilst we're able–that's a simple understanding" (p. 241). Arthur Butler, like a true gentleman, would have accepted the British officer's pledge without question. Yet we must feel that Horse-Shoe's response is an eminently practical and reasonable one and that a certain kind of honor must attach to a character who thinks with such clarity, honesty, and wisdom.

There are indications in the novel that Kennedy sought to enlarge his yeoman figure as Cooper had ennobled the character of Leatherstocking.

Like Leatherstocking, Horse-Shoe expresses his wisdom in long rambling discourses delivered in homely dialect. His entrance into the novel–silhouetted against a door, a venerable hero of a revolution fought forty years before–recalls Cooper's initial description of Leatherstocking in *The Prairie,* silhouetted and enlarged against a setting sun. "What a man I saw!" exclaims the narrator of Kennedy's novel. "With near seventy years upon his poll, time seemed to have broken its bellows over his front only as the ocean breaks over a rock. There he stood–tall, broad, brawny, and erect" (p. 8).

Unlike Cooper's Leatherstocking, however, Kennedy also seems interested in grafting specifically chivalric qualities onto his frontier hero. At one point, as Robinson sets out on an adventure, he is described as riding forth "with as stout a heart as ever went with knight of chivalry to the field of romantic renown" (p. 288). Passages such as this one remind the reader that Horse-Shoe is not a simple reproduction of Leatherstocking. He is not merely a frontier hero. He is a Southern frontier hero, and, as such, he carries with him at least a faint aura of the Cavalier figure. This suggestion of knightly grandeur, however, does not significantly qualify our understanding of his character as a fundamentally pragmatic one. Thus one may question the accuracy of William R. Taylor's description of Robinson as a "mounted knight." But it would be hard to disagree that he is a warrior with "his feet on native ground."

Horse-Shoe Robinson provides an interesting contrast with *Swallow Barn.* Together the two novels might be said to externalize the conflict within Kennedy between romantic and pragmatic attitudes. *Swallow Barn* is completely dominated by the Cavalier stereotype. The yeoman figure is at best shadowy and unsubstantial in this narrative. Three years later, however, Kennedy would write a novel in which the Cavalier type is pushed into the background and in which the plot is dominated by a yeoman hero.

Yet this dichotomy is not so clearly pronounced as it may at first seem. One must remember that even in a novel in which Kennedy celebrates the virtues of the yeoman he feels it necessary to pay proper reverence to the aristocratic ideal. Horse-Shoe dominates the action, but the novel remains essentially the story of aristocratic lovers tragically separated and then, at long last, joyfully reunited. The slighting of Horse-Shoe's character within the scheme of a typically romantic plot is nowhere more evident than at the conclusion. Here Horse-Shoe's story is simply dropped. Instead, the reader is given a description of the death of Mildred Lindsay's father. He also learns that Arthur Butler becomes a colonel and later serves in Virginia. Of course, if anyone is made a colonel it should be Robinson. But Kennedy cannot make Horse-Shoe a colonel because he is not, like Butler, a gentleman. Robinson is fit to fight bravely and to save Butler's life; he is fit to demonstrate resolve, wisdom, and humanity under the most trying of circumstances. But he is categorically denied the option of leading men, for only true gentlemen can lead men. In spite of Kennedy's honest attempt to create a yeoman hero, he cannot ultimately avoid casting his protagonist in an inferior role—for elevating Horse-Shoe above Butler would require either the repudiation or the radical redefinition of the Cavalier ideal, and Kennedy is not willing to tackle either of these tasks. Arthur Butler is not as effective a character as Horse-Shoe. Kennedy must have realized this. Yet Arthur, not Horse-Shoe, must be made colonel, if only because "his sufferings in the cause certainly deserved such a reward" (p. 483). It is a lame excuse for a promotion, but one that Kennedy and his readers no doubt preferred to a more candid explanation.

In the final analysis Horse-Shoe Robinson is not exactly the "Southern Yeoman become Chevalier Bayard" that William R. Taylor describes. Those chivalric aspects of his character that are stressed seem to bear only a superficial relation to his strongest qualities, which are those of the yeoman class from which he comes. Kennedy's problem in *Horse-Shoe Robinson* is that he must pretend that the two mythical types he dramatizes in his narrative are not in fundamental opposition to each other. He seems to illustrate perfectly the Southern paradox that Richard Gray describes. He insists on identifying with both character types in *Horse-Shoe Robinson,* ignoring as best he can the deep gulf between Arthur Butler's perspective and Horse-Shoe Robinson's. Kennedy could have bridged this gulf only by modeling Robinson into a genuine Cavalier-Yeoman. To effect this transformation he would have had to make Horse-Shoe's character, rude though it is, worthy of a lady's love. He would have had to elevate his yeoman to a position of command over others, even over those more conventionally defined as gentlemen. But Kennedy was too committed to the standard definition of Southern Cavalier to attempt to synthesize the best qualities of that type with the best qualities of the yeoman type.

Virginian William Alexander Caruthers' *The Knights of the Golden Horseshoe,* published ten years after *Horse-Shoe Robinson* in 1845, demonstrates that the South's writers continued to struggle unsuccessfully with the Yeoman-Cavalier dilemma. This colorful historical romance set in early eighteenth-century Virginia develops in the course of its narrative two relatively self-contained plots. One, which takes up the first half of the novel, concerns the identity of the mysterious Henry Hall, a tutor to Governor Spotswood's son, who has recently arrived from Scotland. After much confusion Henry reveals himself as Frank Lee, an aristocratic Virginian of noble character who, after traveling to Edinburgh to study at the university there, had unfortunately become involved in a plot to restore the Pretender. The death of Queen Anne produces a general pardon which enables Lee to reveal his true identity. The second and more interesting portion of the novel describes

Governor Spotswood's bold expedition to the height of the Blue Ridge. This expedition drives the Indians westward and opens vast new territories for British colonization. Having disposed of the complicated and excessively melodramatic question of Frank Lee's identity, Caruthers recreates the stirring events of Spotswood's tramontane expedition with a zest and vigor that reveal his writing talent at its best.

In describing this eighteenth-century exploration of western Virginia, an expedition which actually took place, Caruthers fashions Governor Spotswood into a spokesman for nineteenth-century America's ideal of manifest destiny. The governor firmly believes that, if the British colonies are to avoid being hemmed in from the west by the French, Virginians must press an exploratory party to the Appalachian peaks and lay claim to the vast, unknown tramontane region. Although the more conservative planters scoff at his plan, Spotswood tenaciously fights for appropriations from the Burgesses. "Just as sure as the sun shines tomorrow," he declares, "I will lead an expedition over yonder blue mountains, and I will triumph over the French–the Indians, and the Devil, if he chooses to join forces with them."[10] The governor's unwilting determination finally wins him the support he needs from the government as well as the backing of most of the colony's young Cavaliers.

Caruthers attaches profound significance to this expedition, considering it another symbolic step forward in the conquering of a continent. Indeed, he favorably compares Spotswood's achievement with the accomplishments of other American explorers such as Daniel Boone: this march, observes expansionist-minded Caruthers, is but the beginning of a grand procession that, renewed generation after generation, will "transcend the Rio del Norte, and which in half that time may traverse the utmost boundaries of Mexico" (p. 161).

Caruthers' description of the inexorable progression of American civilization toward the south, written on the eve of the Mexican War, suggests that his version of the nation's future growth was a distinctly sectional one shaped to reflect the interests of the Southern planter. For Caruthers, America's inevitable expansion lay not simply toward the Pacific. Implicitly wedded to the idea of the pioneer westward movement is an aristocratic Southern imperialism which, in the words of Rollin Osterweis, offered "the vision of a mighty, *separate,* slave empire, stretching out in a vast golden circle around the Caribbean Sea and the Gulf of Mexico.[11] Though it is doubtful that Caruthers fully recognized the difficulties inherent in this Southern view of the nation's future destiny, his description of a Cavalier march that would "traverse the utmost boundaries of Mexico" articulates a deviant version of manifest destiny that would ultimately be repudiated by civil war.

The Knights of the Golden Horse-shoe obviously intends to introduce a new figure into the nation's pantheon of folk heroes, Alexander Spotswood. It is also obvious that Caruthers intends for Spotswood's character to dominate the portion of the narrative dealing with the tramontane expedition. Yet few who read the book can fail to note that as the expedition progresses Spotswood must share the limelight more and more with a humble, unostentatious, and quite ungentlemanly fellow named Red Jarvis. Jarvis seems to be Caruthers' answer to Natty Bumppo and Horse-Shoe Robinson. Simple, homespun, sententious, humorous, crafty in the ways of the wood–he contrasts vividly with the dandified Cavalier crusaders. In the course of the expedition Spotswood becomes more and more dependent on his guide's advice in the maintenance and provisioning of the army. Indeed, at a crucial point Jarvis literally saves Spotswood's undertaking. Used to the light, sandy Tidewater soil, the army's unshod horses are lamed by sharp, cutting mountain stones. Spotswood bitterly contemplates turning back, but the resourceful Jarvis solves the seemingly unsolvable problem by stripping metal from the supply wagon wheels, molding it into horseshoes, and teaching the noble Cavaliers how to shoe their mounts. In a scene heavy with irony Jarvis stands as supervisor while Frank Lee and Governor Spotswood shoe their horses.

Like Natty, Jarvis is a creature of the wilderness who mourns the destructive forces of civilization. "There's scarce an elk or a buffalo to be found now this side of the hills," he muses, "and he's a gwine to drive them all clean over the ridge" (p. 185). Yet, like Cooper's Leatherstocking, Jarvis is the instrument, the pathfinder, the cutting edge of civilization's advance. Without his knowledge Spotswood's expedition would not have been successfully completed. Jarvis also suggests the leveling influence of the frontier, the democratizing influence of a land where a man can be judged only by his skills and human resources. At the beginning of the expedition the scout rightly predicts that aristocratic trappings will mean little in the wilderness. "You'll see who's the best man among us," he says, "when we get among the mountains, and when neither money nor larnin' can do much for a man" (pp. 185–86).

Of course, there are obvious differences between Caruthers' Jarvis and Cooper's Leatherstocking. Jarvis does not have the nobility and stature that Cooper was able to impart to his hero over a five-novel cycle. Yet for all his ignorance and limitations, Jarvis stands as the most appealing and interesting character in the book. Frank Lee and Alexander Spotswood are two different characters, but essentially they think, feel, and act in distressingly similar and predictable ways. They do not come to life as human beings. They are cardboard characters cut from the pattern of aristocratic gentleman. One feels that one has met them a hundred times before in a hundred mediocre melodramas and romances. Of course, Jarvis himself is not a completely unique characterization, but he does contain a creative spark that the other characters in the novel lack. He is Caruthers' most successful creation, just as Horse-Shoe Robinson was Kennedy's most fully realized character.

Because he likes Jarvis, the reader is apt to be jolted by the character assessment that Frank Lee makes at the end of the expedition. Frank has been closely associated with Jarvis during this perilous journey. The hunter has personally initiated Lee into the mysteries of the forest and the art of surviving in the wilderness. Yet after the army returns to civilization Frank retains essentially the same condescending attitude toward Jarvis he had displayed at the beginning of the expedition. "I have learned to feel somthing like an attachment for the scout," he concludes. "The native soil is a good one, and with judicious attention and skilful guidance, he might be made a useful man in his sphere" (p. 240). Frank speaks of Jarvis as if he were a strange sort of semihuman, to be appreciated at arm's length, to be valued with circumspection. Yet one must assume that the writer stands behind Lee's judgment, for Frank is a hero and a gentleman, and Caruthers' fictional world is structured around the values Lee and men like him represent.

Caruthers' novel ends on a grand scale with Spotswood's investiture of his Cavalier warriors as "Knights of the Horse-shoe." Lee, Page, Randolph, Byrd, Carter, Wythe, Washington, Pendleton, Beverley, Bland, Fitzhugh, Dandridge, Ludwell–each flower of Virginia Cavalierdom receives a golden horseshoe inlaid with precious stones. Spotswood challenges the young men to carry their tokens to King George and to tell him of the new empire they have added to his dominion. "He will recognize you," the governor proclaims, "as a part of the chivalry of the empire–of that glorious band of knights and gentlemen who surround his throne like a bulwark" (p. 245).

Amidst all this pomp and splendor, it is ironic but not surprising that the man most responsible for the success of the undertaking, Red Jarvis, is absent. At this point in the novel Caruthers has no more use for his frontier scout. The Cavaliers take the stage in the final act; all along they have been the destined heroes of the novelist's parable of our nation's destiny–it is not the rude frontiersman, but the polished Virginia aristocrat who most splendidly fulfills his role as leader of the westward continental expansion. The final chapters of *The Knights of the Golden Horse-shoe* serve to remind the reader, in case he has forgotten, that the laurels rest with Governor Spotswood and his Cavalier followers. It is Spotswood that Caruthers celebrates, with his uniformed bodyguard, his powdered footmen, his baronial hall hung with staghorns and war trophies. These are the scenes on which, in the end, Caruthers invites us to rest our eyes.

William Alexander Caruthers was a nationalist, but he could never be considered a champion of American democracy. The task he set for himself in fiction was a difficult one. He sought to create a counter-myth to match the appeal of the myth of the American common man bravely encountering and subduing an uncivilized continent. He accepted the vision of America's manifest destiny, but in his version of our national crusade he substituted as leader and hero the aristocratic Virginia Cavalier for the democratic man of the people. Frank Lee and Alexander Spotswood were his answer to Davy Crockett and Daniel Boone. Caruthers' vision of America's growth was not convincing for the simple reason that aristocratic mythical figures could not be substituted as leaders of a historical movement profoundly democratic in its implications. In a national mythology Spotswood could never be as convincing a figure as Boone. Though he probably did not recognize it, Caruthers stumbled over this very problem in his appealing characterization of Red Jarvis. By the end of *The Knights of the Golden Horse-shoe* Jarvis so threatened Spotswood's supremacy that Caruthers could reestablish it only by the most arbitrary and artificial of means.

There is an obvious and striking similarity between the conclusions of *The Knights of the Golden Horse-shoe* and of *Horse-Shoe Robinson*. In both novels the yeoman character who had come to dominate the action is pushed into the background while the final scene is given to the aristocratic characters. Caruthers' conclusion is even more flamboyantly romantic than Kennedy's. Both narratives, after having displayed the strength and the effectiveness of the yeoman, return in the end to the Cavalier figure and insist on asserting his dominance, even though the vigorous yeomen they have created call into question the validity of the Cavalier concept.

The problem Kennedy and Caruthers faced in their novels was one which all of the South's romance writers had to deal with in their fiction. In response to a mounting chorus of criticism from the North, Southern writers created a mythical aristocratic figure who embodied what were supposedly the highest ideals of their culture. Yet this ideal character was created with the implicit recognition that the values for which he stood were incompatible with the modern doctrines of progress and manifest destiny. Of course this understanding of the Cavalier's anachronism was not clearly articulated in the South's fiction. No antebellum Southern novelist could have managed to admit openly that the aristocratic myth trumpeted in the work was a hollow one. But though the Cavalier's mythic inadequacy was not directly expressed, it was indirectly acknowledged in the yeoman characters who often insinuated themselves into southern romances and who acted as foils, highlighting the fantastic and impractical nature of the Cavalier figure by their own downright pragmatism, their faith in the common man, and their simple integrity.

R. W. B. Lewis has observed that "dominant clashes over ideas"[12] are a prominent feature of the literature of any culture striving to achieve its identity. During the decades before the Civil War the South was engaged in creating such a definition of its culture. In defending itself from outside attack it sought to assert its uniqueness by linking what it believed to be its inimitable virtues with the ideal characterization of the planter-aristocrat. Yet by espousing the Cavalier figure it was forced either to repudiate the yeoman ideal—an ideal just as deeply imbedded in its history as in other sections of the country—or to find some way of reconciling myths that were essentially irreconcilable. Perhaps the most fascinating feature of *Horse-Shoe Robinson* and *The Knights of the Golden Horse-shoe* is the way they unwittingly dramatize "the sometimes bruising contact of opposites," the clash of social ideals through which the South unsuccessfully struggled to forge its own mythology and its cultural independence (Lewis, p. 2). Even as the Cavalier is being most glorified in Kennedy's and Caruthers' novels, a faint voice persistently whispers his doom. Horse-Shoe Robinson and Red Jarvis are yeomen who prophesy the destruction of the Cavalier and of the way of life he represents, a destruction which would come to pass with the Civil War.

NOTES

1. Rollin G. Osterweis, *Romanticism and Nationalism in the Old South* (New Haven, Conn.: Yale Univ. Press, 1949), p. 4.

2. Wilbur Joseph Cash, *The Mind of the South* (New York: Alfred A. Knopf, 1941), pp. 3–5.

3. Clement Eaton, *The Growth of Southern Civilization, 1790–1860* (New York: Harper, 1961), p. 2.

4. Henry Nash Smith, "The South and the Myth of the Garden," in *Myth and Southern History,* ed. Patrick Gerster and Nicholas Cords (Chicago: Rand McNally, 1974), p. 122.

5. Charles S. Sydnor, *The Development of Southern Sectionalism, 1819–1848* (Baton Rouge, Louisiana State Univ. Press, 1948), p. 220.

6. See Howard R. Floan, *The South in Northern Eyes, 1831–1861* (New York: McGraw-Hill, 1958), p. viii.

7. Richard Gray, *The Literature of Memory: Modern Writers of the American South* (Baltimore: Johns Hopkins Univ. Press, 1977), pp. 13–15.

8. William R. Taylor, *Cavalier and Yankee: The Old South and American National Character* (New York: George Braziller, 1961), p. 17. Subsequent references in the text are to this edition.

9. John Pendleton Kennedy, *Horse-Shoe Robinson: A Tale of the Tory Ascendency in South Carolina, in 1780* (1838; reprint, New York: A. L. Burt Company, 1928), p. 218. Subsequent references in the text are to this edition.

10. William Alexander Caruthers, *The Knights of the Golden Horse-shoe: A Traditionary Tale of the Cocked Hat Gentry in the Old Dominion* (1845; reprint, Chapel Hill: Univ. of North Carolina Press, 1970), pp. 28–29. Subsequent references in the text are to this edition.

11. Osterweis, *Romanticism and Nationalism in the Old South,* p. 173.

12. R. W. B. Lewis, *The American Adam: Innocence, Tragedy and Tradition in the Nineteenth Century* (Chicago: Univ. of Chicago Press, 1955), p. 2. Subsequent reference is to this edition.

The Western Novel as Literature of the Last Frontier

DELBERT E. WYLDER

Since the conclusion of World War II, attempts have been made to re-create, or at least to revitalize, the "frontier" concept in American society. There have been many "new frontiers," some denoting social or political movements, some in the areas of science and technology. The most famous of all, of course, is the "new frontier" of space. Evidently, the concept of the frontier, originally thought of in terms of horizontal–rather than vertical–space, remains not only very much a part of the usable American vocabulary, what with all its connotations, but also a part of the American consciousness or, perhaps even more appropriately, the American unconscious. At least the frontier concept appeals to that large part of the population which considers itself descended, not necessarily biologically nor even ethnically, from the Anglo-Saxon invaders of this continent.

Despite the fact that all of America was a frontier for these Western Europeans at one time in our history, the trans-Mississippi West remains the "true" frontier in the American imagination. The towering mountains, the seemingly unending prairies, the hostile deserts–the very magnitude of space that beggared the eighteenth- and nineteenth-century imaginations and that still, despite our ability to fly over it in a matter of hours, has the power to amaze as we see it from thirty thousand feet–are reasons enough. The cast of characters in this drama of expansion and settlement adds further to the longevity of the appeal of the American West. From the Lewis and Clark expedition, through the mountain men and fur traders, through the dogged and deliberate trains of covered wagons, the inexorable progress of the railroads, and later the cattle drives, the American West provided characters in conflict with space, with the elements and, perhaps even more important, with antagonists as romantic as any group of human beings in history, or the history of literature–the native American on horseback.

It is little wonder, then, that the literature of the American West has been such a large part historically oriented, and that it is both a celebration of the heroic activities of those who managed to push a modified Western civilization into the trans-Mississippi West and at the same time a literature filled with nostalgia for the past and what that past meant to the American spirit and a large but decreasing segment of the American people. What becomes more clear in every decade since Turner published his famous thesis is that the settlement of the Western frontier marked the end of that mass-movement of Anglo-Saxons toward the setting sun. When, in *The Great Gatsby,* F. Scott Fitzgerald has Nick Carraway describe World War I as "that delayed Teutonic migration known as the Great War,"[1] we know that he is talking about a reverse migration–a wave, broken against the shore, receding into the sea.

What is true of Western literature in general is particularly true of the first two of three subgenres we might call "Mountain Man," "Cowboy," and "Indian" novels. As with any sweeping generalization, of course, there are some exceptions–even some outstanding exceptions. For the most part, however, Mountain Man and Cowboy novels concentrate on the conquest of space, on battles with the elements, and on the defeat of an enemy within that space. In many of these novels, especially the "popular" novels, there is a celebration of the final conquest by the Anglo-Saxon. In almost all of them, especially the literary novels, there is the constant sadness of the *ubi sunt* theme, for the frontier itself is seen as a land unpeopled by anyone but savages, a virgin land that must be shaped into the Anglo-Saxon man's own image, and that in the shaping has been raped and ravaged–destroyed, in a very important sense, not only ironically for those who have unwittingly destroyed it, but tragically for posterity which will never be able to experience it. The passage of time and its relationship to the activities of people, then, becomes another of the important conflicts in Western novels.

These novels also frequently bewail the loss not only of the virgin land but of a primitive way of life that is extremely masculine in requiring physical strength, adaptability to nature, resourcefulness, courage, and an almost stoic self-control. Both the mountain man and the cowboy must be able to survive alone, although their chances of survival are increased through male-bonding with a relatively few of their own kind, as in primitive hunting societies.

Finally, the novels, for the most part, present protagonists who revel in their freedoms, whose loss creates nostalgia for the way things were. The typical Mountain Man protagonist, for example, has created a life in which he sees himself free from the responsibilities of domesticity, from laws created by communities of men and women, and even from the future. He is motivated by an unreflecting commitment to individualism, a distrust of other human beings in groups, a failure to understand cause and effect relationships, and an almost aboriginal passion for the hunting life. He has, in actuality, left the community of men behind him and not only distrusts that community but hates it.

He detests the lawyer, the merchant, and the farmer. He feels threatened by the lawyer because lawyers represent a legal authoritarian structure that deprives the free-spirited of their freedom through a complex maze of written proscriptions, and by the merchant because he amasses wealth not by work but by financial manipulations. He has contempt for the farmer because the farmer has abandoned the free, more dangerous, style of living of the hunting societies and has substituted, out of fear or weakness or apathy, a life-style typical of agricultural societies. The farmer has betrayed his masculinity by trading the hunter's commitment to male-bonding for family-bonding, and has lost his independence. The farmer tills the soil, making him dependent not only on the weather but on the community and the marketplace. For the mountain-man protagonists, the marketplace is so distant it seems not to exist in reality; its representatives may form the only community that exists with any regularity during the yearly rendezvous, but it does not pervade his life. For the most part, he does not see it as intruding into his life.

The mountain-man protagonists operate within a code that had evolved with very little change from warrior and hunting societies. One of the major tenets of that code was courage in the face of danger. Another was patience and persistence under stress. Another was silence – the acceptance of hardship without complaint, and self-protective silence in dangerous situations. The most important tenet, as demonstrated in Manfred's *Lord Grizzly,* was loyalty to the group, as well as to a way of life that was viewed as masculine and natural.

Whether part of a "code" or not, mountain men and cowboys see woman, at least the Anglo-saxon woman, as threatening to the male, for she embodies the concept of civilization. She carries with her not only the "trappings" of civilization, but is the "trap" that can destroy freedom and the masculine way of life. She must be sheltered from nature, she and her offspring must be provided for, and she brings with her the concept of the future. In this sense, she is more dangerous than the wild animals in the forest.

It is interesting to note that this same code and the attitude toward women exist, for the most part, in the "cowboy" novels as well, and perhaps provide for the tremendous appeal of popular Westerns to the male reading audience. Even in "literary" Westerns, much of the code remains but, as we shall see, the archetypal cowboy novels would serve as transitions into a "contemporary" novel if, indeed, the force of the "last frontier," that tremendous sense of loss, were not so strong.

Aristotle used *Oedipus Rex* as the typical basis for his discussion of tragedy, and any literary critic would have a difficult time selecting a novel other than Guthrie's *The Big Sky* for paradigmatic purposes, for *The Big Sky* is the most typical, the most archetypal of them all. This is not to say that it is necessarily the most successful, but that it is quintessential. It is a celebration of the mountain men and their wilderness, and it also strongly emphasizes the mutability theme. The three males who have bonded together to battle the elements, the Indians, and, on occasion, other mountain men, are an interesting trio. Dick Summers, the oldest, most experienced of them all, is obviously the tutor figure who is gradually replaced by the more dominant Boone Caudill. Caudill has run away from his Kentucky home because his independence and his developing manliness are being threatened, and he fears that he is being trapped and stultified within the confines of civilization. "It wasn't right to set the law on a man, making him feel small and alone, making him run away."[2] Boone escapes to the wilderness. He learns quickly, and is so ego-centered that nothing he does is wrong in his own eyes. Yet, he is bonded closely to both Summers and Jim Deakins, the third member of the group, who is more sensitive and less capable than Caudill. Boone's murder of Deakins, after he has saved his life, is typical of the unthinking Boone, as is his inability to come to grips with his own emotions about Teal Eye or Jim Deakins.

What is most important about the novel in this context, however, is that there is a constant celebration of the immensity and beauty of the country that almost everyone sees except Boone. Even Peabody, the Easterner who has come to map the country, is awed by the power and the beauty. Boone is also almost completely impervious to time and change, two forces which become thematic early in the novel, but most obviously when Zeb Callaway, Boone's uncle, exclaims, "The whole shitaree. Gone, by God, and naught to care savin' some of us who seen her new" (p. 435). The theme is emphasized further as Jim Deakins contemplates the changes he experiences, when Summers thinks about the companions of his younger days who have all now "gone under" and when everyone finally becomes aware of the gradual disappearance of the beaver. All of the ironies implicit in the novel are summed up beautifully in Summers' statement:

> "There was beaver for us and free country and a big way of livin', and everything we done it looks like we done against ourselves and couldn't do different if we knowed. We went to get away and to enj'y ourselves free and easy, but folks was bound to foller and beaver to get scarce and Injuns to be killed or tamed, and all the time the country gettin' safer and better known. We ain't seen the end of it yet, Boone, not to what the mountain man does against hisself. . . . It's like we heired money and had to spend it, and now it's nigh gone." (Pp. 168–69)

John R. Milton, rightly, I believe, identifies *The Big Sky,* Harvey Fergusson's *Wolf Song,* and Frederick Manfred's *Lord Grizzly* as the "three novels being the best fictional treatment of the mountain men,"[3] although I might quarrel with the selection of Fergusson's novel. Fisher's *Mountain Man,* Guthrie's recent novel, *Fair Land, Fair Land,* which was published after Milton's analysis, and even the almost-forgotten *The Shining Mountains,* by Dale Van Every, seem equal in almost all ways, except stylistically, to the Fergusson novel. Another novel published since Milton's evaluation, Bill Hotchkiss' *The Medicine Calf,* a novel based on the life of Jim Beckwourth, must also be considered seriously.

All of these novels are celebratory in nature. The praise is, once again, not only for the land but for the men who, for a short moment in time, made an impression upon it, or at least put a mark on man's record of the passing of time and the changes that occurred. Manfred's *Lord Grizzly* celebrates the courage, hardihood, and the patience of Hugh Glass, the protagonist, in one of the more complex of the mountain-man novels. Glass, true to his calling, does not leave the mountains to return to "civilization" as does, say, the protagonist of *The Shining Mountains,* but his newly found self-understanding and his willingness, as a result, to forgive the companions who, he has thought, have deserted him mark a change from the self-centered lack of awareness of a Boone Caudill and a deviation from the absolutist Old Testament and tribal concept of revenge which, ironically, has kept him alive.

Dick Summers, the mountain-man mentor in *The Big Sky* is, of course, the transitional figure in Guthrie's works. Committed to the ways of mountain men, he instructs Boone Caudill and Jim Deakins in the wiles and ways of this hunting clan. When he realizes, for himself, that the old days are gone and that his own body can no longer cope with the rigors of life in the wilderness, he returns East, only to betray his former companions by leading a wagonload of settlers into the no-longer virgin land in *The Way West.* He had damned Tom Fitzpatrick at the end of *The Big Sky* for just such an undertaking. His understanding of the elements and of the country and of the Indians, learned as a mountain man, is the required knowledge the settlers must have to be successful. And finally, in *Fair Land, Fair Land,* Summers returns to the mountains in an attempt to live out his life in peace and contentment. But it is useless. The beaver is gone, the game is scarce, and his few years of idyllic life with Teal Eye are doomed by the "relentless march" of the Anglo-Saxons. Sam Lash, the protagonist of *Wolf Song,* having established himself within a small hunting group, adjusted to the wilderness and even, in hand-to-hand combat, killed the archetypal enemy, becomes a true mountain man. But Lash trades his passion for the wilderness and the camaraderie of male companions for the love of a Spanish woman, and through the very act of winning her for his bride, he suffers a great loss, for he has been, in a sense, tamed.

Although their roles may not be significant in terms of the space allotted them, women play a significant role in novels about cowboys and the life of the range. It is only in the popular genre, and in cinematic adaptations, that the final scene shows the cowboy hero "riding off into the sunset," thus turning his back on women and the civilized community that she represents. Owen Wister's *The Virginian* is the archetype of the cowboy novel. The protagonist seems perfectly adapted to his life on the range. He is superior in riding, roping, and shooting, and at the beginning of the novel he is carefree, youthfully rebellious, and protective of his freedom. But he is also reflective and ambitious, especially after he falls in love with the schoolteacher who has come from the East. He takes his responsibilities seriously, not only to the owner of the ranch where he finally becomes foreman but to the unwritten laws of the range concerning rustling. He is willing to sacrifice his best friend to the concept of private ownership of cattle. A law higher than the law of the male hunting group becomes operational in the cowboy novels. Boone Caudill would never have betrayed one of his small group; only what he thought was a personal and sexual affront led him to kill Jim Deakins.

The Virginian is no Boone Caudill. He travels to the East and is accepted by the Easterners as almost a model of the reinvigorated man. He has an aesthetic appreciation of the landscape in which he lives. He reads, and he thinks of the future. At the end of the novel, he is finding ways to make the ranching more efficient. Much of his inspiration and motivation comes from his educated Eastern wife, although, one must admit, he is not willing to bow to her pacifism when his integrity is challenged by Trampas. In that sense, he is true to the code of the West.

Constance Ellsworth, in Emerson Hough's *Heart's Desire,* is another Eastern woman who has a dramatic effect upon male-oriented society in a tiny New Mexican town devoid of women except for "the girls from Kansas," who are essentially homemakers and thus not dangerous in Hough's scenario. Even these women cause difficulties, for Curly, a cowboy who has married one of them, is unable to go with a posse to capture Billy the Kid because he has become a "family man" with responsibilities. But the educated, cultured Constance Ellsworth is the real "Eve" in the Garden of Eden, and it is only the weakness of the hero, Dan Anderson, that allows him to invite her into the Garden of Heart's Desire. Dan Anderson is able, by the end of the novel, to arrange something of a compromise between the "corruption" of the railroad representatives from the East and the code that binds him to his friends in the Western hamlet. But *Heart's Desire* is not a typical Western novel. The men who live in the town can hardly be described as energetic, dynamic Westerners; Heart's Desire could be called a "sleepy" town at best.

It would be hard to compile a list of the "best" four or five literary range novels, for there are so many good ones. A. B. Guthrie's *These Thousand Hills* is one of them. Like Wister's Virginian, the protagonist of Guthrie's novel chooses responsibility over his earlier carefree life, but his seeming desertion of the prostitute who has helped him prosper, and his return to his colder but cultured wife is a scene far different from the idyllic honeymoon near the end of *The Virginian,* where the Virginian's bride quite obviously fits very well into the Edenic setting. Perhaps the novel is too realistic to have gained the popularity of Guthrie's other novels, but it illustrates very well the acceptance of a settled way of life and a turning from the masculine society to a family society dominated by a responsibility to women and children. For the most part, the best of the range novels show, if not the actual decay, at least the deterioration of the frontier spirit and the life of freedom. Walter Van Tilburg Clark's *The Ox-Bow Incident* is one, Larry McMurtry's *Horseman, Pass By* another, and Frederick Manfred's *Riders of Judgment* still another. These novels concentrate on human weaknesses or on the "darker side" of human nature as causes of the change, while Jack Shaefer's *Monte Walsh* shows the effect of economic and social changes on the life of the cowboy.

Two highly symbolic novels, Shaefer's *Shane* and Edward Abbey's *The Brave Cowboy,* illustrate quite well the "lastness" of the American frontier. Shane is the epitome of the popular cowboy hero. He rides into the farm and then into town, straightening out the problems that the homesteader and his family are having with the corrupted rancher, and then rides off into the sunset. He has saved the farmers and made a lasting and inspiring impression on the boy narrator and his parents, but he has also caused the beginning of the end of a way of life. The life of the cowboy will be superseded by the life of the farmer and the townsman, an occurrence illustrated in *Monte Walsh*.

In Edward Abbey's *The Brave Cowboy,* made into the cinematically successful *Lonely Are the Brave,* the protagonist Jack Burns is, in a sense, the "last cowboy." He no longer punches cattle but has been reduced to herding sheep and now has come to rescue his friend from a term in prison for aiding "wetbacks." A living champion of freedom, Burns is totally unable to understand his friend's refusal, on philosophical grounds, to escape the punishment of the law. Burns escapes alone, across the mesa and into the mountains on his skittish young horse, Whiskey, only to be killed along with his horse by a truck (although he miraculously reappears in two later Abbey novels), while trying to cross a highway that divides one range of mountains from the range that, he thinks, will provide him with a safe exit to Mexico.

Throughout the novel, Abbey makes it clear that Burns is a ghost from the past. Riding through the modern industrialized Duke City, Burns is seen as an anachronism. The sheriff of the search party trying to capture him speaks of him as a "ghost." Thus the final scene, when he and his horse are hit by the truck carrying flush toilets to Duke City and which throughout the novel has symbolized "over-organized society," depicts the sudden end of a way of life that has been gradually disappearing.

Appropriately to "Indian" novels, such as Frederick Manfred's *Conquering Horse,* in which the capture of a horse is symbolic of the continuation and fulfilling celebration of a way of life—the death of the horse becomes in contrast symbolic in cowboy novels. The cowboy was equally dependent on the horse for his way of life. Another novel in which the death of a horse signals the end of an era is Tom Lea's neglected *The Wonderful Country,* a novel which moves back and forth across the border between Texas and Mexico with descriptions of landscape on both sides, descriptions that are almost unrivaled in their ability to call up southwestern scenes to the mind's eye in order to celebrate the beauty and magnificence of the Southwest.

Lea's novel, of course, is not the only cowboy novel that is celebratory of Western landscapes. As in the mountain-man novels, there is such a concern with descriptions of landscape in cowboy and mountain-man novels that for many critics landscape has almost become a character in the development of individual Westerns. If true, that character is aging; seams and wrinkles show on his face in the cowboy novels. Gone is the purity, the freedom of movement, as towns begin to dot the landscape, and barbed-wire fence and dirt roads divide the land into parcels. Thus, even the descriptions of the land remind the reader of the *ubi sunt* theme that becomes predominant, finally, in the best of both the mountain-man and cowboy novels. There is a sad undertone, even in the otherwise hilarious Max Evans comic novel *The Rounders.*

Gone, too, is the strongly male-bonded hunting group, a victim of both the times and the demands of a hero-oriented, or at least a "protagonist-oriented" novel form. Only in some of the novels of Eugene Manlove Rhodes or in trail narratives like Andy Adams's *The Log of a Cowboy* do we find "men in groups" as the unified hero figure in literature of the range. The Virginian is a hero, as in Dan McMasters in Hough's trail-drive novel *North of 36;* even Jack Burns in *The Brave Cowboy* is a hero.

It would be logical to assume that the "Indian" novel would be the most concerned with the sense of loss—the *ubi sunt* theme—since, at least chronologically, the native-American civilization was the first to inhabit the Western mountains, plains, and deserts, only to be replaced by what Hough called "the relentless march" of the Anglo-Saxons. That would be a mistaken assumption, however; some of the best of the native-American novels concentrate on the human dilemmas of the central characters, and the authors usually depend on the reader's awareness of the loss of the whole native-American culture to the advancing whites. Frank Waters's *The Man Who Killed the Deer,* for example, places the focus on the problems of the protagonist, Martiniano, not only in his attempts to find a place between the white community and the Pueblo community but in his battle with his own ego, and the conclusion, in which Martiniano subordinates his ego to the more important spiritual domination of the tribe and its religion and tradition, is a triumphant affirmation of the human, though particularly native-American, spirit. Frederick Manfred's *Conquering Horse* and the more recent lyrical *Manly Hearted Woman* are both celebrations of the culture of the native American but, even more, novels of the development of the individual but distinctly native-American psyche within that culture.

There have been, of course, many novels, as well as narratives and biographies, which delineate the loss of native-American land and autonomy to the advancing white culture. The story is told in novels as disparate in time and tone as Will Levington Comfort's *Apache* and Thomas Berger's well-researched *Little Big Man,* but the story has been much more emotionally reported in such narratives and collections as Neihardt's *Black Elk Speaks* and Dee Brown's compilation of materials on Wounded Knee.

Novels in which the protagonist attempts to enter the white civilization but finally returns to his native-American heritage are many. The best of these is Waters's *The Man Who Killed the Deer,* although Oliver La Farge's romanticized *Laughing Boy* should certainly not be forgotten. Neither should La Farge's far more naturalistic novel, *The Enemy Gods.* Hal Borland's *When the Legends Die* follows somewhat the same pattern as the latter novel but adds a very symbolic bear for good measure. Leslie Silko's *Ceremony* also deserves mention here, although it belongs to a very distinct group of novels.

This group is written by native-American novelists, and their characters wander, often listlessly, through an almost Kafkaesque landscape and an incomprehensible world until they somehow find themselves and their own Indianness away from the meaningless white culture that surrounds and stifles them. N. Scott Momaday's *House Made of Dawn* is the most complex of these, perceptively showing the conflicts between the Spanish, Mexican, Anglo, and native-American cultures within a contemporary framework, but Jim Welch's *Winter in the Blood* is a beautifully and almost surrealistic depiction of the absurdities, to the native American, of American culture in the West. Silko's novel is far more naturalistic, but also effective, particularly in picturing the despair of native-American males in the twentieth century.

These novels written by native Americans point up most dramatically, in one sense, the loss of freedoms symbolized by the closing of the frontier, for the protagonists find themselves almost totally isolated within an alien culture, with only themselves, their heritage, and their spirituality to save them.

But perhaps the most significant statements about mountain men, cowboys, and native Americans as characters who represent the finality of the frontier is in contemporary novels, which either reject the civilization that has followed the settling of the West or which suggest the incorporation of the mountain man's "clear vision" into the structure of that civilization. Edward Abbey's Hayduke, in *The Monkey Wrench Gang,* is an example, though certainly an atypical one. Hayduke is a "happy-go-lucky" throwback to the mountain man. Careless of the environment himself, he fights against all major attempts to restructure that environment in the name of civilization. Though his cause seems hopeless, his cleverness both in nature and in his understanding of the law allow him to survive both nature and the law. Despite the open-ended conclusion of the novel, however, Abbey's novel presents a pathetic picture of the end of the frontier itself, if not the end of the frontier spirit.

William Eastlake's *The Bronc People* presents another portrait of the mountain-man image which has survived the closing of the frontier. Blue-eyed Billy Peersall is an old Indian fighter who has survived the wars and, by the end of the novel, becomes the tutor for both Little Sant Bowman, the "really cowboy," and his friend Alistair Benjamin, the black boy raised by the Bowmans. The novel celebrates the beauty and the immutability of nature, but the plaintive note of the lost frontier and the last frontier can be found in the following passage when Little Sant and Alistair interview the old Indian fighter.

> "Well, we made the wrong arrangements. We fought the wrong people. We should have joined the Indians, fought the whites, the Easterners. That's why we come here, mountain men, the plainsmen, to escape all that. And then we joined them to fight the people who were the same, who wanted to live like us—the Indians. I don't know why we did it except we were confused by the color of their skins, the Easterners' skins, their language. Because they were the same color, spoke the same language, we must have been confused into thinking, into forgetting we had come out here to escape them."[4]

Eastlake's lament, through his character Blue-eyed Billy Peersall, is a lament that permeates almost all contemporary Western literary novels—the sense of loss of male companionship and the loss of freedom to "do what I please," as Boone Caudill would say.

Blue-eyed Billy's commitment, at the end of *The Bronc People,* to be the inspirational mentor for the young black man, Alistair Benjamin, along with his championing of the Mexican children in the public school system, is highly significant for not only the future of the United States but for the future of Western American literature. The fact that astronauts and scientists have, in the latter decades of the twentieth century, walked on the moon and created a new frontier in space seems much less important to literature than another fact—the complexion of the American people is rapidly changing.

The influx of Eastern and Southern Europeans toward the end of the nineteenth century that so upset hardened Anglo-Saxon Americans like Emerson Hough seems to pale almost into insignificance when compared to immigration statistics since World War II. Refugees came from Korea after the "police action" there, and in even greater numbers from South Vietnam after that unfortunate war, tremendously increasing the numbers of Americans with Asian backgrounds. From the Spanish-speaking countries, there have been refugees from Castro's Cuba, political refugees from Central America, particularly El Salvador, and a stream of Mexicans attempting to find work and a higher standard of living north of the border. Furthermore, though there have been a relatively small number of black immigrants from Haiti, American black citizens have at least made a beginning to finding a measure of equality. To further complicate the situation, American women have insisted on equality of rights, and have, perhaps, made more gains than any of the other groups.

What all this will mean to society is difficult to say. What it means to literature, however, is that it will present a new era of human problems that, though not necessarily new, will be found in different contexts that will appeal not only to naturalistic but romantic writers.

For Western American literature, the shift away from Anglo-Saxon majorities in the reading public may result in a change of interest. The predominant subject matter of Western American literature has been male-oriented, white Anglo-Saxon pantheistic, if not atheistic, hunting or warrior-like societies and individuals who have cherished freedom to live their own way of life despite the rest of society. How such a literature will appeal to the reading public of the future is difficult to guess. Although Western films and television programs seem to be on the decline, the popularity of Westerns where such themes seem to be even more blatantly expressed seems to have remained as strong as ever. And courses in Western American literature seem to be thriving.

But Western American literature has had its Homers, singing of the magnificent days of the past—A. B. Guthrie, Jr., Frank Waters, Frederick Manfred, Vardis Fisher, Harvey Fergusson, Conrad Richter, and many, many more. And it is beginning to see the dilemmas of the contemporary scene through the mixture of the past and the present, as in Wallace Stegner's masterful *Angle of Repose,* or William Eastlake's *Bronc People,* or through a study of the contemporary scene, as we find in some of Larry McMurtry's best novels.

Although the geographical frontier has closed, and there is a strong sense that it was, for Americans at least, the last meaningful frontier on this planet, the possibilities remain great for not only the continued exploration and reinterpretation of that frontier in literature but for an expansion of literature in the social and human problems that change will bring–changes that will cause even greater human problems and conflicts, but also, hopefully, expressions of understanding, tolerance, and love–precisely because the frontier has closed and America must turn in on itself, finally, and find answers to, rather than escape from, its problems.

NOTES

1. F. Scott Fitzgerald, *The Great Gatsby* (New York: Charles Scribner's Sons, 1925), p. 3.
2. A. B. Guthrie, Jr., *The Big Sky* (New York: Cardinal Edition, Pocket Books, Inc., 1962) p. 7. Subsequent references in the text are to this edition.
3. John R. Milton, *The Novel of the American West* (Lincoln: Univ. of Nebraska Press, 1980), p. 234.
4. William Eastlake, *The Bronc People* (Albuquerque: Univ. of New Mexico Press, 1975), p. 156.

Golden State: A Demanding Paradise, an Enduring Frontier

GERALD HASLAM

Somewhere between expectation and experience exists a place, or series of places, called California. People pass their lives here with passion or ennui, with hope or despair, each perhaps affected by where they are because California has never been allowed to be merely a state in the Union. It is also a state of the mind. British journalist Michael Davie acknowledges that "for a hundred years California has been the ultimate frontier of the Western world: the stopping place of man's strange westering urge."[1]

Ironically, one reason that the state remains the "ultimate frontier" is that, unlike the East Coast corridor, whose values have been confused for the nation's, California is relatively free from European yearning; it is a place where the Hispanoamerican concept of *mestizaje*–racial and cultural blending –is much in evidence, a place whose exotic components speak to new forms and new possibilities rather than mere reinforcement of older, Anglo-Saxon patterns. For instance, movie scripts, certainly not a traditional genre, for years constituted a most influential body of literature produced in the state; Nathanael West, F. Scott Fitzgerald, Aldous Huxley, and S. J. Perelman, among many others, wrote them. Moreover, the state's four most important authors have, arguably, been Jack London, Robinson Jeffers, John Steinbeck, and William Saroyan–each a maverick, each misunderstood by mainline critics. Today, California's fiction writers seem increasingly influenced by the powerful magical realism of Latin America, decreasingly by traditional European or American modes. In literature as in life, the Golden State remains *terra incognita,* a place that has escaped domination by the Old World.

European settlement of California is said to have begun in the 1530s, when a few Spaniards ventured onto its southern reaches. In 1542, Juan Rodriguez Cabrillo discovered San Diego Bay and explored the coast north. Nothing those adventurers experienced, however, lived up to the image of California that had already been created by Garci Rodriguez Ordonez de Montalvo in a popular Spanish novel, *Las sergas de Esplandian* (1510):

Know ye that on the right hand of the Indies there is an island called California, very near the Terrestrial Paradise and inhabited by black women without a single man among them and living in the manner of Amazons. They are robust of body, strong and passionate in heart and of great valor. Their island is one of the most rugged in the world with bold rocks and crags. Their arms are all of gold, as is the harness of the wild beasts which, after taming, they ride. In all the island there is no other metal.[2]

Expectation has often preceded and overwhelmed reality here.

California began as a dual frontier: physically, it was sealed by great mountains, by vast deserts, by dense forests; so remote was the area that its first European immigrants approached not from the east but from the south, then the west. Little wonder that today it remains closely linked to Latin America and Asia. As Davie observed, "In California, the European traveler cannot fail to be struck by the absence of the political, social, and religious arrangements the rest of America derived from Europe" (p. 21).

In *The Frontier in American Literature* (1927), Lucy Hazzard suggested that frontier literature had evolved through two stages–the physical frontier, featuring the writing of such as Bret Harte and Mark Twain; the industrial frontier, seen in the work of Frank Norris, Sinclair Lewis, and Edgar Lee Masters–toward a third, the spiritual pioneering for control of self. California writing has not only strongly evidenced the first two of Hazzard's stages, it has virtually defined the third.

As a spiritual frontier, California represents now, as it always has in the American Mind, the possibility of great reward and great disappointment; observed John Bidwell in the nineteenth century, "People generally look on it as the garden of the world, or the most desolate place of Creation."[3] Little room has existed for middle ground in this land of dreams. On Thanksgiving day, 1985, in a San Francisco shelter for the homeless, a migrant named Amos Franklin told a reporter for the *San Francisco Examiner,* "I heard California was about somethin'. But it ain't really about nothin'."

The state continues as an edge where the past abuts the future, and the future is not always as we might wish it to be. Richard Armour states matters:

So leap with joy, be blithe and gay,
  or weep my friends with sorrow.
What California is today,
  The rest will be tomorrow.[4]

The central problem is not that America may become what California is, but that America may become what people *imagine* California is.

California borders the past too. William T. Pilkington and others have noted that Americans continue to believe that once we had an Edenic period full of promise and possibility. For many people, that period of promise remains *now* in California, as evidenced by migrants who continue streaming here: time and place merge on the Pacific shore.

In fact, contemporary illusions concerning the Golden State are largely the product of general misunderstanding fostered by mass media that proclaim versions of Southern California's glittering image to be California's homogeneous reality. California is a large, varied area, multiethnic since earliest settlement; non-white residents are expected to outnumber white residents by 1990. Carey McWilliams points out that the state's diversity of populace is matched by its diversity of environments: "in no other area of the world, of comparable size, is so wide a variety of ecological factors to be found."[5]

Four geo/literary regions have emerged in writing from the Golden State, each of them reflecting regional frontiers, with distinct terrain, patterns of settlement, and literary outputs: The North Coast, extending from Big Sur north toward Oregon, with San Francisco its core—in no other place did the East more dramatically penetrate and influence the West; the Great Central Valley, a state-within-the-state that is among the nation's leaders in agriculture and the production of petroleum and country singers; Wilderness California, a heterogenous catch-all that includes the state's mountains, deserts, and forests—vast tracts still little settled even if widely used; and finally, Southern California, dominated today by the Los Angeles-San Diego freeway culture but which was until the late nineteenth century called the "cow counties"—as wild a West as existed until the end of the nineteenth century.

The North Coast's literary history was dominated by San Francisco Bay, which allowed the development of a rough-hewn imitation of an eastern seaport, attracting to the region during the late 1840s and the 1850s such estimable is largely forgotten early authors as George Horatio Derby (John Phoenix), Alonzo Delano (Old Box), Louisa Smith Clapp (Dame Shirley), and John Rollin Ridge (Yellow Bird). The following decade—San Francisco was by 1860 the fourteenth largest city in the Union—saw the development of a national literary reputation by writers operating in the Bay Area, especially the Golden Gate Trinity (Bret Harte, Ina Coolbrith, and Charles Warren Stoddard, the three editors of the *Overland Monthly*), plus their partner Mark Twain, a high point in American letters. What was most important, perhaps, is that artists of the time reflected a distinctness still associated with the region; "they had defined themselves as a people liberated from the Puritan past," writes Kevin Starr, "glorying in an exuberant lust for life" (p. 241).

Throughout the remainder of the nineteenth century, the San Francisco area remained a cultural magnet, attracting diverse artists: Robert Louis Stevenson, J. Ross Browne, Ambrose Bierce, Gertrude Atherton, Prentice Mulford, Yone Noguchi, Frank Norris, and Joaquin Miller, among others. By the 1870s, the larger North Coast remained frontier, while the Bay Area became a frontier province, complete with its own avant-garde and an association to encourage it. Founded in 1872, the Bohemian Club assembled many of the most creative men of the period—all the authors listed above, save Stevenson—as well as adding earlier masters Harte and Twain; naturalists John Muir and Joseph LeConte; graphic artists William Keith, Virgil Williams, Julian Rix, and Jules Tavenier. It was, as Starr observes, "a gathering place for productive personalities . . . through the turn of the century" (p. 246). Although the Bohemian Club was to become an elitist business and social organization, genuine bohemian movements continued to flourish in the area.

Later in the century, for example, creative people began gathering at Carmel. Some, like Miller, were links to the frontier past; most, however, bespoke a new generation's dynamism: Jack London, Mary Austin, Lincoln Steffens, George Sterling, plus a host of lesser-known writers. Graphic artists Arnold Genthe and Xavier Martinez were also there, and visitors included figures such as Upton Sinclair, Keith, Muir, Coolbrith and Stoddard. By the early twentieth century, then, the North Coast had become one of America's most productive, yet controversial, literary regions. Moreover, it had not only produced literature reflecting all three of Hazzard's stages, but was also the first western area to produce a significant body of writing exploring the spirit and to establish a precedent for the continued examination of that timeless frontier. The North Coast's bohemians real and imagined—Jack Kerouac and the Beats, Ken Kesey and his Merry Pranksters, Richard Brautigan and the Hippies—have been, among other things, navel-gazers.

One distinguished novel that captures the sense of the churning North Coast—and California—during the nineteenth century, as well as the recent past, is Wallace Stegner's *Angle of Repose.* Employing contemporary historian Lyman Ward, who is writing a novel about his grandparents, as narrative voice, Stegner powerfully links the past and present. The novel's central figure is prototypical of earlier North Coast immigrants: "The West began for Susan Burling on the last day of 1868, more than a century ago. She was in love with Art, New York, and Augusta Drake." Stegner has his narrator explore the nature of the novel being written within *Angle of Repose,* so that the work expresses not only history but also Hazzard's third frontier, the human spirit as it actually is, linked with all that has shaped it. Ward complains that modern people "have suffered empathectomy, their computers hum no ghostly feedback of Home, Sweet Home." In its innovative form, as well as in its revealing exploration of lives that shaped and were shaped by the state, *Angle of Repose* illustrates North Coast writing at its finest.

Although it boasted virtually no literary history of note prior to the 1930s, California's Great Central Valley, the state's heartland, has become in the past fifty years a literary region. Well over four hundred miles long and fifty miles wide, the valley is bounded on all sides by mountains. When William Henry Brewer passed through it in 1861, he described the area as "a plain of absolute desolation" relieved only by icy Sierra rivers that flowed into it at intervals.[6] Damming those rivers and channeling their waters for irrigation helped convert the valley into the world's richest agricultural region. In turn, that richness has attracted an ethnically and socially diverse series of migrants to work its fields: Chinese, Japanese, Italian, Portuguese, Sikh, German, Filipino, Mexican, black, and various poor whites, among others.

If it appears that the valley has typified the California Dream, however, there is a difference, for in it virtually the only path to a better life has been hard physical labor, whether on the farms or in the oil fields that sprouted shortly after the turn of the century. This is not the California most dreamers have envisioned, so it has tended to attract the tough, the determined, possibly the desperate. Some have suggested that it has also attracted the unimaginative, but since the emergence of two native sons, William Saroyan and William Everson, and the area's centrality during the thirties in two classic books by nonvalley natives, *The Grapes of Wrath* by John Steinbeck and *Factories in the Fields* by Carey McWilliams, it has produced a steady stream of innovative literature that defies the state's stereotype. Much of this writing starts with the soil, the physical reality from which so many valley dwellers wrest their livings.

Just as hard urban realities have shaped much writing from California's cities, so have the valley's harsh rural realities shaped literature produced there, limiting illusion without harming expression. Or limiting most illusion, for, as native Joan Didion shows, parochialism and xenophobia are not unknown, especially among the "old families" which no longer toil in the fields:

> I remember being taken to call upon a very old woman, a rancher's widow, who was reminiscing (the favored conversational mode in Sacramento) about the son of some contemporaries of hers. "That Johnston boy never did amount to much," she said. Desultorily, my mother protested: Alva Johnston, she said, had won the Pulitzer Prize, when he was working for *The New York Times*. Our hostess looked at us impassively. "He never amounted to anything in Sacramento," she said.[7]

On the other side of the tracks, however, a different ethos endures, one more concerned with survival than with acceptance by San Francisco's society. In his visionary play *Bernabe* for example, Luis Valdez allows his central character to be tempted and taunted by La Tierra, the Earth herself: "All your life you work for nothing como un perro, para que? The patron at least has me, Bernabe–what do you have?" Leonard Gardner, in his story "Christ Has Returned to Earth and Preaches Here Nightly," describes a young worthy this way:

> On one forearm beneath a dagger piercing his profusely bleeding skin was written DEATH BEFORE DISHONOR, and on the other, HARRY AMES and U.S.M.C. curved around the Marine Corps emblem–an anchor and the world with a boil in its northern hemisphere. He had obtained these in his thirteenth year from a Hawaiian who had come up from Stockton on a motor scooter with his needles in the tool box.[8]

In his sketch "Going Short," Chester Seltzer (Amado Muro) quotes a field laborer: "'It's never popular to be poor–only in the Bible,' he said. 'A man must have invented stoop labor because a snake never would.'" Humor is frequently employed by this region's authors in their unflinching view of life; Wilma Elizabeth McDaniel writes in "Transportation" about the funeral of Okie migrant Dolita Owens:

> I knowed her in them days
> model T's
> model A's
> and right on down the list,
> I hope she's satisfied riding in a Cadillac today . . .

Can these be voices from Calilfornia? They can be and are voices from what Powell has called "the *cor cordium* of the state."[9]

Less than a hundred miles south of the valley exists a separate nation, Southern California. To proceed there, however, a traveler must climb the Grapevine grade into the Tehachapi Mountains, the state's major east-west range and one of the diverse manifestations of still another literary region, Wilderness California. Outsiders do not always understand the dimensions of the Golden State's open, uncultivated land. The Mojave and Colorado deserts border it to the east and south. A remarkable and varied coastline marks the west. The north is Bigfoot country: both virgin and second-growth forests as dense as any in America grow here. Northeast is a volcanic moonscape. Moreover, the state is spined by mountains: the Sierra Nevada, the Cascades, the Coast Ranges, the Tehachapis.

What is most interesting in the distinguished body of writing produced about Wilderness California is that it combines elements of Hazzard's first and third stages of frontier; that is, in the work of the finest writers, the topography of the land is never far from the topography of the soul. Look, for example, at the literary reclamation of the desert. Those barren lands had once been crossed by pioneers too intent on survival to notice the unique beauty surrounding them. By the turn of the century, however, the arid lands could be studied and sometimes romanticized. It was one of those interesting cases where changing circumstances allowed people to *re-vision* an area.

John C. Van Dyke's *The Desert* (1901) was the first in a series of books that changed the way those ostensible wastelands were viewed. An art professor, he saw the arid land as a painter might: "Pure sunlight requires for existence pure air, and the Old World has little of it left. The chief glory of the desert is its broad blaze of omnipresent light." He also demonstrated keen ecological intuition: "The deserts should never be reclaimed. They are the breathing-spaces of the west and should be preserved forever."[10]

Other major works in the literary reclamation of the arid regions were A. J. Burdick's *The Mystic Mid-Region* (1904), George Wharton James's *The Wonders of the Colorado Desert* (1906), and J. Smeaton Chase's *California Desert Trails* (1919). The finest of all desert books, however, the most mystical and eloquent, is Mary Hunter Austin's *The Land of Little Rain* (1903). While her nature writing was both accurate and rhapsodic, it was her recognition of the desert's symbolic power that made her book special. "Out there where the boundary of soul and sense is as faint as a trail in a sand-storm," she wrote, "I have seen things happen that I do not believe myself. . . . Great souls that go into the desert come out mystics."

California's mountains and forests boast as distinguished a cadre of authors as do its deserts. The master here, of course, is John Muir. His work ranged from romantic to scientific. In his books, such as *The Mountains of California* (1894), Muir wrote prose that soared toward poetry. Of the Sierra, he wrote:

> After ten years spent in the heart of it, rejoicing and wondering, bathing in the glorious floods of light, seeing the sunbursts of morning among the icy peaks, the noonday radiance on the trees and rocks and snow, the flush of the alpen-glow, and a thousand dashing waterfalls with their marvelous abundance of irised spray, it still seems to me above all other the Range of Light, the most divinely beautiful of all the mountain chains I have seen.[11]

Other distinguished books in the same tradition include Clarence King's *Mountaineering in the Sierra Nevadas* (1871), Joseph LeConte's *A Journal of Ramblings through the High Sierra* (1875), William Henry Brewer's *Up and Down California, 1860–64* (1930), and Robert Wood's *Mountain Cabin* (1974).

The northern wilderness is the setting of one of the state's more interesting recent books, *The Klamath Knot* (1983), by David Rains Wallace, a volume blending evolutionary theory with mythic realizations, hinting at a new synthesis. He writes, for example, of "the bear's deep ancestry": "I was seeing a bear as it really is, not only a black animal in a forest, but part of a long wave of black animals surging upward from depths of time imperceptible to normal senses." Perhaps more to the point is that only a wilderness at least as deep as the bear's continuum could have triggered such challenging perceptions, and it exists in northern California, waiting, waiting. . . .

Sometimes ignored when considering Wilderness California is its impact on poets and novelists; yet it has inspired some of the state's finest literature. For instance, much of Robinson Jeffers's finest poetry—say, "Roan Stallion"—demonstrates the symbolic power of California's coastline and hills. George R. Stewart wrote of Sierra forest when he produced two of his most memorable novels, *Storm* (1941) and *Fire* (1949), and one of Walter Van Tilburg Clark's most magical works, *The Track of the Cat* (1949), is set in eastern Sierra cattle country.

A particularly interesting example is *The Ford* (1917), a novel that Mary Austin set in fictitious Tierra Longa, which resembles the Owens Valley. Austin's story closely follows the controversial diversion of the Owens River at the turn of the century, an action that turned verdant ranchland into a desert in order to provide water for Los Angeles, allowing that city to boom. In *Southern California: An Island on the Land* (1973) Carey McWilliams called it, "the Owens Valley tragedy." Water and the politics of water have been more important than gold in California's development. The region that drained the Owens Valley, Southern California (aka, The Southland) is a desert-turned-city as a result of water piped—some say stolen—from elsewhere. The absence of local water resources is California's eternal problem. Before water became available, both another frontier and another *type* of frontier fermented in the arid southland: the "cow counties," little touched by the gold rush, had remained largely Spanish speaking until 1860, and they harbored a strong movement to split the state to avoid dominance by the economically and culturally advanced north. "At that time," Lawrence Clark Powell observes, "Los Angeles was the toughest town in the West, a cesspool of frontier scum."[12] But it was definitely a frontier, not an eastern enclave, as was San Francisco.

How tough was it? Brewer explains his precautions in 1860:

> We all continually wear arms—each wears both bowie knife and pistol, while we have always for game or otherwise, a Sharp's rifle, Sharp's carbine, and two double-barrelled shotguns. Fifty or sixty murders per year have been so common here in Los Angeles . . . as I write this there are at least six heavy loaded revolvers in the tent, besides bowie knives and other arms. (P. 14)

An article in the *Southern Californian* of May 30, 1855, began: "The past week or two have been tolerable good for killing."[13]

While hardly the literary outpost that San Francisco was, the region did produce an interesting body of writing in the nineteenth century, writing that exemplifies principally the first of Hazzard's three stages. Most interesting are Richard Henry Dana's early glimpses of Spanish California in *Two Years before the Mast* (1840), a book that views the area as the first American settlers did, from the sea; William Manley's *Death Valley in '49* (1894), which approaches overland (after surviving the terrible desert–not everyone in his party did–Manley wrote, ". . . [W]e came to the sea shore, the grandest sight in the world to me, for I had never before seen the ocean. What a wide piece of water it was!"[14]); and the first clothbound book to be printed in Los Angeles, *The Reminiscences of a Ranger* (1881), which describes that municipality as "a place where every man carried his code strapped to his posterior" and whose author, Horace Bell, a contemporary called a murderer and houseburner, among other vile things.[15] Powell included all three of those titles in his book *California Classics* (1971).

The pivotal work in Southern California's literary history is Helen Hunt Jackson's *Ramona* (1884). Intended to expose the plight of Mission Indians, the novel ironically became the major factor in the creation of a romanticized mission past. *Ramona* created a mythic history, which promoters and developers exploited. In *A Literary History of Southern California* (1950), Franklin Walker explains the response to *Ramona* this way: "The readers were, it is feared, much more interested in building up a glorious tradition than in doing anything to protect the helpless Indians from importunate and ruthless squatters." Judging by the number of people who today claim to believe the myth of the mission past as embodied in Jackson's novel, this remains one of those instances where a literary work became a major factor in the post-hoc invention of a romantic frontier past. Three years after the publication of Jackson's book, rate wars between the Santa Fe and Southern Pacific Railroads dropped the fare from the Missouri Valley to Southern California to one dollar, and the boom was on. As John Gregory Dunne so eloquently summarizes it, "And still they came, a generation on every trainload. If New York was the melting pot of Europe, Los Angeles was the melting pot of the United States."[16] It still is.

The second of Hazzard's stages did not emerge from southland writing until much later, the 1930s, but when it did a powerful new force in American fiction was the product. Although other strong, more conventional approaches to industrialization were produced in the state–work by Edwin Markham, Steinbeck, McWilliams, and Sinclair, for example–and although Dashiell Hammett's work in the Bay Area may be said to be a precursor, it was nonetheless in Southern California that detective novels became a major mode of examining the effect of industrialization and the emerging society it produced. James M. Cain (*Mildred Pierce, The Postman Always Rings Twice,* etc.), Raymond Chandler (*The Lady in the Lake, Farewell My Lovely,* etc.), and Ross Macdonald (*The Drowning Pool, Underground Man,* etc.) produced novels significant enough to force serious critical attention as well as a new sense of the price exacted by obdurate urban reality. Chandler's Philip Marlowe, for example, reflects lost innocence in, as Chandler himself explains, "a world gone wrong where the law was something to manipulate for profit and power."[17]

Southern California's link to Hazzard's third frontier, and to the turmoil that often attends self-realization, may be best exemplified in literature dealing with Hollywood, that land of dreams. Since the southland was the only place that *could* produce such writing, it remains a unique regional literature. As Walker points out in *A Literary History of Southern California,* although the nearly two thousand novels about the movie industry vary greatly, "nearly all agree that the life in the movie colony is artificial, the art meretricious, and the industry the graveyard of talent." The most distinguished of such efforts are Harry Leon Wilson's *Merton of the Movies* (1922), Aldous Huxley's *After Many a Summer Dies the Swan* (1939), Budd Schulberg's *What Makes Sammy Run?* (1941), and F. Scott Fitzgerald's *The Last Tycoon* (1941). What many writers—especially outsiders who originally moved to Hollywood to write movie scripts—don't admit is that they are reflecting their own senses of guilt for having sold out as they criticize the industry which made it possible. This is a literary netherworld where fantasy and fact spar, the most visible border with Fantasy California.

Because much interesting writing about California deals not with real place and real people but with the gap between what newcomers expect and what they find, a body of writing has grown that explores, not a particular locale, but a region of the mind that might be Fantasy California: the boundary where time and space merge, where expectation and realization blur. It is this fabled region that remains an open and dangerous frontier with disappointment looming like a prairie coulee, because in it dwells, not the state's reality, but its symbolic power.

Fantasy California's existence entered the popular American mind, as Starr has documented, in the very first English-language writing about the province, early nineteenth-century travel literature:

> An ideal California—a California of the mind—underwent composite definition: the elusive possibility of a new American alternative; the belief, the suggestion (or perhaps only the hope), that here on Pacific shores Americans might search out for themselves new values and ways of living. In this sense—as a concept and as an imaginative goal—California showed the beginnings of becoming the cutting edge of the American Dream. (P. 45)

For many, Fantasy California is the *only* California, a land of sun-bleached blondes on roller skates hurrying to hot tubs after working in their marijuana fields or, in the last century, a place where gold nuggets could be scooped up by the shovelful and fruit burgeoned year round. In a film of the mid-forties Deanna Durbin and Robert Paige sang of California's superior qualities–wetter oceans, drier deserts, and girls with more gender. Such hyperbole frequently leads to disillusionment; wrote Alonzo Delano in 1849: "the greatness of California! Faugh!"[18] Both extremes, while nonsensical, may accurately reflect some individual's state of mind, the churning of an unclosed conceptual frontier.

Fantasy California has, in any case, produced an intriguing body of literature, including Evelyn Waugh's bitingly humorous *The Loved One* (1948), Robert Roper's dark comedy *Royo County* (1974), Ernest Callenbach's fancifully visionary *Ecotopia* (1975), and Cyra McFadden's trendy satire *The Serial* (1977), as wel as such pioneering works as Bret Harte's romanticized gold rush tales and Mark Twain's "stretchers" in *Roughing It*. The apotheosis of Fantasy California's literature, however, is Nathanael West's *The Day of the Locust* (1939).

As Lawrence Clark Powell explains in *California Classics,* West wrote the novel "to formalize a tragic view of life. He perceived Hollywood and its product as the pure epitome of all that is wrong with life in the United States." *The Day of the Locust* is not a book about California; it is a book about Nathanael West's *response* to the world in which he found himself. A hint of his attitude may be gleaned from a letter he wrote to Josephine Herbst in 1933 shortly after he had become a screenwriter: "This place is Asbury Park, New Jersey. . . . In other words, phooey on Cal. Another thing, this stuff about easy work is all wrong. My hours are from ten in the morning to six at night with a full day on Saturdays. There's no fooling here."[19] "Cal" turned out to be a real place, not wonderland, and a chasm between expectation and realization yawned; it was that interstice, not Hollywood, that provided the actual setting of West's masterpiece, Fantasy California's greatest novel. As West demonstrates, artists can find in the Golden State's complexity vehicles for writing about virtually anything, because "There's no fooling here."

There is a real California, of course, and it is both varied and different. The old saying that the state is "full of nuts" is actually a grudging acknowledgment of the state's tolerance of individual variation. If this has allowed cults to proliferate on the one hand, it has on the other hand allowed more ethnically mixed marriages than any other mainland state, tremendous upward socioeconomic mobility because of an excellent and inexpensive system of higher education, and it has allowed people to pursue their personal fulfillments to the extent that they don't infringe upon the rights of others; this is the state that produced Richard Nixon and Earl Warren, Jerry Brown and Jerry Garcia, Joseph DiGiorgio and Cesar Chavez. "The old way" is considered neither automatically correct nor incorrect in California; it is one option. Moreover, California invites expansion of the concept of frontier.

James D. Houston has suggested that "we now have entered the third phase in the image history of this state." He points out that in phase one, which comprised approximately the first hundred years, "the prevailing tone in books about California was high enthusiasm for its various resources and fresh opportunities"; books such as Charles Nordhoff's *California for Health, Pleasure and Residence* (1872) typify early boosterism. In the mid-1960s, however, phase two emerges when anti-California backlash burgeoned in books such as Didion's *Slouching toward Bethlehem* (1968) or Kenneth Lamont's *California: Our First Para-Fascist State* (1971) among many others: a prolonged age of innocence seemed at an end, Houston summarized. Phase three, he concludes, was signaled by the 1978 publication of James D. Hart's *A Companion to California,* which documents the range of life in this state. Houston's own *Californians* (1983) is a distinguished entry in the new, more complicated, more empirical approach. This state has produced fake experts on itself–frequently transplants–faster than mosquitos breeding in meadow ponds, but Houston looks with hope at native-born writers who accept California's reality.[20]

As the nation's number-one *destination,* the Golden State has suffered because it has sometimes failed to live up to the unrealistic expectations of migrants, yet they keep coming. W. H. Hutchinson remarks in his book *California: The Golden Shore by the Sundown Sea* (1981) that even though more people are born in California than migrate there, more than a third of its population is non-native. It remains a seeker's state. Those who would limit the frontier to a static time of trappers or cowboys or schoolmarms misunderstand that such were only symptoms of a far deeper quest, a quest for the possible.

If the closing of the physical frontier in 1890 created a pervasive sense of loss, it did so principally among those who required a tangible boundary to evoke spiritual limits; however, the physical frontier was an effect, while the spiritual frontier was a cause: the quest itself. The sense of loss in California is less for missed historical opportunities than for the forfeiture of cherished illusions. Unfortunately, the same may often be said for the sense of exultation the state can stimulate: it, too, is often chimerical. In 1985 a Fresno County farmer told a reporter for the *San Francisco Examiner* when his land and property were lost to foreclosure, "None of us ever thought this sort of thing would happen in California. We thought this was something that only happened in the Midwest."

But in areas and among people who have faced the state's varied realities—who have sought to reclaim the land as William Saroyan's Uncle Melik did in "The Pomegranate Trees," who like Lily have frayed as the old order disintegrated in Joan Didion's *Run River,* who have outlasted adversity as did Sula Parkington in Wilma McDaniel's "The Entertainer"—and who recognize that toughness is a necessary ingredient for triumph in this demanding paradise, an enduring satisfaction can result. Little wonder that a hard edge capable of rupturing dreams characterizes the state's finest literature.

The quest continues. Some may mourn the romanticized trappings of earlier excursions but they fail to realize that Natty Bumppo and Tamsen Donner and Ma Joad were embarked on a continuing human expedition; as the last says, "[W]e're the people—we go on." Even today, it is people like Ma Joad who not only venture to California but who also "go on," because they have the necessary grit and because this new El Dorado has come to represent the cusp of the possible, a physical correlate for the spirit's enduring frontier.

NOTES

1. Michael Davie, *California* (New York: Dodd, Mead, 1972), pp. 10–11. Subsequent reference in the text is to this edition.

2. Excerpted in "The California of Queen Califa," in *California Heritage,* ed. John Caughey and LaRee Caughey (Los Angeles: Ward Ritchie Press, 1962), p. 48.

3. Quoted in Kevin Starr, *Americans and the California Dream, 1850–1915* (New York: Oxford Univ. Press, 1973), p. 13. Subsequent references in the text are to this edition.

4. Quoted in Davie, *California,* p. vii.

5. See Carey McWilliams's comments in *California: The Great Exception* (Santa Barbara, Calif.: Peregrine Smith, 1979), pp. 83–88.

6. William Henry Brewer, *Up and Down California in 1860–64,* ed. Francis P. Farquahr (1930; reprint, Berkeley and Los Angeles: Univ. of California Press, 1966), p. 379. Subsequent references in the text are to this edition.

7. Joan Didion, "Notes of a Native Daughter," in *California Heartland,* ed. Gerald Haslam and James D. Houston (Santa Barbara, Calif.: Capra Press, 1978), pp. 99–100.

8. Gardner, "Christ Has Returned to Earth and Preaches Here Nightly," quoted in *California Heartland,* p. 112.

9. Lawrence Clark Powell, foreword, in *California Heartland,* p. ix.

10. Quoted in Franklin Walker, *A Literary History of Southern California* (Berkeley: Univ. of California Press, 1950), p. 186.

11. John Muir, *The Mountains of California* (1894).

12. Powell, foreword, *California Heartland.*

13. Cited in Walker, *Literary History of Southern California,* p. 51.

14. Quoted in Powell, *California Heartland,* p. 37.

15. Cited in Walker, *Literary History of Southern California,* pp. 51, 56.

16. John Gregory Dunne, "Eureka! A Celebration of California," in *Unknown California,* ed. Jonathon Eisen and David Fine with Kim Eisen (New York: Macmillan, 1985), p. 20.

17. Raymond Chandler, quoted in *West Coast Fiction,* ed. James D. Houston (New York: Bantam, 1979), p. xviii.

18. Alonzo Delano, cited in Franklin Walker, *San Francisco's Literary Frontier* (Seattle: Univ. of Washington Press, 1969).

19. Quoted in Powell, *California Heartland,* p. 351.

20. James D. Houston, "The New Anatomy of California," *California History* 63, no. 3 (Summer, 1984): 256–59.

PART FOUR
Multicultural Perspectives

Homeward Bound: Wilderness and Frontier in American Indian Literature

MICK McALLISTER

"We need to learn that this is home."

To understand the meaning of the frontier in American Indian literature, we must examine the frontier's meaning in the male Anglo-American consciousness that has shaped most of our literary history. The American frontier has been the base for an essentially American idea, the idea that the direction of our lives and culture is infinitely linear. In the folklore of most cultures, one basic story tells of the adolescent who goes out from the community on a quest. These adolescents, often three sons in our Western traditions, undertake their quest to prove their value to the community, and the quest is successfully completed when they return in triumph. This is a pattern you will find in American Indian traditions as well; in the Plains cultures, the seeker is a young man who goes alone looking for spiritual guidance, and in the desert Southwest heroic twins often comprise the seeker, and their collaboration offers a folk lesson in the value of cooperative rather than competitive life.

Unlike the circular trip of the quester, permanent, linear departure is negative in meaning for most folk cultures: banishment, exile, divorce from one's community–they are, for the Greeks and the Hebrews as much as for most non-Western cultures, fates equal to death. Expansion, the spreading of a people, was normal, but the uprooting of a community, the casting out of an individual, the severance of one tribe's connection to its parent stock–our very metaphors illustrate how undesirable they were. Of course, great migrations had occurred prior to the transatlantic invasion of the Americas, and many Indian traditions even corroborate the generally accepted theory that Indian Americans crossed over the Bering Strait to people the American continents. But while the migrations were remembered –by the Hopis, for instance–no infrastructure of traditions and values endorsed such migrations, and for most cultures the metaphorical beginnings were not migratory but emergent. The Hopis are a case in point; their history and myth resemble in detail and in apparent self-contradiction those of the Aztecs, the Navajo, the Siouan peoples.

Each people was, like the Greeks and Lombards, an immigrating invader. The Aztecs of northern Mexico descended upon the peoples of the Mexican highlands like a barbarian horde, bearing their hummingbird wargod and carving a short-lived empire out of one of the era's most technologically advanced civilizations. Historically, the Navajos were very late arrivals in the Southwest, and their popular name is Tanoan (Tewa Pueblo) for "foreign enemies, raiders." The Sioux and their Siouan relatives may once have been farmers on the Atlantic coast, if the demography of language families is reliable evidence, and have slowly moved west in response to population pressures. During the period the Sioux were observed by whites, this impulse took them across western Wisconsin and Minnesota and on into western Dakota Territory. The "sedentary" Hopis tell of Hebraic migrations, great cyclic whorls that took them to all the various American environments, after which roving they returned to their desert, sure that where they had emerged into the world was where they belonged: First, Second, and Third Mesa.

The history of the Hopi mesas is a record, for the last century, of dissension and intravillage conflict resolved by fragmentation: Oraibi split from Shungopovi, then fragmented to form Hotevilla and Kikuechmovi; Hotevilla was then split by the founders of Kikuechmovi and Oraibi again to create Bakavi. Each splinter weakened the moral spine of the culture, according to the old men of Oraibi, and the economic devastation at contemporary Third Mesa is a result of this rending of the spiritual community. And the Kiowas popularized by Scott Momaday have a story of a seventh band whose leader lost an argument over a prestigious hunting trophy and, in his anger, took his people from the camp circle. This happened in the mid-eighteenth century, and there is no historical clue regarding the fate of these renegades, the Tepda, or "Pulling out" people.

Indians define themselves by their place in the land, by their homes. All the tribes mentioned–Hopi and Kiowa, Aztec and Navajo–describe creation as an emergence. They came from the earth, through holes in trees, from caves, from lakes. They began under the earth, and most of them define themselves in relation to the place of the beginning. When I taught Indian students at the University of North Dakota, I asked a female student one day where she was from. "Standing Rock" was the answer. She told me she had been born in Los Angeles, had lived all her life in California, and had only been to Standing Rock that summer, on her way to Grand Forks. But she was from Standing Rock, a place she'd never seen. My Indian students went home every weekend, to Belcourt, Four Bears, Fort Yates,

St. Michaels, journeys of two and three hundred miles, some of them. Reading Jim Welch's early novels (*Winter in the Blood, The Death of Jim Loney*), we will find in them paralyzed, trapped narrators, young Indians incapable of rescuing themselves from the spiritual and material poverty of their lives on their reservations, but we must temper our reading of these alienated modern men with the understanding that Indians can go home, not can, but must, and sacrificing one's relationship to the land for some personal gain is as unthinkable as sacrificing one's children or parents.

Daniel Boone–not the wealthy land speculator but the self-created legendary frontiersman–once said he moved on when the neighbors got too close, meaning when he could see their smoke from his door. The frontier has been a "steam valve" for social unrest, an escape route for the discontented, whether one was orphan boy, draft-dodger, or environmentalist. For very few has it been a home, a place one lives upon and gives back to in the same measure one takes from it. There are four ways to relate to the land: as raider, as tourist, as scavenger, or as symbiot, giving and taking in equal measure.

The raider comes in the folktale manner to make his fortune and return to civilization: he is the gold miner, land speculator, cattleman, moviemaker, oilman. He falls upon the land as if it were a rich village, loots it, and returns to his homeland with the spoils of conquest. He is the president of Standard Oil, Union Carbide, United Fruit. He is the carpetbagger who never unpacks. He appears in the story we maintain of the Tabors and Strattons and Hills, the Huntingtons and Stanfords who made their fortunes and returned to "the real world," Samuel Johnson's world of cities and conversation.

The tourist is a looter of the spirit, the backpacker who recreates himself with a weekend at Big Bend, the photographer who goes to Crow Fair or Anadarko every summer, the English gentleman whose Wyoming ranch is a retreat from the social rigors of Victoria's court. He comes to look, taste, smell, possibly to take a bit of pottery or a few feathers, a trophy or two–hardly worth calling loot. At his best he is Melville, Catlin, Burroughs, Parkman or Audubon, carrying home the message that there is spiritual bounty waiting for pillage, teaching new understanding of the nature and meaning of the wilderness.

The scavenger and the symbiot are faces of one coin. The Indians are the true symbiots, the Indians and the mountain men who came as looters and like children seduced by bears grew hairy, uncommunicative, Esau-brown. The symbiot is an ideal type, one who accepts the wilderness on its own terms and barters his needs and values for the right of domain. A good film, *Jeremiah Johnson,* the finest novels on the fur trade and the Indians, and a few good biographies capture this character for all time: Fred

Manfred's *Lord Grizzly* and *Conquering Horse,* Dorothy Johnson's *Buffalo Woman,* LeRoy Hafen's *Broken Hand,* Black Elk and John Neihardt's *Black Elk Speaks.* The scavenger is as apparently permanent on the land, but I chose this noun for him to put his connection to the land in its starkest perspective. He is the emigrant pioneer, Ishmael Bush, Beret Hansa, prepared to live on the land, but unable to understand the need for new values, new priorities.

The scavenger is the most ardent believer in the myth of the frontier. He is that "leading edge" of common folk celebrated in histories of America thirty or forty years ago, the yeoman poor and the white trash a few steps ahead of Enclosure, the Potato Famine, the tax collector. The frontier as escape valve. What escapes? When the city is polluted, with sewage, crime, government, then move on, take civilization over the next hill. Is the community unjust? Create a new community on land free for the taking. Go west, make Salem, make Utah, lay out Greeley, build Arcosanti. And when we stand like whimsied leaders of the people on the lee edge of California, left with no more land to move westward into, faced not just with the widest ocean on the planet but, on its other side, a four-billion-head argument against proceeding west again when population and its discontents need to be left behind, then look to Vandenberg Space Center and the New Frontier: untouched moonsoil, uncreated Marslands, future cities of Titan waiting for us.

When Gary Snyder accepted the 1984 Distinguished Achievement Award from the Western Literature Association, he spoke on the especially American unwillingness to commit to a home, to, in Frost's brilliant image, "be the land's rather than call it ours," to perceive this tiny planet as our home, not merely our base of operations. The American mind always has a suitcase packed, and that, as much as any shaping and essential concept, makes it so difficult for us to respect the rights of the land and our fellow creatures, makes it almost impossible for us to understand the Indian.

"Beyond freedom and dignity": the right to conform.

Frank Waters' *The Man Who Killed the Deer* is generally acknowledged as the finest novel about the American Indian prior to the Indian Renaissance which began in 1968 with the publication of *Custer Died for Your Sins* and *House Made of Dawn.* It is still used in Indian literature classes and, with the author's *Masked Gods, The Book of the Hopi,* and *Pumpkin Seed Point,* it remains an important if controversial work on the Indians of the Southwest. What is seldom mentioned in discussions of the authenticity of the book is Waters's tacit endorsement of theocratic totalitarianism. Mentioning it requires discussing the implicit–no, explicit–totalitarianism in American Indian traditional cultures.

The protagonist of *The Man Who Killed the Deer,* Taos Indian Martiniano, is dragged off to "away school" by the white government, taught a trade and civilized values, and then dumped like a rape victim on the doorstep of his home pueblo. He has learned that the demands of the village elders are wasteful and illogical. He has learned that venison tastes just as good if you do not lay the deer's head facing eastward and dust it with pollen. He has learned that his pants fit fine without cutting out the seat and that wrapping a blanket around the resulting nakedness means buying two garments instead of one. He brings reason into a community of unreason, economies into a wasteful community racked with poverty. He is–I would have said not welcome, but that is not true. He is tolerated, in the strongest sense of that word; his new ways are not held against him. He is punished for his disrespect to the deer–a justice done the deer if an injustice to him; he is ostracized for refusing to take time from his own planting to clean the mother ditch.

He is the victim of a tiny dictatorship. Adolf Bandelier, writing in 1890, like the line of his literary godchildren stretching into the present, has seen in the theocratic tribal structure repression, sexism, self-serving demagoguery, what it is no longer fashionable to call "backwardness." Tribal values, Indian values, the social structure of all "primitive" cultures, conflict with what we regard as the basic essentials of humanism. When the needs of the community come before the needs of the individual, then inevitably the individual will suffer. Martiniano suffers. He suffers the repression of his personal needs and desires. He is materially harmed by the community's refusal to allow him the freedom to conduct his life in the manner he chooses.

Surely one of the cruelest realities of the frontier is that it is the grinding edge of civilization, the debris-cluttered crest of the wave of civilization. With notable exceptions like the Iroquois Confederation, most Indian cultures were totalitarian cultures. The pueblos were theocracies, communities ruled by the "will of the gods." As civilized humanists, we must disapprove such governments; when we see similar communities in our own culture we abhor them. But are civilized dictatorships similar? I think not. Theocracy, totalitarianism, in a context of Blakean innocence, are not the same as the similar repression of an individual in an experienced society, a society of individuals who have discovered that they are individuals, have decided that their values are significant independently of the community with which those values might conflict.

When Martiniano chooses to subordinate his personal self-interest to the interests of the community, he gains freedom and strength from that self-subjugation. This resolution is, of course, an outsider's romantic view of the possibility of regaining innocence. Waters is enough of a realist, and knows the Taos people well enough, to show us that Martiniano can only return to the village as a welcome but crippled prodigal. He can never enter directly into the ceremonial life of the village because he was gone during the adolescent years when he should have been training his spiritual self.

No tribal group has struggled more heroically, nor against more imposing adversaries, to retain its intellectual and spiritual innocence than the Pueblos. Santo Domingo is famous for the integrity of the tribe's stand against the influence of white culture, and the Hopis of Oraibi once "closed" their village to tourists, posting a No Trespassing sign at the boundary. The sign barred visitors from the Snake Dance, citing the white disrespect for Hopi religion. The decision cut off a significant source of tribal revenue. If a community is small enough and closed tightly enough against immigration that it can reasonably expect the experience of the individuals to be homogeneous, and if a community exists in an environment hostile enough that the welfare of each individual is intimately tangled into the welfare of the community, then there is nothing pernicious in a theocratic totalitarian government, a government in which a very few people govern, but govern only insofar as their behavior is consistent with the community's understanding of the will of the gods as it is known, in its broad strokes, by all the community.

The Aztecs are no exception to this idea. Their community became too big to maintain the consensus that must endorse the actions of the leaders, and their leaders too separated from the lives and needs of the community. But a successful community of this sort is a fragile ecosystem, vulnerable to both technological pollution and the insidious cult of the individual. There is a certain heroism in the fictional resistance and ultimate victory manifest by the Taos council in *The Man Who Killed the Deer* and in the fierce consistency of the conservative Santo Domingos. The Hopis' resistance to progress has stood up to electricity, education, and elections, and their legendary closure is so intransigent that they still regard the Hano, Pueblos who traveled two hundred years ago from the Rio Grande to settle at the foot of the Hopi mesas, as neighbors, a separate people. And the Hano, on their part, still speak their own language. But such successes are shadowed by apparent defeat and outnumbered by the failures elsewhere to maintain tribal values successfully in the white light of European technological advances.

The tragedy of Jim Welch's nihilistic heroes is double: on the one hand, there is no society for them to sacrifice their wills to; on the other, once those wills exist, we cannot part with them, any more than we can regain any other lost virginity. Welch's protagonists are flawed by knowledge, marred by truth, and they can find no cultural community on which to pin their solitary existences. Jim Loney has no one, not even a wife; and the unnamed hero of *Winter in the Blood* has only his nuclear family, memories of a senile grandmother, and a blind old man who in one revelatory scene gives the boy a grandfather and takes away his tribal identity.

"The White Man has his Ways."

Two novels any work of American fiction must be measured against are Scott Momaday's *House Made of Dawn* and Leslie Silko's *Ceremony.* Each deals, like *The Man Who Killed the Deer,* with an individual spiritually dissociated from his home, and each offers its own resolution for the conflict faced by the protagonist. For Scott Momaday, a Kiowa writing about the closed society of Jemez Pueblo, Abel's tragedy is his inability to accept a place in the culture of his pueblo. His troubles begin before he goes away to war. He is a mixed blood and, as such, a pariah. More than that, he is an individuated consciousness, a man incapable, even from his childhood, of playing the games of communal consciousness. Sent to catch an eagle for a ceremonial sacrifice, he sees his captive as nothing more than a ruined creature and he kills it unceremonially, in a fit of disgust.

Abel's every act, however primitive, however tribal in its effects, is vitiated by personal judgment. He kills the eagle. It would have died anyway, but a ceremonial death would have been meaningful; the snuffing out of its life by the repulsed boy is a meaningless waste. He kills a witch, a frightening albino whose snake nature is even more manifest in death than in his life. But he kills the albino for besting him in a semireligious contest, for defeating and humiliating him. He goes home finally, from his disastrous relocation in Los Angeles, but he goes home defeated, physically and emotionally beaten, and many readings will leave unresolved the question of whether his return to Walatowa is a defeat, a last admission of failure merely underscored by his apparent death on the final pages of the novel, or an achievement of grace, a resolution of personal conflict that renders the question of his physical survival on that last page inconsequential.

Abel's place in the world is a central issue of *House Made of Dawn,* and the tragic tension of the novel pits the spiritual values of the Pueblo community against the secular needs of a modern citizen of a world where such values are embattled if not destroyed for all time. He is a man without a community, almost as much so as Jim Welch's protagonists. He is a man without a language, and his recovery of that language in the final paragraph is an uplifting, positive note to a conclusion so filled with despair and defeat, uplifting even if we know that the word he utters, the formulaic ending for telling a story at Jemez, means "It is finished," with precisely the ambiguity of Christ's last words.

Ceremony is less an outsider's book, and less pessimistic in its analysis of the survival of Indian values. The novel itself is a ceremony of healing, at once a story and an act of magic, speaking and making real by speaking. Silko's healer, the old Navajo Betonie, offers an explanation of the organic survival of tradition when he explains to the protagonist, Tayo, how certain change is inevitable and natural:

> [L]ong ago when the people were given these ceremonies, the changing began, if only in the aging of the yellow gourd rattle or the shrinking of the skin around the eagle's claw, if only in the different voices from generation to generation, singing the chants. . . . [A]fter the white people came, elements in this world began to shift; and it became necessary to create new ceremonies. I have made changes in the rituals. The people mistrust this greatly, but only this growth keeps the ceremonies strong. . . . [T]hings which don't shift and grow are dead things. They are the things the witchery people want.[1]

Tayo's Uncle Josiah works secular change that Betonie connects to Tayo's cure. Josiah buys Mexican cattle thinking they will be more hardy than the white man's Herefords, capable of surviving both the temporary drought and the dry normal conditions of the reservation. Tayo "saw" his Uncle Josiah in the face of a Japanese soldier killed in the Philippines, and his uncle dies while Tayo is overseas. For Betonie, the connection is real, and the hallucination in the Philippines not insane but prophetic, because Josiah is a potential agent for community survival, and his enemy is witchery. "It isn't surprising you saw him with them. You saw who they were. Thirty thousand years ago they were not strangers. You saw what the evil had done: you saw the witchery ranging wide as this world" (p. 124). Tayo was on the Bataan Death March, and as he watched his brother die in the mud of the jungle, he cursed the rain. But when he returns to Laguna, he brings the curse with him, and the land is without rain. To curse the rain was an act of madness, as mad as swinging an ax at the scorpion on your foot, and the consequences reach far beyond Tayo's imagining. Until he is taken by his desperate family to the crazy Navajo Betonie, he is paralyzed with his sickness. Betonie gives him back his sanity. From Betonie he relearns his proper relationship to the land. He has come back with the bitterness of the veteran, who has seen what the white man took from the Indian, the magnitude of the theft and the profit from that theft. The other veterans in the novel live lives of futile bitterness, telling stories of how it was when their country needed them. Betonie explains, standing on the lip of a mesa overlooking the Indian Hell, Gallup, New Mexico. He points east to Mount

Taylor: "They only fool themselves when they think it is theirs. The deeds and papers don't mean anything. It is the people who belong to the mountain" (p. 128).

Gallup is Betonie's home. In one of the most horrifying passages in the novel, Silko describes what must be Betonie's childhood in the most squalid outskirts of the city. But it is Betonie's home: "It strikes me funny, . . . people wondering why I live so close to this filthy town. But see, this hogan was here first. Built long before the white people ever came. It is that town down there which is out of place" (p. 118).

Tayo's Uncle Josiah similarly recognizes the permanent meaning of the land. As he says, "there are some things worth more than money. . . . This earth keeps us going" (p. 45). To survive, Tayo must learn his place in the land; he must understand his connection to the people, and he must learn that to be separate from the land and separate from the people on the land is a kind of death. The doctors in the mental hospital try to cure him of the madness brought on by his brother's death, but their cure requires that he stop thinking of "we" and "us," and he cannot, because medicine doesn't work that way. His sickness, Betonie confirms, is part of something larger, and the cure is something great and inclusive.

"Who Will Bring the Rain?": Objects for Witchery.

Tayo's participation in the larger cure of the land gives him meaning, not merely as an individual but as a member of his community. The great thing is larger than white people, larger than America, a thing more evil than governments and wars, a way of looking at the world, a way that Silko calls witchery. It is glib and easy to identify virtue with a race or community. Silko does not, no more than Waters or Momaday. In *Ceremony,* the white man is instrument, not agent, for a life-denying force present in all cultures. Witches are anarchs, slaves of self-love, creatures who have so lost touch with the land that animals recognize and fear them. Witchery is the prying impulse, the need to try the next bomb, the curiosity that stirs up ant hills, that tortures in order to learn how pain manifests itself, that imagines horrors for entertainment. Witchery could curse the rain, or witches could manipulate a good man into cursing the rain, because witchery is the impulsive, the act untainted with reflection, unentangled with any sense of implication, of ends, of responsibility.

Witchery is the ultimate denial of the home place, the absolute denial of community values, the utter rejection of meaning. Historically, the Pueblo peoples found little evidence of witches among the whites. Witchery was internal, and therefore the cure was internal. Betonie rejects the fatalism of Tayo's view when Tayo wonders "what good Indian ceremonies can do against the sickness which comes from their wars, their bombs, their lies?" (p. 132). Sitting on that hill above Gallup, west of Laguna, west of the huge uranium mine which will be the scene of the conclusion of this novel, Betonie has a terrible answer:

> That is the trickery of the witchcraft. . . . They want us to believe all evil resides with white people. Then we will look no further to see what is really happening. They want us to separate ourselves from white people, to be ignorant and helpless as we watch our own destruction. But white people are only tools that the witchery manipulates; and I tell you, we can deal with white people, with their machines and their beliefs. We can because we invented white people; it was Indian witchery that made white people in the first place. (P. 132)

The white man is not cause but symbol and tool of the true spirit of denial. Witchery is that spirit. What Tayo must learn is that he can grow and change rooted in his home place. His brother Rocky is programmed for "escape." A good student, football star, he has been trained to believe that he should leave home, go into the white world. The war, a Japanese hand grenade, days of flesh-rotting jungle rain conspire to stop him.

The novel climaxes at the abandoned uranium mine (closed in August 1945, when the bomb fell on Hiroshima). It ends not with an act of violence against the witches, but in two scenes of self-destruction. The first Tayo sees. He watches the four veterans he has hung out with all through the novel as they drink and dance around a fire. Suddenly the drunken party becomes a nearly hallucinatory nightmare as two of the men seize the other two, bind them, and murder them in a ritual manner, punishing them for failing to find and kill Tayo in his retreat above the village where he is keeping the Mexican cattle. A few days later the ringleader, Emo, "accidentally" shoots and kills his surviving henchman. The village banishes him, and he goes to California, "a good place for him," as Tayo says.

A threat to the land is a threat to the community. For the Indian mind, everything centers upon home; home defines, home creates the individual. A man is never without a home, and if he chooses to deny the home, he denies by implication everything, he joins the spirits of denial, the witches working. Witchery. It brought the object-creating white man to America. It set in motion the whorls of destruction that bloomed into deadly spores at Hiroshima. It brought us here, and now witchery turns our heads toward the stars, our backs to the land.

NOTE

1. Leslie Silko, *Ceremony* (New York: Viking, 1977), p. 126. Subsequent references in the text are to this edition.

La frontera, Aztlán, el barrio: Frontiers in Chicano Literature

JOAN PENZENSTADLER

Until now, little attention has been paid to the question of a frontier motif in the literature of American ethnic minorities, on the assumption perhaps that the experience of non-Anglo-Saxons provides no basis for such a concept or, possibly, that any thinking about a frontier would simply echo the white man's notion of it. In this essay, however, we will find a frontier experience in Chicano literature that is not the same as that of mainstream American, or Anglo, myth. If the essence of "frontier" is a border between civilization and savagery, then Chicano fiction contains a frontier, but one that divides a relatively civilized Chicano world from a relatively barbaric Anglo world. If the frontier is a moving line of conquest by a superior race, then in Chicano literature it is seen from the obverse side, from the point of view of the conquered. If the frontier is envisioned as a danger zone in which various forces threaten the inhabitants with harm, captivity, or death, such a zone appears in Chicano literature, but the danger seldom comes from native Americans or natural phenomena; rather, it comes from Anglos and alien systems. Traditional frontier themes in Anglo literature, such as the struggle against nature or against treacherous "redskins," are rare in Chicano fiction; in their own world view Chicanos live in comparative peace with nature, and the native American is usually embraced as an ethnic relative, despite occasional misunderstandings.

It takes only a small acquaintance with history to know that the Spanish conquistadors from whom Chicanos are descended were as brutal a lot as any Anglo-Saxon desperadoes; we can imagine that creating ranches, farms, and cities in the Southwest must have been just as dirty, dangerous, and discouraging for Mexican settlers as it was for the later Anglos. We know that Chicano culture and people have as many flaws as Anglo culture and people. But Chicano fiction, following its own mythical view of things, chooses virtually to ignore the Spaniards as progenitors and to concentrate on the native-American side of the ancestry, to downplay struggle against the wilderness and its inhabitants in favor of struggle against threats posed by urban culture, and to assert Chicano cultural values in preference to Anglo attitudes and behavior. This is not surprising; myth is by nature ethnocentric, stressing the chosen values of the tribe.

Depicting the American experience from a Chicano perspective is neither more nor less biased than what has been done by Anglo-Saxon writers. But we cannot conclude from this that the Chicano version must be a presentation of the same experience with a slightly different cultural flavor. The fact which strongly colors the Chicano frontier myth is that this group has been oppressed, for the most part, by the other group, and a key element—we could almost say the instrument—of that oppression has been the mental construct that Anglos call "the frontier." The Anglo notion of a superior civilization improving the wilderness, together with its contradictory ideal of solitary union with nature (after displacing the previous inhabitants) is at odds with the views of many cultures. The Anglo frontier has been defined at the expense of other groups; it has acquired much of its meaning by depreciating or misunderstanding other peoples. Moreover, Anglo culture has attempted to prove its validity by force of arms, a fact not lost on the other racial groups. Hence the line between Chicano and Anglo culture is associated, in the Chicano mythical view, with a good deal of hostility.

The line dividing Mexican-American culture from Anglo culture is both physical and mental. As a historical and geographical entity, the line is an Anglo creation, a result of the invasion and conquest by Anglos of Mexican-Americans; it is a boundary imposed by one group which maintains control over the other. As a psychological, or mythical, line it is a social barrier that Mexican-Americans are challenged to cross, but at a price. This line exists because the mainstream culture refuses to assimilate Mexican-Americans but also because Mexican-Americans refuse to be assimilated—a position which received its fullest articulation during the Chicano movement of the 1970s.

The border between the two groups exists in several versions, which came into existence as a result of various historical situations. Chicano literature deals with several spatial forms of frontier (although, as stated earlier, not with all possible ones). First is the "other side" of the Anglo frontier. During the nineteenth century, although westward-moving Americans may have felt they were bringing order into an empty wilderness, in fact they were rolling into and over established civilizations—not only native-American cultures but also the two-century-old agrarian society developed in the Southwest by Mexicans descended from Spaniards and native Americans. The significance of the Anglo frontier for the dispossessed Mexicans—and for their descendants who have learned this history—has been the destruction of their property, their way of life, and their dignity. Hence modern

Chicanos are ambivalent about the heroism of much classic Western fiction, in which Mexicans are portrayed in unrelenting negative stereotype.[1]

The acquisition of the Southwest by the United States created another boundary–the southern border. This border, consisting of the Rio Grande and a line westward across the desert to the sea, became an all-important barrier in the eyes of the Anglos. Henceforth many legal and cultural difficulties were to attend the crossing of *la frontera,* as it was known. Nonetheless, for the Mexicans who remained in the Southwest as second-class citizens, if not virtual serfs, the southern frontier was irrelevant. The artificially created dividing line failed to interrupt the Spanish-speaking culture they had in common with Mexico. Later, during the Chicano movement, this fundamental continuity was officially baptized *Aztlán,* after the mythical homeland of the Aztecs, which includes the Hispanic parts of the Southwest and most of northern Mexico.

La frontera took on great significance, however, in the first decades of this century, when huge numbers of refugees fled Mexico to the U.S. It became a symbol of escape into relative safety and prosperity after the repressions and violence of the Díaz regime and the revolution. But even then, as we shall see in Chicano literature, the Rio Grande was not the River Jordan.

La frontera solidified to the south as generations of Mexican descendants in the United States began to distance themselves from the parent country economically, politically, and culturally, while increasing their identification with the United States. But because they did not easily assimilate into the Anglo scheme of things, and tended to stay in familiar territory, their culture remained concentrated in whole counties, even significant portions of entire states–areas nonetheless controlled politically or economically by an Anglo minority. Thus we can conceive of a kind of invisible edge between the territory where Chicanos were in the majority–the poor but stable backwater area we will call *Chicanía*–and the rest of the country where they felt unwelcome–*Gringuía.*[2]

In urban areas, both in the Southwest and elsewhere, a similar clustering and intensification took place: Chicanos occupied specific localities, often bounded in part by visible markers such as railroad tracks (later, freeways), forming ghettoes. The Hispanic neighborhood, or *barrio,* existed as a confined space surrounded by a frontier–and outside was unknown, hostile territory.

The "frontier" dividing Mexican-Americans from Anglos has been a line largely created by Anglos, either to drive Chicanos out or to keep them "in their place." The pressure exerted from the Chicano side has been used, until recent times, primarily to counteract the sense of pressure from without, rather than to expand or to move the frontier further. Because of the unequal balance of power and the different natures of the two cultures, we should expect that the significance for Mexican-Americans of living near such a line, of crossing it, or of trying to push it in the opposite direction, should turn out to be quite different in Chicano literature from Anglo descriptions of their own frontier.

Let us examine more closely the dividing line between the two cultures in terms of the worlds it separates. In all the versions of the Mexican-American frontier we have outlined, the significant interface is between Hispanic and Anglo culture. *Chicanía,* an intermediate zone, is perceived in terms of Anglo-Hispanic contrasts at either of its edges. Fronting Mexico, *Chicanía* and its Mexican-American inhabitants have a relatively Anglo character; fronting the rest of the United States–*Gringuía–Chicanía* is by comparison "Mexican."

The cultural differences are perceived similarly by Anglos and Hispanics. Even specific pairs of adjectives such as are used on semantic differential scales are agreed upon by both groups in describing themselves to each other. A noteworthy difference, however, is that characteristics perceived with negative connotations by one group may be viewed positively by the other. Table 1 gives an oversimplified (i.e., mythical) scheme of differences between Anglos and Hispanics which was consistently agreed to by a variety of respondents, combined with additional contrasts revealed in Chicano literature. In addition to the contrasts shown on the table are some differences in concepts of space and time. To Hispanics (as well as to other observers of American culture), Anglos view time and space as uniform entities, divisible into discrete quantities, and in limited supply. In the Hispanic culture these continua are comparatively fluid, and there is plenty to go around. While from an Anglo point of view time and space will be "wasted" if they are not filled and used (their value being assigned by humans), in the Hispanic world view these matters will take care of themselves. Space and time, according to Hispanic attitudes, can be enjoyed without being put to a pragmatic "use"; the real waste would be to employ them for unpleasant or destructive purposes. Hence there is still another type of frontier between the two cultures, psychic rather than socioeconomic or historical, which nonetheless can act as a barrier to understanding.

In examining "frontier" in Chicano literature, then, we will be looking for a sense of a boundary which has a constraining but challenging effect; on the other side is something alien. Most works of Chicano literature deal quite explicitly with the forms of frontier outlined above. We will examine in turn the literary treatment of the Western frontier, the U.S.–Mexican border, Aztlán, the territory of *Chicanía,* and the limits of the barrio.[3] Whatever forms the barrier, the characters in the fiction to be discussed feel the presence of such a border and are under pressure to cross it. They

Table 1. Characteristics of Anglo and Chicano Culture in Chicano Myth

Anglos	Chicanos
disciplined	anarchic
controlled	impetuous
indifferent	passionate
organized	disorganized
intolerant	tolerant
disloyal	loyal
hypocritical	sincere
cold	affectionate
artificial	natural
proud	humble
brusque	courteous
aggressive	passive
materialistic	idealistic
stingy	generous
practical	dreamy
rich	poor
sophisticated	simple
atheistic	religious
rational	intuitive
legalistic	personalistic
verbal	non-verbal
print-based	orality-based
literal	symbolic
mechanistic	organic
high-tech	low-tech
product-oriented	process-oriented
fast	slow
urban	rural
colorless	colorful
isolated	social
greedy	moderate
independent	dependent
scornful of past	respectful of past

Note: This list is composed of items from several sources. The first eighteen items are taken from a semantic differential used to compare mutual and self-perceptions of Hispanics and Anglos in a variety of countries in this hemisphere. "In general, adjectives considered important in the characterization of Hispanos are considered to represent emotive, personal, and concrete values, and those considered important in the characterization of Anglos to represent cognitive, collective, and abstract values." Chester Christian, "The Analysis of Linguistic and Cultural Differences: A Proposed Model," in *Bilingualism and Language Contact: Anthropological, Linguistic, Psychological and Social Aspects,* ed. James Alatis (Washington, D.C.: Georgetown University, 1970), pp. 149–62. The remainder of the items are derived from personal observation and from analysis of Hispanic literature.

can be destroyed in known ways if they stay where they are, but they may be destroyed in unknown ways if they cross.

The negative side of the westward-moving Anglo frontier is depicted in Chicano oral tradition and in several historical novels. Américo Paredes' study of South Texas Chicano balladry, *"With His Pistol in His Hand:" A Border Ballad and Its Hero,* details the contrast between two myths: the Anglo glorification of the "quintessential Texan"–the Ranger–and the viewpoint of the border dwellers.[4] Paredes states that the Rangers (*los rinches*), who helped implement the Anglo takeover of land from old Mexican families, "created in the Border Mexican a deep and understandable hostility for American authority. . . . Terror cowed the more inoffensive Mexican, but it also added to the roll of bandits and raiders" (p. 32). Thus were born the heroes of the ballads in Spanish called *corridos;* these songs form an interesting countermyth to the Anglo one–they supply a lone Mexican counterpart of the Lone Ranger:

> The hero is always the peaceful man, finally goaded into violence by the *rinches* and rising in his wrath to kill great numbers of his enemy. His defeat is assured: at the best he can escape across the border, and often he is killed or captured. But whatever his fate, he has stood up for his right. (P. 149)

Two recent Chicano novels about living on the wrong side of the Western frontier continue this theme of strength in defeat. *Not by the Sword* by Nash Candelaria (1982) deals with the impact of incoming Anglos on the Hispanics in New Mexico.[5] Abandoned by Mexico and by their own local government, some of the landowners try to fight the American troops. The main characters are twin brothers, one a priest, the other a rancher who joins the resistance. Shot in the ensuing extermination of rebels, the fallen rancher maintains to the last, "Before I die I want to kill one more Yankee" (p. 200). The priest, seeing the legal maneuvers by which the Anglos are getting the Mexicans' land, leaves the priesthood and becomes a rancher, organizing with the others to protect their property titles. He commits himself to the task of simply surviving to pass down land to his heirs, though his chances of success are in doubt as the book ends.

Reto en el paraíso by Alejandro Morales (1983, Spanish), draws a brutal picture of California, where gringos drive Mexicans from their gold claims, lands, and political or economic positions.[6] The protagonist, a young twentieth-century Mexican-American architect, recalls his ancestors: a prosperous landowner and his rebel neighbor, both of whom fight against Anglo takeovers –unsuccessfully. The huge holdings go to an ambitious Anglo entrepreneur, and the descendants of the original owners become laborers–"slaves and strangers in their own country" (p. 156; my translation). Their only heritage, transmitted to the twentieth-century protagonist through oral and written accounts, is an implacable hatred of the gringo. Ironically employed by the Anglo's descendants for the design of a "planned community" on his ancestor's land–a utopia that will exclude most of his own race–the architect assumes a rebellious philosophy within his restricted role: "I think alienation feels good. I am alone and I love it, motherfuckers" (p. 105). The movement of the Anglo frontier, with its victors, has produced on the other side defiant heroes who resist to the bitter end.

The next form of frontier, the crossing of *la frontera* from Mexico into the United States, is treated as a major life-event in several key Chicano works. José Antonio Villareal's *Pocho* (1959) and Richard Vásquez's *Chicano* (1970) both devote considerable space to describing the life of the first-generation protagonist in Mexico before he travels north.[7] In both novels the character is compelled to leave by a life-endangering situation resulting from the Mexican Revolution. The works then continue with treatments of life in the United States for the immigrant and his descendants. The net result seems to be loss–of spiritual values, of family cohesiveness, of self-esteem. The immigrant turns to drink, his children reject his authority, his wife becomes dissatisfied. Villareal's novel takes us only to the next generation: a son who refuses to identify himself with "the Mexican cause" does not want to stay at home to support his mother and siblings and leaves for the Navy, feeling that "for him there would never be a coming back (p. 187)." Despite his apparent conversion to an individualistic Anglo mentality his victory is ambiguous. The young man finds that his own goals are unclear, compared with those of his father, about whom he reflects: "for him life was worthwhile, but he had never been unaware what his fight was (p. 187)."

In Vásquez's *Chicano* the story of the immigrant's descendants continues to the third generation in the United States; we see the native-born American generation gain in prosperity but lose in other areas. One branch of the family grows wealthy through drug smuggling, the other becomes materialistic and vulgar. The last generation depicted, consisting of a brother and sister who are twins, is destroyed in late adolescence–she dies of an illegal abortion, he is sent to prison for drug-dealing. Both of these novels, then, are antithetical to the American Dream; there is a question as to whether the trip across the border was even a fair trade of one type of misery for another.

Related to the theme of crossing into the United States are the Chicano works which focus on the Mexican Revolution: Villareal's *The Fifth Horseman* (1974) and Lawrence Gonzales' *El Vago* (1983).[8] The effect of these adventurous accounts of riding with Pancho Villa and other famous figures of the time is to offset American stereotypes concerning that period. People abandoned Mexico in droves in the early twentieth century not merely because the place was poor, or dirty, or corrupt, but because it was dangerous. Furthermore, the fiction shows some Mexicans joining the revolution for reasons of honor or humanitarianism, others joining out of desperation. Not all revolutionaries, in other words, were the bandits or buffoons portrayed in American mythology. On the other hand, these novels do not try to simplify the confusion, cross-purposes, and betrayals that made the revolution such a frustrating experience for those who were supposed to benefit–its outcome was the opposite, in other words, of the success story of the American Revolution.

At the same time, the books portray the culture of old Mexico as having such praiseworthy qualities as attachment to the earth, order, faith, loyalty, creativity, joy. In these works, as in the early sections of *Pocho* and *Chicano,* readers are given to understand that the Mexican heritage is nothing to be ashamed of. As a result, crossing into the United States is depicted as a poignant experience because emigrants are not in a hurry to reject that past. In this fiction, moreover, what lies ahead in America does not offer as glittering a prospect as it may have for European immigrants. Mexicans, exposed to a constant flow of information circling back to them from across the border, know what they face: second-class status because of their dark skins. Hence in Chicano works we will find an occasional character who prefers to return to Mexico, not in failure but in relief.

Bringing the border-crossing theme closer to the present, fiction dealing with immigration later in the twentieth century emphasizes the motive that still holds today for Mexican illegals–hunger. It is not so much an illusion of prosperity and equality in the United States that draws these characters across the border as their disillusion with poverty and inequity in Mexico. Since the border has been tightened, they take much greater risks than any previous immigrants. In the Spanish-language fiction, especially, we find a nightmarish portrayal of the southwestern United States as filled with trigger-happy police; exploitative employers who arrange INS raids just before payday; *coyotes* (venal opportunists who charge exorbitant fees to arrange border crossings, jobs, and papers); and assorted racists who delight in harassing the fugitive who is virtually devoid of rights. The most negative description of the experience of *mojados* (wetbacks) is found in a work by a Mexican, Luis Spota, *Murieron a mitad del río* (1948, Spanish).[9] The novel is based on the author's experiences in South Texas, "perhaps the world's biggest concentration camp" (preface). After a series of misadventures that include the deaths of several companions, the protagonist returns to Mexico "embittered, hardened, frustrated" (p. 219).

In Chicano works, sympathetic treatments of the unfortunate *mojado* appear in the Spanish-language fiction *Peregrinos de Aztlán* (1974), *El diablo en Texas* (1976), and *Chulifeas fronteras* (1981).[10] These works include scenes such as the "accidental" shooting of an alien youth by arresting officers; farm workers, warned by the cry, "*agua!*" running from the fields to splash back across the Rio Grande whenever the Border Patrol arrives; a businesswoman who rates herself a saint because the low-paid illegal aliens in her employ get to use toilet paper for the first time in their lives; a night crossing where the fugitive wades across to the United States over a riverbed strewn with human bones.[11] And in the English-language novel *The Road to Tamazunchale* by Ron Arias (1975), the dying protagonist is so moved by the plight of the illegals that he resists death a little longer to fantasize organizing a mass border crossing for them, with their eventual assumption into the never-never land of Tamazunchale.[12] The emphasis in all these works is on the human needs of *mojados*. As Méndez points out in *Peregrinos de Aztlán*, "These emaciated men are not on a quest for gold: they are led by the life-or-death search for protein" (p. 51; my translation). In Chicano literature, those who cross the border are heroes, not because they have acquired property or knowledge, but because they have simply survived. Their motive is not glory but the welfare of their families. Their accomplishment is relatively unglamorous but no less difficult than that of the pioneers of Anglo myth.

Sympathy for those who cross the frontier into the United States is related to the concept of Aztlán–the mythical Hispanic homeland embracing both northern Mexico and the American Southwest. A continuous cultural region in previous centuries, even now it is not effectively divided by American attempts to "seal the border" to immigrants. The efforts of U.S. officials to dam the northward flow is often treated satirically in Chicano fiction. *Chulifeas fronteras* contains a story about a Border Patrol officer who goes insane in his fear of Mexican blood polluting the United States. *El diablo en Texas* describes the devil's favorite game as watching a cat and a rat play hide-and-seek. "The joke is to be careful of the drop of water that divides two lands, as though they weren't the same. The patrol cat with knitted brow waits in ambush for the rat, who carries his defense in his stomach in the form of hunger" (p. 69).[13]

In *Peregrinos de Aztlán* the protagonist, an old Yaqui who washes cars in a Mexican border city, sums up in his life experiences the sorrows of Aztlán: the futile efforts of the Yaquis during and after the Mexican Revolution to save their lands, the struggles of field laborers to find a living, all ending in alcoholism, starvation, or violent death on both sides of the border. He has a vision of the desert lands extending across the Southwestern frontier: "I saw the cosmic solitude of the Sonora Yuma desert, the republic which we would inhabit–the wetbacks, the Indians sunken in misfortune, and the enslaved Chicanos. Ours would be the 'Republic of Despised Mexicans'" (p. 101; my translation). Once again, the frontier is presented as an entity imposed by Anglos that creates additional difficulties for people who already suffer. It is paradoxical, however, because the same border that divides people is the one that protects those who escape across it from the ills of old Mexico.

Now we turn to literature set primarily in the area north of the border, populated by Mexican-Americans: *Chicanía,* surrounded by *Gringuía.* There are several works which serve to establish and document the unique culture which has emerged in this area; at times they show a virtually closed world with a minimum of Anglo presence. The borderline seems far away and barely relevant. The best-known example of such fiction is Rudolfo Anaya's *Bless Me, Ultima* (1972), which creates an almost totally Hispanic agrarian environment in an elegy for a mythical past.[14] The few traces of Anglo culture are an ineffective schoolteacher, an Irish priest, and the distant war that takes young men away and returns them mysteriously rebellious. The world is not idyllic–evil individuals exist–but within the Christian–Moorish–Native-American world view that comes with the Mexican healing tradition of *curanderismo,* the evil can be counteracted. There is barely a hint of the huge systemic evils of racism and economic exploitation that surround this island community and wait to destroy it. Only the *curandera* Ultima and the child protagonist sense that a new form of healer, a new type of priest, will be needed in the coming world.

Another New Mexican work, more idyllic than Anaya's, is Sabine Ulibarri's *Tierra Amarilla* (1971), a collection of gentle, reminiscent short stories where the only Anglo is a beloved priest with fractured Spanish, and the worst crimes are social ostracism. A continuation of memories of rural New Mexico is Ulibarri's 1977 collection *Mi abuela fumaba puros.*[15] In these works, there is little friction with the Anglo world. Ulibarri's later *Primeros Encuentros/First Encounters* (1982) focuses on interactions with the Anglos who move into the rural Chicano-populated area.[16] These are isolated arrivals rather than conquests, and difficulties surrounding them are usually resolved amicably by adaptation on both sides, usually by the acceptance of the Anglo into the Chicano community rather than vice versa. While stressing the positive aspects of *Chicanía,* however, Ulibarri is not oblivious to injustice. He contrasts his people's experience with the Anglo frontier tradition:

> We never left our native land. New Mexico is our native land. . . . We never set out in search of the American Dream. The American Dream came to us unannounced and uninvited [and] remains just that, a dream, unfulfilled and unrealized. The mainstream has marginalized us.[17]

Another relatively closed world, but one not as positively described, is Tomás Rivera's *". . . y no se lo tragó la tierra"–". . . and the earth did not part"* (1971), which follows a group of Chicanos for a year on the cycle between their Texas homes and their migrant work.[18] The few Anglos who appear are not pleasant–a boss who shoots a child by accident; school officials who expel a boy for fighting. The walls of prejudice fit much more tightly around this world, yet they are never referred to explicitly. Without a direct look at racism as a system, we see its effects in the sufferings caused by poverty: illness, violence, ignorance. The people are mostly victims but are drawn with dignity and defined by their own values in relation to their community, not in relation to the Anglos'.

Rolando Hinojosa's *Estampas del Valle y otras obras* (1973) and *Klail City y sus alrededores* (1976) present many characters, mostly Chicano, who populate a fictional Belken County in the Rio Grande Valley—the Yoknapatawpha of South Texas.[19] Despite the dominating presence of the Anglos, the Chicanos in *Klail City* manage their own affairs with some control. Hinojosa describes the relationship between the groups:

> The gringos are . . . at the margin of these events. The Chicano people of Belken don't pay attention to the gringos. Meanwhile the gringos, obviously, because they are in power, pay attention to the Chicanos when it suits them—elections, war, economic scare, etc. (P. 11).

As a Chicano expression puts it, the two groups are "*juntos, pero no revueltos*" (together, but not mingled). The barriers in Hinojosa's work consist less of geographical lines than of differences in world views. Good and bad qualities are relatively evenly distributed between the two groups, although identification and sympathy clearly lie with the Mexican-Americans.

In these works of the "Chicano Renaissance," the world of Mexican-Americans is shown as rich and relatively complete, drawing its life from itself rather than from the residues of other cultures. The writers emphasize the communal, organic aspects of this culture, especially such values as family solidarity, honesty, hard work, attachment to the land, and the role of oral tradition—the last-named shown particularly in the Spanish-language works. Rivera and Hinojosa use a literary form combining short stories, anecdotes, vignettes, and dialogues which makes the community itself the subject of their writing. Anaya's novel, while focusing on its protagonist, incorporates many important aspects of Chicano culture, adding an examination of religious tradition and native-American heritage to the list of values already mentioned.

Nonetheless the Chicano world, surrounded or governed by a different culture hostile to it, is a prison. Unlike works of Anglo frontier fiction that assume free protagonists who may, indeed, risk captivity as they approach the frontier but who may also hope for release, Chicano fiction has to assume protagonists who, if born in the Southwest, are born in captivity. Escape is unlikely unless one becomes something, or someone, else. The prison-like aspects of being Chicano are most noticeable in Rivera's book, in which the characters' freedom is limited not only at home in Texas but even while they work in other parts of the country. Migrant farm workers, in fact, take a kind of portable *barrio* with them. The sense of separation felt in migrant camps, or at work in the fields, is developed by contrast with the lives of Anglos in Barrio's *The Plum Plum Pickers* (1969). Saul Sánchez's descriptions of migrant life in *Hay plesha lichans tu di flac* (1979) include a piece titled "The Field Next to the Golf Course," which describes the resentment felt by Chicano workers doing stoop labor while the Anglos recreate nearby.[20]

Fiction dealing with the urban *barrio* shows much more claustrophobic characteristics; the sense of a surrounding barrier is always present, and to cross it is to enter hostile territory. But staying inside is not always pleasant either. Life in the barrio is less attractive than the previous rural life in Chicanía. As in the country, the place where Chicanos live is poor and undeveloped; now, however, it is also crowded, ugly, and far more dangerous. Even so, many Chicano writers manage to portray the barrio experience as quite positive.

A Spanish-language work, Morales' *Caras viejas y vino nuevo* (1975), now in English as *Old Faces and New Wine* (1981), provides what seems to be a predominantly negative picture of a California barrio.[21] Alcoholics and directionless youth spend their lives getting drunk or high, whoring, and fighting, in a cycle most do not escape. Yet the protagonist, who plans to leave, associates with the gang to learn from them. He concludes the book with an expression of nostalgia for "the magnificence and enchantment of days already past" (p. 132). A similar ambivalence toward the barrio occurs in *Pocho:* the protagonist travels with youth of other races and plans to escape his barrio surroundings, but he also befriends the tough Chicano gangs, the *pachucos,* for what they can teach him. *Chicano* depicts the conflicts people encounter who try to leave the barrio: when the American-born family moves into a better neighborhood the Anglos drive them out; a Chicana is accepted as an Anglo's lover, but cannot be his wife. The negative portrayals of the barrio show characters who want to leave but are pushed back or still attached to the cultural womb.

Positive images of the barrio as warm, accepting, rich, and exciting appear in *The Road to Tamazunchale* and Sandra Cisneros' *The House on Mango Street* (1983).[22] Set in Los Angeles and Chicago, respectively, these works show barrio residents who mingle sociably, help each other out, and take a matter-of-fact view of trouble and death. *Mango Street,* written from a feminist perspective, shows the various ways the barrio traps girls and women, as the stories intermingle scenes of sexual abuse, violence, and emotional illness with pleasant memories. When characters in both works venture temporarily outside the barrio there is some nervousness, but, with caution, no major conflicts occur. Nonetheless, in *Mango,* the narrator plans to leave her barrio: "One day I will say goodbye to Mango. I am too strong for her to keep me here forever." But she adds, "I have gone away to come back . . . for the ones who cannot get out" (pp. 101–102). It is interesting to note that in both the positive and negative treatments of the barrio, its redeeming values are the same: cooperation, family support, and group solidarity. In the case of the negative barrio, these features make life at least bearable, and in the positive barrio they provide an experience superior to what seem to Chicanos the cold, prejudiced, uniform, and dull neighborhoods of Anglos.

At this point we should be able to make some generalizations comparing Anglo and Chicano frontiers. Both Anglo and Chicano cultures agree in viewing the Hispanic environment as closer to nature. On one side of the line dividing them is a relatively rural, simple, natural, tolerant, cohesive, nontechnological region; on the other, a more urban, complex, artificial, judgmental, individualistic, and technological one. But the Chicanos have to move in the *opposite direction* across this line from the frontier-seeking Anglos. Nonetheless, for Chicanos as well as Anglos, crossing the frontier represents going from a familiar order into unknown chaos, from the relatively safe to the difficult and dangerous.

Over generations, Chicanos have had to cross frontiers in this "reverse" direction several times: from Mexico to the United States, from rural *Chicanía* to the barrio, and from the barrio to mainstream American life. Each time it is, for them, a move in the direction of increased urbanization and limitation. Some would say that Chicanos are merely "catching up" with the Anglos and hence should be eager to cross these barriers. Yet, as we have seen in the fiction, Chicanos often move in that direction reluctantly, perforce. In fact, the Chicano and Anglo frontier myths agree in taking a negative view of the urban rat race.

The frontier hero, also, differs in the two sets of myths. Unlike Anglo heroes, Chicano heroes seldom win. Their manliness is established by how bravely, even senselessly, they fight before they fall. Many Chicano heroes are not achievers so much as survivors. When unable to fight, they endure misfortune with dignity. The strength of simple people is celebrated time and again in Chicano literature.

Another important heroic quality in the Hispanic myth is loyalty–to a person or to a commitment, often maintained at the expense of pragmatic considerations. The venerable tradition goes all the way back to the literary figures El Cid and Don Quixote. Chicano literature contains such devoted heroes as faithful adherents of Villa, self-appointed guardians of an admired person, laborers who choose poverty over dishonesty, families who are patient with their senile or insane members.[23]

The theme of loyalty helps explain the role in Chicano literature of Anaya's novel *The Legend of La Llorona* (1984), a fictional rehabilitation of Cortez's mistress, the much-maligned Malinche, considered a traitor in Mexican tradition.[24] Anaya shows her as making an initial commitment to the Spanish conquistador both in love and under the impression he would benefit her people. Ultimately she is not the betrayer, but the betrayed. She does not abandon Cortez (she is virtually his prisoner) but perfers to kill her sons by him rather than let him take them back to Spain. Thus she becomes the original *la llorona*—the ghostly woman who haunts Chicano folklore, wailing for the children she has killed. She is also a prototype of the Mexican identity conflict: what to do when the enemy is someone you have accepted, who is now part of you? Mexicans refer to themselves as *hijos de la chingada*—children of her who was screwed—defiantly acknowledging their origins from Indians raped by Spaniards. This novel shows that *la llorona* and *la chingada* are the same. Representing native Americans, she receives the stranger in good faith and is exploited; after fighting in vain to remove the oppression she suffers the consequences nobly. In classical terms, her tragic flaw is the excess of a good quality—trust.

Now we will look at some Chicano novels which deal with the effort to push the Anglo frontier *backward*—the Chicano liberation movement. In contrast to the advance of the Anglo frontier by means of superior technology and with convictions of superior culture and divine support, the Chicano *movimiento* in these works is characterized by the desperation and unconventional methods of a less powerful group. The most vivid documentation of the action in California in the late sixties is found in Oscar Zeta Acosta's books, which should be read as a pair: *The Autobiography of a Brown Buffalo* (1972) and *The Revolt of the Cockroach People* (1973).[25] In addition to a candid account of people and activities in the movement, the works also record the lawyer-protagonist's personal journey from overachieving individualist to directionless hippie to Chicano militant. The author's self-mockery and frankness, the absurdity and illegality of the events he reports, give an impression of discounting the Chicano revolution, but the books maintain a strong theme of commitment to justice. The best image of the reversing of the frontier appears in *Revolt,* where demonstrators push into the wealthiest Catholic church in Los Angeles, leading to the removal of the local archbishop. The methods used to force back the barriers include legal action, media attention, and as a last resort, destruction of property to alarm those in power.

Another Anaya novel, *Heart of Aztlán* (1976), deals indirectly with the *movimiento* by setting the novel in an earlier time, portraying railroad union struggles in New Mexico.[26] The protagonist, significantly named Chávez, undertakes a dangerous purification rite to find the "heart of Aztlán" and learns that this key element resides in his people. The novel ends with the Christlike figure leading demonstrators in nonviolent protest, using the weapon of love against the unfair system. Meanwhile his unnamed baby grandson is prophesied to emerge as a great leader.

A writer who is not Chicano but deals sympathetically with Chicano activism is John Nichols. In *The Milagro Beanfield War* (1974) and *The Magic Journey* (1978) he presents Chicanos in a small New Mexican community trying to protect their land from developers.[27] The rebels are aided by a few supportive Anglos and by supernatural forces, such as the spirits of Mexican revolutionaries. The barriers are pushed back not only by solidarity and strategy but also by sabotage and a little bit of luck.

Despite the variety of weapons used, all these works end without conclusive victories. The frontier seems to be pushed back, or broken, but questions remain: Are the gains here to stay? What will it take to maintain the pressure against a restless force that seems unable to accept equilibrium, much less retreat? The Chicano frontier is not, like the Anglo one, based on a concept of moving into a relative vacuum and accomplishing permanent change; this one feels resistance and senses the possibility of losing ground. A Spanish-language work that illustrates the treacherousness of an only partially dissolved frontier is Sergio Elizondo's *Muerte en una estrella* (1984).[28] Two Chicano youths, one with considerable promise as a poet, visit Austin on leave from their Job Corps center during the late sixties. The antipoverty program has given them new opportunities and fresh hope, but all this ends when they are shot to death by police after stealing a car. Parts of the frontier are still fatal.

Fiction focusing on individual attempts to break through the barrier of cultural discrimination shows not only resistance from the surrounding society but strong inertia from within. One's "Mexicanness" cannot be sloughed off; one cannot escape the powerful hand of the past. The protagonist of *Pocho,* for example, like Stephen Dedalus in *Ulysses,* feels he has outgrown his cultural milieu and cannot wait to leave it; yet once he leaves, that milieu is what the author writes about, just as Joyce in exile never lost his fascination with Ireland. In Chicano literature, the past is too vital a part of the self to cut off without that individual suffering harm.

Chicano protagonists who try to break through barriers without bringing along their past only meet disaster. An Ulibarri story in *Tierra Amarilla,* "Hombre sin nombre" ("Man without a Name"), tells how a writer who has just written successfully about his father is visited by the older man's ghost, who wants to coexist with the son in the son's body. The son refuses, is stricken ill, and the father takes over completely. Villareal's *Clemente Chacón* (1984) tells of a self-made man, son of a Mexican prostitute, who crosses the border and by shrewdness and opportunism rises to a high position in his company.[29] He gains a promotion, only to find it has been obtained through his wife's sleeping with his boss—an irony which suggests the failure to escape not only his Mexicanness but also his childhood taint of prostitution. Candelaria's *Memories of the Alhambra* (1977) portrays a successful Chicano who in his later years attempts to trace his ancestry to Spain, totally rejecting any connection with a Mexican, or worse, Indian, heritage.[30] He dies without satisfactorily establishing a connection with the *conquistadores,* but he achieves a partial reconciliation with his New World past when he meets a descendant of the Spanish Moors who exemplifies in the graceful acceptance of his origins the pride one can take in ancestors, even when they have been defeated.

Coming to terms with one's past is accomplished more successfully in other novels. In *The Road to Tamazunchale,* when his wife's ghost protests against his concern over "all these *mejicanos,*" the old protagonist asks, "What are we? Chinese?" (p. 72). He does not forget he once swept streets in Mexico. In Hinojosa's continuing Belken County stories, one protagonist leaves to fight in Korea, the other, his friend, becomes the first Mexican-American bank officer in the area. Two books deal with their absence from the Rio Grande Valley: *Korean Love Songs* (1978) contains letters home from the soldier at war; *Mi querido Rafa* (1981) portrays the adventures of the bank officer, ending with his disappearance from the area, headed for graduate school.[31] But by the time of *Partners in Crime* (1985), set several years later, both are back in the Valley, the one again in the bank, the other a police detective.[32] Both are highly effective and respected in their positions, able to get along with Anglos as well as Chicanos of all generations. They seem to have integrated their pasts with their present.

Some fiction by Chicanos deals not so much with the cultural boundaries deriving from group membership as with the limitations surrounding an individual. Although these works do not explicitly deal with Chicano issues, they nevertheless portray attempts by a protagonist to remove some barrier that applies individually, a sort of "personal frontier." Four Chicano novels of the 1980s fit this category. In the first, Anaya's *Tortuga* (1982), the protagonist, a youth crippled in an auto accident, faces not ethnic discrimination but a combination of physical handicap, self-doubt, and societal attitudes toward the disabled.[33] In two other novels, written by Chicanas, individuals cross personal frontiers created by prejudice. *Faultline* by Sheila Ortiz Taylor (1982) tells of a woman who struggles to win custody of her children after she has left her husband to enter a lesbian relationship.[34] By means of alliances with a somewhat bizarre assortment of friends, she succeeds. Cecile Pineda's *Face* (1985) narrates the sufferings and final victory of a Brazilian who, horribly disfigured in a fall, is treated as a pariah until he reconstructs his own face and reenters society.[35] These novels can be considered analogous to other Chicano works in that they identify with the victim of social rejection and show such traditional values as faithfulness in spite of suffering and the importance of tolerance and solidarity.

Finally, Arturo Islas's *The Rain God* (1984) presents a Chicano family's struggle against an emotional handicap which has persisted through several generations.[36] The desert is the recurring metaphor for emotional dryness, inability to confer affection—a disability passed from parent to child that tragically damages the sensitive souls of others, driving them to illness, insanity, or suicide. The protagonist, a writer barely escaped from death, strives to understand the various perverted, repressed, or aborted forms of love in his family heritage so that he can cope with them. He crosses his personal frontier with an acceptance of death, of vulnerability, of the painful experiences of his past.

Of the characters who try to cross frontiers, the difference between those who survive as integrated persons and those who fail is to be found in their choice of identity concepts. One way of viewing ethnic identity is as an "either/or": one must decide to be either a Mexican or an American. This view often originates with Anglos; when imposed upon Chicanos by schools, government officials, and the media, it creates a frantic effort among many Chicanos to prove themselves all-American. Unfortunately, as most Chicano works show, the Pygmalion-like transformation falls short. The failure may be due to an imperfect adaptation, as with the family in *Chicano* whose members own a Cadillac and use cake mix but are unaware that middle-class people don't urinate in the front yard. Or the failure to integrate is beyond one's control; the individual cannot escape his Mexican exterior which continues to be held against him, as in *Pocho* and many other works. The cost is so great, and the odds so slim, that few manage to achieve the American Dream. An allegory of an either/or situation is Alarcón's story "El resbaladero" ("The Slide") in *Chulifeas fronteras,* in which six million members of *la raza* try to climb the mountain of success. At each stage all but a tenth are sent back to the bottom on a huge slide. Only six climbers reach the palace at the top, and they have in the process lost their cultural heritage.

Another way to look at a cultural identity is "neither/nor": neither Mexican nor American. This, too, is a source of great stress, and Chicano fiction contains numerous scenes in which a Chicano, rejected in the United States as a backward "Mexican" who can't speak English, finds himself also rejected in Mexico as a gringified *pocho* who doesn't know his mother tongue. Or, accustomed to cursing the racist American justice system, he undergoes an even worse experience with the corrupt police and courts of Mexico. Caught between two groups which practice neither/nor thinking, the protagonist finds himself in a void.[37]

Whereas earlier Chicano fiction like *Pocho* and *Chicano* reflected the "either/or" or "neither/nor" views of being Mexican-American, what emerges from works of the Chicano movement is the definition of a third alternative –*chicanismo*. The need to establish the uniqueness of Chicano culture explains the literary and artistic interest in the *pachucos,* who created their own style of dress and speech different from that of either Mexico or the United States. The peculiar flavor of pachuco speech is a high point in several works, especially in Spanish ones, where it can be displayed fully.[38] During this same period Chicano poets began to employ a mixture of English and Spanish that performed on a literary level what colloquial "Tex-Mex" achieved on the street–utilizing the best expressions from each language, forming unique combinations.[39] The majority of writers, however, simply began to document the lives of Chicanos, their practices and myths, thereby establishing the integrity and validity of their world as a distinct culture.

Most recently, however, we are seeing the emergence of what may be the full fruit of the Chicano Renaissance–the concept of "both/and": the Chicano, as a bilingual, bicultural person, is a citizen of both the Anglo and Hispanic worlds–the entire Western hemisphere, and significant parts of the Eastern one, are open to him.[40] He can easily cross frontiers that are serious obstacles to monolingual, monocultural people.

The earliest example of a character achieving some degree of success in the Anglo world while being faithful to his origins appears in an episode of *Chicano,* in which a Mexican-American cement finisher triumphs as a foreman by following the Spanish instructions of an old Mexican. The sequence is allegorical; maintaining solidarity with one's culture is a help, not a hindrance. Later we see the appearance of fully bilingual characters who can function almost anywhere; some turn up in Hinojosa's works of the seventies. In *The Road to Tamazunchale* we encounter a protagonist who embraces the hemisphere in his fantasies; the dying encyclopedia salesman travels mentally through all the Americas, speaking with a Peruvian shepherd one moment, reciting Roosevelt's death announcement the next. He does not seem to feel alienated anywhere. Similarly, in Hinojosa's *Partners in Crime* the Chicano detective fares better than the others on the force because of his ease in dealing with people on both sides of the border.

Another indication of the direction in which the Chicano self-concept is moving is found in publication decisions. *Revista Chicano-Requeña,* for thirteen years a literary magazine in Spanish and English featuring Chicano and Puerto Rican literature, in 1986 changed its name to *The Americas Review* in order to include "all U.S. Hispanic groups in creative brotherhood" and stated that it is "committed to [their] inclusion in the tradition of American letters."[41] Reinforcing this vision is the continuation of the practice of writing Chicano works in Spanish as well as in English, as is evident in noting the dates of the Spanish-language works cited here. The population of Spanish readers is increasing in the United States; moreover, the potential Spanish audience in the hemisphere is vast. Chicanos and other American Hispanics may be able to lead the way to improved international consciousness in this country, since they already have a transcultural identity and bilingual skills.

Looking back over our survey of Chicano literary frontiers, we see several general trends over the years: from overt physical barriers to more subtle psychological ones; from boundaries applying to large groups to those surrounding an individual; from struggles with separatist, oppositional thinking to explorations of synthesis and complementarity. Nonetheless, a consistent tone in Chicano fiction has been to question the Anglo American Dream—not only as to whether it is attainable by Mexican-Americans but as to whether it is worth attaining at all. While some features of Chicano frontier heroics and heroes are shared with Anglo myths, as they are with myths everywhere, a major effect of Chicano myths is to help define the Anglo mentality. And naturally the interface between the Anglo myth and the Chicano culture has helped Chicano culture define itself. It is possible that understanding both sets of myths will lead to a higher view of human reality, as suggested in this observation of Alan Watts: "Things are joined together by the boundaries we ordinarily take to separate them, and are, indeed, definable as themselves only in terms of other things that differ from them."[42]

It is fascinating to speculate: if there had been no blacks, native Americans, or Hispanics from whom Anglos could differentiate themselves, how would the American character have been delineated? But of course it is too late to find out; these other groups have already played their role as Others in the Jungian sense, helping Anglo-Saxons define their identity. Now a different question becomes importunate: When will the literary myths of these minority groups be recognized as integral, rather than peripheral, to American studies? After all, as we have seen, such alternate myths are not just "local color"; rather, they provide a type of three-dimensional modeling necessary to a truthful self-portrait of this country.

NOTES

1. Arthur G. Pettit documents Anglo portrayals of Mexicans and Mexican-Americans in *Images of the Mexican American in Fiction and Film* (College Station: Texas A&M Univ. Press, 1980).

2. The term *Gringuía,* meaning "Gringoland," is borrowed from Miguel Méndez M., who uses it in his stories to refer to the United States. Here it refers simply to the area where gringos are in the majority. *Chicanía* is a term coined to match and stands for the area where Chicanos are in the majority, namely, the Southwest.

3. Because of space limitations, I will confine the notes to citations of primary works in order to include as many examples of Chicano fiction as possible. For the same reason,

summaries of the better-known works will not be as detailed as those of other, less available works.

4. Américo Paredes, *"With His Pistol in His Hand:" A Border Ballad and Its Hero* (Austin: Univ. of Texas Press, 1971). Subsequent references in the text are to this edition.

5. Nash Candelaria, *Not by the Sword* (Ypsilanti, Mich.: Bilingual Press, 1982). Subsequent references in the text are to this edition.

6. Alejandro Morales, *Reto en el paraíso* (Ypsilanti, Mich.: Bilingual Press, 1983). The title means "Challenge/Risk in Paradise." Parts of the novel are in English. Subsequent references in the text are to this edition.

7. José Antonio Villareal, *Pocho* (1959; reprint, Garden City, N.Y.: Doubleday, 1970). The title is the Mexican term of contempt for a Mexican who has emigrated to the United States and lost his own culture. Richard Vásquez, *Chicano* (Garden City, N.Y.: Doubleday, 1970). Subsequent references in the text are to these editions.

8. José Antonio Villareal, *The Fifth Horseman* (Binghamton, N.Y.: Bilingual Press, 1974). Lawrence Gonzales, *El Vago* (New York: Atheneum, 1983). Although titled in Spanish ("The Wanderer"), the work is in English.

9. Luis Spota, *Murieron a mitad del río* (Mexico City: Talleres Gráficos de la Nación, 1948). The title reads: "They died halfway across the river." Subsequent references in the text are to this edition; the translations are my own.

10. Miguel Méndez M., *Peregrinos de Aztlán* (Tucson: Editorial Peregrinos, 1974); Aristeo Brito, *El diablo en Texas* (Tucson: Editorial Peregrinos, 1976); Justo S. Alarcón, *Chulifeas fronteras: cuentos* (Albuquerque: Pajarito Publications, 1981). The titles translate respectively, "Pilgrims of Aztlán," "The Devil in Texas," and "Pretty/Ugly Frontiers: Stories."

11. These incidents are found in the following works: the first two in *El diablo en Texas,* the third in *Peregrinos de Aztlán,* and the last in "El Puente" ("The Bridge"), a story in *Chulifeas fronteras.*

12. Ron Arias, *The Road to Tamazunchale* (Reno: West Coast Poetry Review, 1975). Although a real place, in this fantasy Tamazunchale is used as an imaginary destination.

13. My translation. Alarcón's border patrol story is aptly titled "Contaminación."

14. Rudolfo A. Anaya, *Bless Me, Ultima* (1972; reprint Berkeley, Calif.: Tonatiuh-Quinto Sol, 1984).

15. Sabine R. Ulibarri, *Tierra Amarilla: Stories of New Mexico,* trans. Thelma Campbell Nason (Albuquerque: Univ. of New Mexico Press, 1971). *Mi abuela fumaba puros/ My Grandma Smoked Cigars* (Berkeley, Calif.: Quinto Sol, 1977). Bilingual edition.

16. Sabine R. Ulibarri, *Primeros Encuentros/First Encounters* (Ypsilanti, Mich.: Bilingual Press, 1982).

17. Sabine R. Ulibarri, *La fragua sin fuego/No Fire for the Forge* (Cerrillos, N.Mex.: San Marcos Press, 1971).

18. Tomás Rivera, *. . . y no se lo tragó la tierra/ . . . and the earth did not part,* trans. Herminio Rios (Berkeley, Calif.: Editorial Justa, 1977). Bilingual edition.

19. Rolando Hinojosa, *Estampas del Valle y otras obras* (Berkeley, Calif.: Editorial Justa, 1973) and *Klail City y sus alrededores* (Havana: Casa de las Américas, 1976). The titles translate as: "Images of the Valley and Other Works" and "Klail City and Its Environs." English-language editions of these works are *The Valley* (Tempe, Ariz.: Bilingual Review Press, 1983) and *Klail City* (Houston: Arte Público Press, 1986).

20. Raymond Barrio, *The Plum Plum Pickers* (Sunnyvale, Calif.: Ventura, 1969) and Saul Sánchez, *Hay plesha lichans tu di flac* (Berkeley, Calif.: Editorial Justa, 1979). The latter title renders, in Spanish phonetic spelling, a Hispanic-accented pronunciation of the Pledge of Allegiance.

21. Alejandro Morales, *Old Faces and New Wine,* trans. Max Martinez (San Diego, Calif.: Maize Press, 1981). Subsequent references in the text are to this edition.

22. Sandra Cisneros, *The House on Mango Street* (Houston: Arte Público Press, 1983). Subsequent references in the text are to this edition.

23. These are found, respectively, in *Pocho, The Fifth Horseman,* and *El Vago;* in *The Road to Tamazunchale* and *The Autobiography of a Brown Buffalo;* in *Chicano* and *El diablo en Texas;* and in *Heart of Aztlán* and *. . . y no se lo tragó la tierra.*

24. Rudolfo A. Anaya, *The Legend of La Llorona* (Berkeley, Calif.: Tonatiuh-Quinto Sol, 1984).

25. Oscar Zeta Acosta, *The Autobiography of a Brown Buffalo* (San Francisco: Straight Arrow, 1972), and *The Revolt of the Cockroach People* (San Francisco: Straight Arrow, 1973).

26. Rudolfo A. Anaya, *Heart of Aztlán* (1976; reprint, Berkeley: Editorial Justa, 1982).

27. John Nichols, *The Milagro Beanfield War* (New York: Holt, Rinehart and Winston, 1974) and *The Magic Journey* (New York: Holt, Rinehart and Winston, 1978).

28. Sergio D. Elizondo, *Muerte en una estrella* (Mexico City: Tinta Negra, 1984). The title translates, "Death on [or in] a Star."

29. José Antonio Villareal, *Clemente Chacón* (Binghamton, N.Y.: Bilingual Press, 1984).

30. Nash Candelaria, *Memories of the Alhambra* (Palo Alto, Calif.: Cibola Press, 1977).

31. Rolando Hinojosa, *Korean Love Songs* (Berkeley: Editorial Justa, 1978) and *Mi querido Rafa* (Houston: Arte Público Press, 1981). The latter title translates as "My Dear Rafe."

32. Rolando Hinojosa, *Partners in Crime* (Houston: Arte Público Press, 1985).

33. Rudolfo A. Anaya, *Tortuga* (Berkeley, Calif.: Editorial Justa, 1982). The title means "Turtle."

34. Sheila Ortiz Taylor, *Faultline* (Shelburne Falls, Mass.: Naiad Press, 1982).

35. Cecile Pineda, *Face* (New York: Viking Penguin, 1985).

36. Arturo Islas, *The Rain God* (Palo Alto, Calif.: Alexandrian Press, 1984).

37. Scenes of bafflement and rejection in Mexico occur in *Chicano, The Autobiography of a Brown Buffalo,* and *Memories of the Alhambra.*

38. Passages of *pachucano* appear in *Chulifeas fronteras, El diablo en Texas,* and *Peregrinos de Aztlán;* English approximations of it appear in *The Revolt of the Cockroach People* and *The Road to Tamazunchale.*

39. During this period linguists began to interpret the "code-switching" features of Chicano speech as a valid language form following its own rules; it is no longer considered simply a combination of defective English and defective Spanish. A survey of such research is in Fernando Peñalosa, *Chicano Sociolinguistics: A Brief Introduction* (Rowley, Mass.: Newbury House, 1980).

40. Even the far East is becoming accessible to Spanish-speakers. In Korean schools and universities, Spanish is replacing French and German as the principal foreign language—after English—in anticipation of expanded trade relations with Latin America.

41. *The Americas Review* 14, no. 1 (Spring, 1986), inside cover.

42. Alan Watts, *The Two Hands of God: The Myths of Polarity* (New York: Collier, 1963), p. 212.

An American Chicano in King Arthur's Court

RUDOLFO A. ANAYA

The literature of the Southwest comprises a variety of voices. Writers from each of the cultural groups write from their particular perspective. Eventually these different perspectives will form the body of work we call Southwestern Literature. I say eventually, because as of now the contemporary writings of the Chicano and Native-American communities–while they are flourishing–have not yet been widely disseminated and have not yet made their final impact on the region.[1]

It is understood that whenever cultural groups as different as the Anglo American, the Chicano, and the Native American exist side by side, cultural sharing takes place; but also each group will develop a set of biases or stereotypes about the other groups. This is unfortunate, but it is a substantiated historical fact. The problem is compounded, of course, when one of the groups holds social, political, and economic power over the other groups. Then prejudices will affect in an adverse manner the members of the minority groups.

How do we make the literature of the Southwest a truly multicultural literature which informs the public about the variety of voices which reflect the cultures of the Southwest? Can our different literatures help to lessen the negative effect of cultural stereotypes?

I am an American Chicano, and I have titled my essay "An American Chicano in King Arthur's Court." For me, King Arthur's Court represents an archetypal time and experience in English memory, an archetype transplanted onto American soil by the first English colonists. It is an archetype which is very much alive. (Remember the Kennedy administration reviving the dreams of Camelot?) In other words, King Arthur's Court represents a "foreign" archetype that is not indigenous to the Native-American memory.

There is no judgmental value attached to what I have just said. King Arthur's Court has a right to exist in the communal memory of the British and the Anglo Americans. It is part of their history, part of their identity.

And communal memory is a force which defines a group. Camelot and King Arthur's Court are "real" forces in as much as they define part of the evolution of this group's eventual worldview.

In 1848, King Arthur's Court moved to what we now call the Southwest United States. During the war with Mexico the United States occupied and finally took Mexico's northern territories. In so doing the United States acquired a large population of native Americans and Mexicanos. Suddenly a very different social, economic, and political system was placed over the social system of the Mexicanos. The Mexicanos became Mexican Americans. A different worldview, with its particular archetypes, was imposed over the communal memory of the Mexicanos. In the area of artistic impulse and creation, this element of the Anglo culture would cause as many problems for the Mexicanos as did the new language and value system with which they now had to contend.

The Mexicano of the Southwest had his own vision of the world when the Anglo Americans came. The view was principally Hispanic and Catholic, but it was also imbued with strains of belief from the Native-American cultures. The culture was Hispanic, but in its soul and memory resided not only Western European thought, Greek mythology, and the Judeo-Christian mythology and religious thought, but also the thought and mythology of Indian Mexico. The Mexicano culture was, with few and isolated exceptions, a mestizo population. Therefore, its worldview was biased by the memory of the indigenous, American cultures.

The Mexican-American community sought economic and political justice in the 1960s. It also needed an artistic infusion of fresh, creative energy. We had to take a look at ourselves and acknowledge the Indo-hispano tradition for hundreds of years. This is precisely what the Chicano Movement of the 1960s and 1970s did. The Chicano Movement of those decades fought battles in the social, economic, and political arenas, and in the artistic camp. Taking up pen and paintbrushes, we found we could joust against King Arthur's knights and hold our own. In fact, we often did extremely well because we were on our soil, we knew the turf. Quite simply, what we were saying was that we wanted to assert our own rights, we wanted to define ourselves, we believed that our worldview was as important as any other in terms of sustaining the individual and the culture.

We engaged actively in large-scale production of creative literature. We insisted that a definition of our community was in the arts, in poetry and stories. A wealth of literature was produced which was labeled the Chicano Renaissance. This view of the writers working from within the Chicano community helped to dispel some of the old stereotypes and prejudices. We could think, we could write, we did honor parents and family, we did have a set of moral values, we were as rich and as complex a cultural group as any other group in the country, and so the old, one-dimensional stereotypes began to crumble.

We explained to the broader "mainstream" culture that we are American Chicanos; we are an inherently American, indigenous people. We are Hispanic from our European heritage, we are Native American from our American heritage. We are heirs to the mythologies and religions and philosophic thought of Western civilization, but we are also heirs to the mythologies, religions, and thought of the Americas. A renewed pride in our American heritage defined us.

Out of the Native-American world flowed a rich mythology and symbology which the poets and writers began to tap and use. We confronted our mestizo heritage and proudly identified with this New World person. The idea of an original homeland, typified by the concept of Aztlán, became a prevalent idea. The homeland was indigenous, it was recorded in Native-American legend. For the Chicano consciousness of the sixties it provided a psychological and spiritual center. One of the most positive aspects of the Chicano movement was its definition of a Chicano consciousness. Spiritually and psychologically, Chicanos had found their center; they could define their universe with a new set of symbols, new metaphors. They had tapped once again into their native experience and recovered the important, archetypal symbols of their experience.

That consciousness which was defined in the art, poetry, and stories of the Chicano writers continues to exist not just as a historical phenomenon that happened in the sixties and seventies. It continues to define the Chicano collective memory. The power of literature, the power of story and legend is great. True, the Chicano Movement has waned in social action, but the renewed consciousness born in the literature of those decades survives in art, writing, history, and in the language and the oral tradition of the people. In a broader sense, its humanistic principles of brotherhood, its desire for justice, its positive cultural identification, its definition of historic values, and its concern for the oppressed continue to be guiding principles in the thought and conduct of American Chicanos. Chicano consciousness continues to center us, to instruct us, and to define us.

The evolution of Chicano consciousness created a new perspective in humanistic philosophy. It took nothing away from our Hispanic European and Mexican heritage, it took nothing away from other western influences; on the contrary, it expanded the worldview of the Americas. But we are still involved in the struggle to define ourselves, to define our community. Evolution is a slow process. Once the definition of Chicano consciousness has worked itself into the society, then we will not have to be so sensitive about the concept of King Arthur's Court. After all, we understand its right to exist as a mythology, we understand it as part of the definition of a particular group. The challenge for us, for the writers of the Southwest from all cultural groups, is to understand and accept those views which define groups and the individuals from all communities.

Since 1848, King Arthur's Court has been the social and legal authority in the Southwest. It has exercised its power, not always in a fair and judicious way. My concern here is to explore how the Anglo-American value system affected the artistic impulse of the Mexicano. Did it impede and stifle the creative impulse of the Mexicano, and if so did it interfere in the Mexicano's self-identity and artistic impulse?

The artistic impulse is an energy most intricately bound to the soul of the people. Art and literature reflect the cultural group, and in reflecting the group they not only deal with the surface reality but with that substratum of thought which is the group memory. The entire spectrum of history, language, soul, voice, and the symbols of the collective memory affect the writer. A writer becomes a prism to reflect those elements which are at the roots of the value system. We write to analyze the past, explore the present, and anticipate the future, and in so doing we utilize the collective memory of the group. We seek new visions and symbols to chart the future, and yet we are bound to the mythologies and symbols of our past.

I remember when I started writing as a young man, fresh out of the university, my mind teeming with the great works I had read as a student. I was affected, as were most of my generation, by the poetry of Dylan Thomas, Eliot, Pound, Wallace Stevens. I had devoured the works of world authors, as well as the more contemporary Hemingway, Faulkner, Steinbeck, and Thomas Wolfe, and I felt I had learned a little about style and technique. I tried to imitate the work of those great writers, but that was not effective for the stories I had to tell. I made a simple discovery. I found I needed to write in *my* voice about my characters, using my indigenous symbols. I needed to write about my culture, my history, the collective experience of my cultural group. But I had not been prepared to explore *my* indigenous, American experience; I had been prepared to deal with King Arthur's Court. I discovered that the underlying worldview of King Arthur's Court could not serve to tell the stories about my communal group.

I suppose Ultima saved me. That strong, old curandera of my first novel *Bless Me, Ultima* came to me one night and pointed the way. That is, she came to me from my subconscious, a guide and mentor who was to lead me into the world of my Native-American experience. Write what you know, she said. Do not fear to explore the workings of your soul, your dreams, your memory. Dive deep into the lake of your subconsciousness and your memory, find the symbols, unlock the secrets, learn who you really are. You can't be a writer of any merit if you don't know who you are.[2]

I took her kind and wise advice. I dove into the common memory, into the dark and hidden past which was a lake full of treasure. The symbols I discovered had very little to do with the symbols I knew from King Arthur's Court–they were new symbols, symbols I did not fully understand, but symbols which I was sure spoke of the indigenous American experience. The symbols and patterns I found connected me to the past, and that past was not only my Hispanic, Catholic heritage; that past was also Indian Mexico. I did what I had never been taught to do at the university. I got in touch with myself, I explored myself, and found I was a reflection of that totality of life which had worked for eons to produce me.

All writers have to go through the process of liberating themselves and finding their own true stream of creative energy. For Chicano writers it has been doubly difficult because in the formative years we were not presented with the opportunity to study our culture, our history, our language.

My generation will receive at least some thanks from the future, if only because we dared to write from the perspective of our experience, our culture. Of course a steady stream of Southwestern Hispanic writers had been producing works all along. Before and after 1848, poetry, novels, and newspapers were produced, but those works were never part of the school curriculum. The oral tradition was alive and well, and its artistic impulse was invigorating to those of us lucky enough to grow up in its bounty. But by the 1960s the Hispanic culture had reached a crisis point. Not only were the old prejudices affecting us adversely, but the very core of the culture was under threat.

Part of our task is to keep reminding each other that each cultural community has an inherent right to its own definition, and Aztlán does define us more accurately than Camelot. Hildalgo and Morelos and Zapata are as valuable as Washington, Jefferson, and Lincoln. The mythology of Mesoamerica is as interesting and informing as Greek mythology. Mexico's settlement of her northern colonies is as dramatic and challenging as the settlement of the thirteen United States colonies. As American Chicanos, we have a multilayered history on which to draw. To be complete individuals we must draw on all the world traditions and beliefs, and we must continue to understand and strengthen our own heritage. We seek not to exclude, but to build our base as we seek to understand the interrelated nature of the Americas. Our eventual goal is to incorporate the world into our understanding. But in the span of world time, the Chicano community is a young community. It is still growing, still exploring, still defining itself. Our history has already made valuable contributions to American thought and growth, and we will continue to make more. What we seek now, in our relationship to the broader society is to eliminate the mindless prejudices which hamper our evolution and to encourage people of goodwill who do not fear a pluralistic society and who understand that, as a group of people define themselves in a positive way, the greater the contribution they make to mankind.

For a century American Chicanos have been influenced by the beliefs imposed by a King Arthur's Court scenario. We have learned the language, we have learned the rules of the game. We have adopted part of the cultural trappings of Arthur's Court, but we also insist on keeping true to our culture. The American Southwest is a big land, a unique land. It has room for many communities. It should have no room for the old, negative prejudices of the past. When we, each one of us, impede the fulfillment of any person's abilities and dreams, we impede our own humanity.

NOTES

1. This presentation was given in Tucson in October, 1984, as part of a lecture series for the Writers of the Purple Sage project. My talk at the Old Southwest/New Southwest Conference, "The Voice of the Chicano in the New Southwest," continued this theme.
2. Rudolfo A. Anaya, *Bless Me, Ultima* (Berkeley, Calif.: Tonatiuh-Quinto Sol, 1972).

"O Beautiful for Spacious Guys": An Essay on the "Legitimate Inclinations of the Sexes"

MELODY GRAULICH

> *Given . . . the legitimate inclinations of the sexes, it was natural that the West should find this theme strong in its history. . . . It is inescapable. . . . Male freedom and aspiration versus female domesticity, wilderness versus civilization, violence and danger versus the safe and tamed.*[1]

In a satiric line, "O Beautiful for Spacious Guys," Jean Stafford suggests that America's fruited plains and majestic mountains are the domain of "spacious guys" and mocks one of the most cherished myths in American Studies: the tale of the self-reliant rebel who escapes civilization and heads West to find the freedom from authority and tradition that Turner–and many others–associated with the frontier.[2] Such creative and influential cultural historians as Bernard De Voto, Henry Nash Smith, Leslie Fiedler, and R. W. B. Lewis have explored America's "collective fantasy," the obsession with the rugged individualist who rejects society's conformity for a quest in nature in search of his identity and moral values. From Rip Van Winkle to Natty Bumppo, Deadeye Dick, Huck Finn, Isaac McCaslin, John Wayne, and the Sundance Kid, this rebellious man has become a significant hero in American culture; in fact, the "frontier myth" and the "American Dream" that it expresses have often been elevated into a megamyth, becoming a theoretical framework through which critics come to understand American culture.

This classic American story offers boys heroism and "space" in return for rebellion and nonconformity, but in the American literature that myth criticism has canonized, the West's legendary freedom is not promised to girls. In fact, the "false" values of society, with its constrictions, obligations, and capitulations, are assigned to white women, the hypocritical Miss Watsons who force Huck to wear shoes and go to school, the Molly Woods who learn in the West to acknowledge their desires for dominant men, or the Victorian gentlewomen who are unable to respond to the West's egalitarian grandeur. Adventure, independence, and freedom belong to male characters, while women "endure," as does the long-suffering pioneer helpmate who tries to re-create "home" in the West, memorialized as the Madonna of the plains. Thus, what has come to be the quintessential American plot, what Nina Baym calls the "melodrama of beset manhood," not only denies women the hero's role but defines them as obstacles to the male hero's freedom.[3]

At the heart of this "archetypal" American story is an opposition of values symbolized by gender conflict, the "inescapable" opposition summarized so neatly by Wallace Stegner: "male freedom and aspiration versus female domesticity, wilderness versus civilization, violence and danger versus the safe and tamed." Male characters are frequently allowed to bridge the two worlds, but female characters, very seldom (except, of course, in the works of women writers). Few feminists would be so certain as is Stegner that these are the "legitimate inclinations of the sexes," that what Henry Nash Smith has called the myth's "drastic simplifications" represent fundamental female and male dreams.[4] This rigid dichotomizing of sex roles has often handicapped and confused male as well as female writers, yet the myth of the frontier dream has been formulated from the male point of view, as if the male is the subject of all experience, the female an object in *his* story, the antagonist to the story's implicit values. (While female values may sometimes win out in the end, it is with a profound sense of loss.)

Judith Fetterley has described the woman reader's response to such plots: disallowed identification with the hero and presented with repressive and symbolic façades of womanhood, she becomes a "resisting reader" to avoid being forced to reject herself.[5] Women writers, too, resist this powerful cultural tradition. Seeking ways to write about their own and other women's experience in the West, they challenge and revise the dichotomized sex roles and the values associated with them. Often aspiring to escape and rebellion, to nonconformity and adventure, they create women whose imaginations *do* respond to the West's limitlessness, but they also acknowledge and seek to understand the real restrictions in women's lives, to redefine the ways in which we understand such concepts as "individualism" and "freedom." Women writers thus try to liberate for themselves western literary traditions by claiming male territory as their own *and* by reclaiming from stereotyping the significance of traditional women's values.

This essay will explore some of the effects of the complex relationship of the woman writer to the rebellious male/civilizing female convention and suggest some of the problems of using the myth, with its simplified and schematized view of female and male needs and values, as a framework for understanding women's themes and culture. This is too large a topic for a single essay; I do not pretend that my speculations are inclusive, and most readers will find exceptions to my rules springing to mind. I recognize that some male western writers like Hamlin Garland and Stegner have also questioned the values associated with the polarized sex roles, that their relationship to these roles is more complex than the myth allows, but they are subjects for other essays. Finally, while the frontier dream of escape to freedom *is* a significant recurring pattern in American literature, it is only one of many and has often been too widely applied in defining the essential qualities of American literature. As Nina Baym has persuasively shown, the critical obsession with the frontier fantasy has excluded from the American literature canon not only women writers, whose works it could not adequately interpret, and minority writers, but also male writers who did not respond to the call of the wild.[6] Therefore I will discuss the frontier myth only in relation to those texts in which women writers present the wilderness or frontier as a literal setting or image.[7]

The centrality of the frontier myth in defining the essential "Americanness" of American literature was established by a series of trailblazers in American studies: Smith, Lewis, Chase, Marx, Fussell, Fiedler, and a host of followers.[8] Like Turner, these influential writers, with the exception of Smith, present this expression of our collective fantasies in male terms and draw their conclusions almost entirely from male texts. Lewis, Fussell, and Marx do not discuss a woman writer, though women writers were far more widely read in the periods upon which they focus than those they claim captured the American imagination. In *The Return of the Vanishing American,* as in much of his work, Fiedler discusses women at length, not as creators, but as destroyers. Describing the "Basic Myths" in "archetypal American tales," he defines the "real West" as

> the place to which White male Americans flee from their own women into the arms of Indian males, but which those White women, in their inexorable advance from coast to coast, destroy. (P. 50)

While it is perfectly legitimate to focus on male experience, the ***unacknowledged*** androcentric bias of these texts suggests that male voices give us a universal myth and dream. Thus we get an incomplete—and therefore false—view of the fantasies the frontier has nurtured in all Americans, a reduction of the complexity of themes associated with the West. I will return to this point near the end of this essay, after looking at how the woman writer responds to the universalizing of male needs and values.

Like Stafford, Joanna Russ has parodied the centrality of the myth and women's exclusion from the hero's role. In "What Can a Heroine Do? or Why Women Can't Write," she begins with two plot summaries: (1) Two strong women battle for supremacy in the early West; (2) a young girl in Minnesota finds her womanhood by killing a bear.[9] The absurdity of her recast plots suggests to Russ that "authors do not make their plots up out of thin air. . . . These very familiar plots simply will not work [because] they are tales for heroes, not heroines, and one of the things that handicaps women writers in our—and every other—culture is that there are so very few stories in which women can figure as protagonists" (p. 4). As Russ implies, despite rare exceptions, the frontier myth "simply will not work" for women writers. Few women writers are likely to cast themselves in the roles allowed them: civilizing and/or repressive agent; submissive helpmate; compliant sexual savage; or feminized sexual landscape. How can a woman writer use the western plots and still convey her understanding of women's experiences and fantasies of the West?

Our response is illustrated by both Stafford and Russ: make fun of the "spacious guys," parody their plots, and satirize the West's mythic freedom. This Stafford effectively does in *The Mountain Lion,* a western tale so stereotypically "classic" that it represents a comment on the western tradition. She creates two sets of contrasting images that mock the "archetypal" thematic pairings in American literature: female/male; civilization/wilderness; culture/nature; conformity/rebellion. The story moves between the points of view of a brother and sister, Ralph and Molly Fawcett, youngsters trying to grow up in the West. Both children are obsessed with two patriarchal symbols: the long-dead Grandfather Bonney, their mother's father, an effeminate man so cultured that he orchestrated dinner table conversations about Tennyson, wore "a pink carnation in the lapel of his morning coat; a silk hat and a gold-headed stick, a black Chesterfield and a pair of white gloves" (p. 49), and after dying reposes in an urn on the mantel; and Grandpa Kenyon, a tall-tale–telling rancher who looks like an Indian, dresses like Jesse James, and reminds his grandson of a "big river." Subsequent generations take on the symbolic—and hilariously clichéd—values of these forefathers. Mrs. Fawcett, née Bonney, talks about "our sort of people" (who don't own cows or linoleum) (p. 57), appreciates elevated conversations, and gets sick headaches, while her half-brother Claude, who rides and shoots with authority, tries to eat his sherbet out of his fingerbowl and reads only gun catalogues. The dichotomy is further drawn through the story's two settings. Mrs. Fawcett creates a cultural enclave at Covina, California, which is *not,* Grandpa Kenyon says, the *real* West. Life there is mannered and controlled, defined by what one is "not allowed" to do. At Claude's "Bar K," "lawlessness seemed natural" (p. 97). Ralph responds to his dichotomized world by categorizing everyone as either "Bonney merchants" or "Kenyon men," the "fundamental distinction [being] their attitude toward horses and vice versa, the attitude of horses toward them" (p. 114).

By reducing the two worlds, in a novel of growing up, to rigid male and female stereotypes, as cluttered with comic cultural symbols as the Grangerford house, Stafford mocks gender expectations frozen into cultural myths. But there is a darker side to her western fable. The western plot, she makes clear, belongs finally to the male, to Ralph, who leaves behind "the sissy life he had had to lead" with his refined mother for the "Ride 'em, cowboy" world of the Bar K, where he hunts a golden mountain lion, whose death will initiate him into the mysteries of nature and sexuality, while proving his superior power, his manhood. Yet at the climax, Ralph "accidentally" kills, not "Goldilocks," but Molly, with whom he has shared such a close relationship that the two had felt "themselves . . . split in half" (115). Through Ralph's story, Stafford implies that the fable of the West is predicated on the destruction of the feminine, in nature and within the masculine self. But Molly's story is as important as Ralph's. Her ironic viewpoint reveals that life at the Bar K, life in the "real West," limits mature growth, that "Claude" is aptly named. Her story, in counterpoint to her brother's, shows that the West welcomes only male rebels and misfits; that to those women who, for whatever reason, dream the American dream of rebellion and escape from the stultifying social world, the frontier and its "liberating" myths have always been closed.[10]

Stafford "resists" the very themes that she employs, and she achieves some liberation from the myths through her mockery of them. Yet Molly is clearly her creator's alter ego, and Stafford can find no place for her or her rebelliousness in the West. Her black humor masks a real sense of pain at her exclusion.

While some women writers respond to their exclusion through satire, others retell the classic stories to undermine the male values and point of view. In Adrienne Rich's term, they "re-vision":

> Re-vision – the act of looking back, of seeing with fresh eyes, of entering an old text from a new critical direction – is for women more than a chapter in cultural history: it is an act of survival. Until we can understand the assumptions in which we are drenched we cannot know ourselves. . . . We need to know the writing of the past, and know it differently than we have ever known it; not to pass on a tradition but to break its hold over us.[11]

In "The Return of Mr. Wills," Mary Austin challenges the assumptions of one of the patriarchs of the rebellious-male/civilizing-female tradition, for her little-known story revises from a woman's point of view that classic story of escape into the wilderness, "Rip Van Winkle."

Austin focuses on how the actions of the wandering male affect his wife's character. Initially Mr. Wills is a likable enough fellow, a dreamer who becomes obsessed with searching for lost mines, but his obsession, the female narrator tells us, is "the baldest of excuses merely to be out and away from everything that savored of definiteness and responsibility." Meanwhile his family, like Rip's, suffers; his actions "struck" at them, and his wife becomes "hopeless."[12] Finally, like Rip, he disappears.

At this point the story stays with Mrs. Wills rather than following her husband into the wilderness, and Austin shows that she is not inherently weak, only rendered powerless by her culture. Having "lived so long with the tradition that a husband is a natural provider," she at first feels abandoned (p. 59). But soon she and the children discover that they can support themselves, with "a little over." She realizes that "she not only did not need Mr. Wills, but got on better without him" and finds a "new sense of independence and power" (p. 59).

Unfortunately, Mr. Wills does not stay away for twenty years but returns to the home his family has built without him, and settles on them "like a blight," announcing that "'There's no place like home' . . . or something to that effect" (p. 62). The story ends with a covert expression of Mrs. Wills's new-found independence when she happily realizes that her husband will inevitably wander off again, perhaps forever. While "Rip Van Winkle" implies that women inhibit men's freedom and stifle their characters, "The Return of Mr. Wills" asserts that men inhibit women's independence and stifle *their* growth. If "The Return of Mr. Wills" were accepted as an archetypal expression of the relations between the sexes, as "Rip Van Winkle" has been, then men as well as women would be forced to acknowledge their own role as antagonists and obstacles to freedom.

Stafford and Austin provide two rather positive and successful examples of the woman writer's efforts to resist the western myth. And yet, resist as she might, no writer, no woman, can wholly escape her cultural traditions: in mocking them or challenging them, she reaffirms their centrality to her way of understanding the West and women's experience there. Although these writers will readily make fun of the West's "spacious guys," they are less certain about how to claim for women a *sweet* land of liberty, and their writings show a good deal of ambivalence about how to wed the West's liberating spirit and individualism with traditional women's values of connection and care.

Some women writers found it impossible to make the "familiar plots" work with female protagonists, to discover space within the western themes for a positive treatment of their own values. The masculine, turbulent West was the setting for heroic exploits, danger, conflict, and adventure, not of sisterhood, nurturing, or artistic aspiration, the subjects of much of nineteenth-century women's literature. The life of the "real" West was closed to them, as experience and as subject matter, yet their own lives could not be the subject of fiction set in the wild, wild West. Although they were often attracted to the promised freedom and independence (and found it in their own lives), many could not make up out of the thin air that Russ describes a plot which would allow a woman character to merge the values of the dichotomized roles.

Nor could women writers grant a woman's concerns legitimacy and significance, a home in the West. Such a writer is Mary Hallock Foote, whose major theme as an illustrator and writer is the effect of the West on those for whom it became home.[13] A contemporary of Owen Wister, whose *The Virginian* consolidated the supremacy of the male myth by popularizing the image of the cowboy, Foote believed that the West was male territory, territory she, who called herself "one of the 'protected' women of that time," could neither fully inhabit nor claim as her own.[14] She described one of her books as

> not a woman's story. *How* I wish I had a son who would put his name to my stories. One could write so much better if one were not a woman–a wife and mother of small girls–the fields beyond which only men may tread. I know as much about the men who tread those fields as a man could–more–but I don't know the fields and don't wish to appear to.[15]

Foote felt that "the men who tread those fields" were the legitimate subjects of western fiction. Although she discovered in the West the "desire that life shall not satisfy," she found her own fiction inadequate because she could not effectively use the male plots, nor could she twist the sentimental conventions of eastern women's fiction to convey the depth and complexity of her own western experiences.[16] These experiences are richly and fully rendered in the 540 or so letters she wrote to her closest friend over a period of thirty-five years; this private audience, Foote was sure, would be interested in how a western woman practiced birth control and gave birth, how she expressed her sexuality and fought with her husband, how she felt about her work and satisfied her ambitions, subjects Foote could find no way to convert to fiction.[17] The themes of female exclusion and alienation from the West present in her fiction may be as much a rendering of her response to her cultural traditions as to her life in the West.

Foote's confidence in her subject matter as truly "western" was undermined by her belief that the western literary landscape was a masculine one. She did not identify with the male values, yet she recognized that she would feel more comfortable as a western writer, that spaces would open to her, if she were a man. Many women writers follow the pattern for success described by Carolyn Heilbrun in *Reinventing Womanhood:* "those women who *did* have the courage, self-confidence, and autonomy to make their way in the male-dominated world did so by identifying themselves with male ideals and role models, . . . by not identifying themselves . . . as women."[18] This "choice" demonstrates the difficulty of bridging the polarized sex roles and reveals the psychological anxieties which result from them.

Mari Sandoz, who claimed she found her "emotional identity" in the landscape and culture of the West, was unable to decide whether to identify with the masculine or feminine Wests, clearly separate worlds in her family autobiography, *Old Jules*. Although Sandoz's book purports to be a biography of her pioneer father, a famous character in frontier Nebraska, its covert subject is a woman's history of the West. Through telling the story of her mother and her mother's friends, Sandoz reveals themes generally overlooked in conventional western history: frontier marriage and its institutionalization of male power; family violence and the resulting personal and social scars; and the exploitation of pioneer women, supported by tradition, by law, and by simple brute force. Sandoz's women lead seemingly unbearable lives, and she is clearly fearful and angry that her mother is preparing her to follow in her own footsteps.

Yet Sandoz chooses to present her brutal, abusive father as her story's hero for he, after all, possesses the traits of the hero of the western myth. Jules Sandoz found the freedom Turner described, though the West did not offer his wife Mary the same bargain. After exposing in *Old Jules* the violent and circumscribed lives of her mother and other plains women, Sandoz turns in her later histories to the classic masculine West and its themes, to what she calls "the romantic days."[19] Interested in heroism, individualism, and power, which she sees as the natural subjects of history, Sandoz never again gives woman a starring role in western history, though in one of her late novels, *Miss Morissa,* she manages to allow a female protagonist, a nurturing and adventurous doctor, the best of both worlds.

Sandoz suggests that American Dream and nightmare can be inextricably mixed. Yet she wanted to claim the dream for herself–and to escape the nightmare. Sandoz saw her mother's life as circumscribed and powerless; she coveted the freedom, power, and vision the West seemed to give to her father. *Old Jules* suggests one of the major problems facing feminist writers as they try to reconstruct women's history. Some search for literary foremothers who rebel and manage to achieve in their lives the measure of freedom the cultural myth promises the male; others acknowledge some truth in the stereotype of the reluctant woman pioneer and, like Sandoz, explore the differences in power and independence in men's and women's lives. Sandoz's fine book reveals her uncertainty about whether to identify with her father's or her mother's West. Her desire to take over male territory is one shared by a number of writers. Yet she knows she cannot escape from being a woman. Her split viewpoint is the inevitable result of the myth's dichotomizing, and it reveals the difficulties of writing about women while aspiring to male freedom.

Sandoz's uncertainty about how to assess and respond to the differences in men's and women's lives in the West is shared by critics schooled in the American Studies tradition. The liberated male/domestic female convention is as "inescapable" for critics as for fiction writers, and feminist scholars have been sorely confused about how to decide just what are "the legitimate inclinations of the sexes." The answers are not yet in, but I will take a look at a few possible directions and implications.

The "seminal" books of the male myth – in fiction, history, and criticism – have encouraged women to purchase their self-esteem, power, and freedom by suppressing their attraction to the domestic, the civilized, the safe and the tame, reduced to stereotypical terms. Fetterley hints at the causes of this response when she describes the "powerlessness" of the female reader of "classic American literature," who is "asked to identify with a selfhood that defines itself in opposition to her. . . . Our literature neither leaves women alone nor allows them to participate. It insists on its universality at the same time that it defines that universality in specifically male terms" (xii–xiii). Her point is poignantly illustrated in a fine essay, "Eve among the Indians," which Dawn Lander opens by describing her own liberated western childhood:

> I did not identify myself with houses, churches, and fences. I loved to be outdoors. I loved the space, energy, and passion of the landscape. . . . Repeatedly, however, I could find no place for myself and for my pleasure in the wilderness in the traditionally recorded images of women on the frontier. Tradition gives us the figure of a woman, strong, brave and often heroic, whose endurance and perseverance are legendary. It may seem strange that I find it difficult to identify with this much praised figure. But I can almost hear her teeth grinding behind her tight-set lips; her stiff spine makes me tired and her clenched fists sad. Victimization and martyrdom are the bone and muscle of every statue, picture, and word portrait of a frontier woman. She is celebrated because she stoically transcended a situation she never would have freely chosen. She submits to the wilderness just as – supposedly – she submits to sex. But she needn't enjoy it, and her whole posture is in rigid opposition to the wilderness experience: to the land, to the Indians. Her glory, we are told, is that she carried the family, religion, fences, the warmth of the hearth and steaming washtubs inviolate to the [West].[20]

I have shared Lander's bitterness at our exclusion from the liberating myth. Like her I identified with the values associated with western males and sought heroines who shared our response, whose lives satisfy our own needs – and discovered them in Caroline Kirkland, Eliza Farnham, Isabella Bird, Elinore Pruitt Stewart, Agnes Cleaveland, Abigail Scott Duniway, Agnes Smedley, and others. Like Lander, throughout this essay I have found male writers and critics responsible for creating what she calls "the discrepancy between women's actual feelings and the received tradition" (p. 197). We might have learned this rebellious response to cultural prescriptions of gender roles from the writers I have already discussed or from those listed above: it is a part of a western women's tradition.

It is natural for feminist scholars who yearn for the freedom promised the frontiersman to attack the stereotyping of women in male texts and to search for women who share their feelings of rebellion. The promise of the frontier is, after all, a human fantasy. And yet we cannot claim that fantasy for women by denigrating traditional female values, the "warmth of the hearth," simply because they have been reduced and stereotyped within the masculine myth. As early as 1932, Mary Austin suggested that the western feminist's revolt must be built upon an understanding of the influence and power of the "happenings of the hearth." Writing her autobiography in the third person, she said of her foremothers:

> Whatever in Mary makes her worth so much writing about has its roots in the saga of Polly [McAdams] and Hannah and Susanna Savilla, in the nurture of which she grew up. . . . It is to the things that the Polly McAdamses discovered in their westward trek that Mary's generation owed the success of their revolt against the traditional estimate of women. . . . Chief of the discoveries of the Polly McAdamses, as it was told to Mary, was the predominance of the happenings of the hearth, as against what happens on the battlefield and in the market-place, as the determinant of events. What they found out was that the hope of America . . . depended precisely on the capacity of the Polly McAdamses to coordinate society, to establish a civilization, to cause a culture to eventuate out of their own wit and the work of their hands, out of what they could carry with them into the wilderness.[21]

Throughout her life Austin tried to understand the relationship between what Lander calls the "space, energy, and passion of the landscape" and the "warmth of the hearth," to reconcile the two. Her recognition of a women's culture as "the determinant of events" yields a revisionist view of Western history. In these insights, as in much else, she presages later feminist concerns.

In the past few years, this dialectical understanding of female and male values, initially attacked as stereotyping, has gained legitimacy among feminist writers. Like Susan Armitage, who in 1981 described the "central question" in western women's history as whether the frontier liberated women, they have initially attempted to evaluate women's experience in relation to male patterns, to claim male territory for women. Many–not all–have come to acknowledge, as did Armitage, that "there were two Wests: a female and a male one."[22] More recently Armitage has argued that while the "frontier myth" has been shaped by male preoccupations with courage, honor, violence, and individualism, attention to women's lives and concerns will provide historians with the basis for a major reinterpretation of western history.[23] Instead of simply appropriating male freedom and male patterns of heroism for women characters–and for themselves–feminist literary critics can now map a female territory and tradition, as Annette Kolodny has recently shown. The overlap in the two traditions will suggest that just as the male fantasies of freedom and self-determination are universal human–and not exclusively male–dreams, so are the female concerns with human interdependence and obligation universal human needs which have been undervalued.

Like Smith's *Virgin Land,* Kolodny's *The Land before Her: Fantasy and Experience of the American Frontiers, 1630–1860* explores the mythologies writers create to express collective desires. These desires, Kolodny implies, are shaped by gender. Describing "women's developing literary response to the West," Kolodny argues that "women claimed the frontiers as a potential sanctuary for an idealized domesticity," and that in creating a nurturing, homey garden, a feminine Eden, "women reveal themselves healed, renewed, revitalized–and even psychically reborn."[24] Like the male hero, these women find psychic health in the West, yet they do so not by leaving behind civilization and domesticity but by creating through them.

One of the roles of women's culture, as Gerda Lerner and others have argued, is to turn subordination into complementarity and then redefine it in positive ways.[25] Thus, Kolodny's description of the female fantasy of "idealized domesticity" in some ways resembles the role women are assigned in the male myth, seen from a healing, renewing vantage point. As Kolodny acknowledges:

> The forms a fantasy may take, after all, are constrained by what the culture makes available to imagination. During the formative years traced here, women's fantasies about the west took shape within a culture in which men's fantasies had already attained the status of cultural myth and at a time when woman's sphere was being progressively delimited to home and family. What women eventually projected onto the prairie garden, therefore, were idealizing and corrective configurations drawn from the spheres in which their culture had allowed them imaginative play. (P. 12)

Thus, the women's tradition Kolodny describes is not only an expression of women's emotional needs but also a response to the male tradition.

Yet Kolodny's tradition never gained the "status of a cultural myth" except as it was reduced within the male myth, in which the domesticity the women writers saw as fruitful and renewing became limiting and constricting–to female as well as male characters. This women's tradition of western fantasy was largely lost to late nineteenth- and twentieth-century writers, particularly after Wister's cowboys solidified the grasp of the male fantasy on our culture. Certainly women writers continued to express the fantasies Kolodny describes, but increasingly the male myth got in the way of the woman writer's ability to tell her own story and form her own values, as my examples have shown. Kolodny's book begins the process of counterbalancing the male tradition with a female tradition of frontier and western dreaming.

The recovery of a woman's tradition can help us to understand women writers and to shape the concerns of feminist literary criticism. As Elaine Showalter has argued in "Feminist Criticism in the Wilderness," a woman's text confronts both paternal and maternal precursors and must deal with the problems and advantages of both lines of inheritance."[26] Women writers, she says, "are not inside and outside of the male tradition; they are inside two traditions simultaneously" (p. 202). In claiming Showalter's "two traditions," the woman writer seeks to reconcile Armitage's "two Wests." For many of the writers I have discussed, they are in conflict. And yet most women's texts work toward their resolution, toward a marriage of the two value systems. Although critics like R. W. B. Lewis have focused on the male "individual standing alone," this character has often been allowed to unite the values of the two worlds. One has only to think of Hawkeye grasping Chingachgook's hand across Uncas's grave or Huck's decision to go to hell for Jim to recognize that male characters have been allowed both a yearning for freedom and independence and an understanding of human interdependence and companionship. A more thorough look at the woman writer's relationship to her two traditions will eventually reveal, I think, that most women writers attempt to merge "the space, energy, and passion of the landscape" with "the warmth of the hearth," that they have always claimed the wider range of self-expression usually granted only to the male in our canonized literature.

Attention to the two traditions can also allow feminist critics to combine the two approaches in vogue in recent years. It is not enough to focus on women's exclusion, to reveal how women have been oppressed and handicapped by a dominant male culture (as I have done throughout this essay). But in writing about women's texts and validating the traditional women's values of nurturing and care, we must not imply that a women's tradition existed apart from, unhampered by, male culture. Many western women saw their gender as both a strength and a limitation. Like Austin, Elinore Pruitt Stewart and Agnes Cleaveland responded to the energy and passion of the landscape of the West *and* to the warmth of the hearth. Stewart recreated "home" in the West, where she found the space she needed. Exulting that she led "no life for a lady," Cleaveland nevertheless was an early graduate of the West's most prestigious university, Stanford. Neither could entirely evade gender roles, but both saw more possibilities in being a woman than in being a man. The points of view of these two independent women present a new definition of the West's freedom.[27]

The recovery of a women's tradition will allow for a fuller understanding of the gender-role dichotomies of the mythic West. Only a synthesis of the history of both men's and women's cultures, Lerner argues, will yield a truly universal history–or a universal mythology. One of America's foremost historians of the American character, David Potter, made this same point in 1962 in "American Women and the American Character." Regretfully acknowledging that "masculine orientation is to be expected, of course, in a society which is traditionally and culturally male-dominated," Potter goes on to suggest that "many of our social generalizations which are stated sweepingly to cover the entire society are in fact based on the masculine population, and that if we took the feminine population into account, the generalization might have to be qualified, or even run in an entirely different direction." Potter's first "notable example" is "Frederick Jackson Turner's famous frontier thesis."[28]

Potter is certainly right that the frontier "generalizations" would be qualified by attention to women's voices, as one example will suggest. Richard Slotkin has demonstrated that the male hero of the mythic West often regenerates himself–or proves his manhood–through violence.[29] When women characters like Molly Wood resist this violence, they are told by various avatars of the Virginian that they don't adequately understand "how it must be about a man."[30]

While it would be an oversimplification to suggest that violence is a wholly positive force within the myth, it is clearly a necessity, a measure of a man's power within his world. And yet the most cursory look at violence within western women's literature, where it is also a major theme, reveals a largely unexplored consequence of the western male's obsession with violence: that women are often the victims of the frontier's celebrated freedom. In works by Agnes Cleaveland, Mary Austin, Agnes Smedley, Mari Sandoz, Meridel Le Sueur, and Tillie Olsen, the writers focus on what they present as the widespread physical and emotional abuse of pioneer women, abuse that Sandoz calls "every husband's right."[31] Today this is hardly a surprising subject, since recent sociologists of wife abuse have suggested that violence occurs in over half of all marriages. Woman abuse was an undercover subject in our literary canon, as it was in our society. The frontier's mythic sex roles appear darker when we question whether the frontiersman or pioneer might have been a woman abuser, whether the "real" Davy Crocketts, Natty Bumppos, Virginians, and Ben Cartwrights took for granted a patriarchal authority that sanctioned woman abuse, whether the frontier's cherished freedom and individualism, which the myth claims as shapers of American character and culture, might have encouraged the violent domination of women.

This example suggests that attention to women's voices will lead to the reinterpretation of western experience Armitage calls for. Freedom and self-determination, interdependence and obligation–these are the positive expressions of the opposed values of the "two Wests." While much of the gender dichotomizing represents a facile oversimplification of men's and women's needs and characters, such studies as Carol Gilligan's *In a Different Voice* show that there are indeed real differences in the development of female and male values, providing new angles from which to approach the old myth. Gilligan suggests that

> relationships, and particularly issues of dependency, are experienced differently by women and men. For boys and men, separation and individuation are critically tied to gender identity since separation from the mother is essential for the development of masculinity. For girls and women, issues of femininity or feminine identity do not depend on the achievement of separation from the mother or on the progress of individuation. Since masculinity is defined through separation while femininity is defined through attachment, male gender identity is threatened by intimacy while female gender identity is threatened by separation. Thus males tend to have difficulty with relationships, while females tend to have problems with individuation.[32]

While Gilligan finds that male voices express a concern for separation and female voices a need for connection, she argues that a psychological balance of the two needs is essential to full human growth. Her discovery of these two modes of psychological development certainly illuminates the myth's dichotomies, but I don't think we are yet ready to say what are the "legitimate inclinations of the sexes." What we can say Mary Austin already knew in 1918: "This is what women have to stand on squarely, not their ability to see the world in the way men see it, but the importance and validity of their seeing it in some other way."[33]

NOTES

1. Wallace Stegner, "History, Myth, and the Western Writer," in *The Sound of Mountain Water* (New York: Dutton, 1980), p. 195.
2. Jean Stafford, *The Mountain Lion* (1949; reprint, Albuquerque: University of New Mexico Press, 1972), p. 32. Subsequent references in the text are to this edition.
3. Nina Baym, "Melodramas of Beset Manhood: How Theories of American Fiction Exclude Women Authors," *American Quarterly* 33, no. 2 (Summer, 1981): 123–29.
4. Henry Nash Smith, *Virgin Land* (Cambridge, Mass.: Harvard Univ. Press, 1950), p. ix.
5. Judith Fetterley, *The Resisting Reader: A Feminist Approach to American Literature*

(Bloomington: Indiana Univ. Press, 1978). Subsequent references in the text are to this edition.

6. Baym, "Melodramas of Beset Manhood." Had our literary history been told from a female point of view, had we searched the major female texts of the nineteenth century for a myth of equal weight to the male fantasy of the call of the wild, our cultural traditions would look quite different. Although the frontier myth has been widely applied in interpreting male texts, it is not useful in interpreting the work of many important nineteenth century women writers, such as the so-called "domestic novelists," or Alcott, Stowe, Phelps, Jewett, and Freeman.

7. I have also limited my examples in this essay to white women because native-American and Hispanic women suffer under different stereotypes and have a more complicated relationship to the myth, and any attempt to simplify it for the purposes of a short essay like this is inevitably reductive. Certainly alienated from the white male's western myths, Indian women of many tribes can look to such cultural traditions as the tribal grandmother, spider woman, for myths of female heroism. Any attempt to formulate a history or mythology of the West should, of course, attend particularly to the voices of native Americans and Hispanics. I plan to give this subject the attention it deserves in my forthcoming book on western women writers.

8. Smith, *Virgin Land;* R. W. B. Lewis, *The American Adam* (Chicago: Univ. of Chicago Press, 1955); Richard Chase, *The American Novel and Its Tradition* (Garden City, N.Y.: Doubleday, 1957); Leo Marx, *The Machine in the Garden* (New York: Oxford Univ. Press, 1964); Edwin Fussell, *Frontier: American Literature and the American West* (Princeton, N.J.: Princeton Univ. Press, 1965); Leslie A. Fiedler, *The Return of the Vanishing American* (New York: Stein and Day, 1968). Subsequent references in the text are to these editions.

9. Joanna Russ, "What Can a Heroine Do? or Why Women Can't Write," in *Images of Women in Fiction: Feminist Perspectives,* ed. Susan K. Cornillon (Bowling Green, Ohio: Bowling Green Univ. Press, 1972), p. 4. Subsequent references in the text are to this edition.

10. For a fuller discussion of this novel, see my "Jean Stafford's Western Childhood: Huck Finn Joins the Camp Fire Girls," *Denver Quarterly* (Spring, 1983), pp. 39–55.

11. Adrienne Rich, "When We Dead Awaken: Writing as Re-Vision," in *On Lies, Secrets, and Silences* (New York: W. W. Norton, 1979), p. 35.

12. Mary Austin, "The Return of Mr. Wills," in *Lost Borders,* (New York: Harper & Brothers, 1909), p. 58. Subsequent references in the text are to this edition.

13. This theme has also been identified by Lee Ann Johnson in *Mary Hallock Foote* (Boston: Twayne Publishers, 1980).

14. Levette Jay Davidson, "Letters from Authors," *Colorado Magazine* 19 (July, 1942): 123.

15. Quoted in Johnson, p. 116.

16. Mary Hallock Foote, *John Bodewin's Testimony* (Boston: Ticknor and Fields, 1886), p. 344.

17. These letters are in the Stanford University Library collection. Xeroxed copies are in the Huntington Library Collection.

18. Carolyn Heilbrun, *Reinventing Womanhood* (New York: W. W. Norton, 1979), p. 31.

19. Mari Sandoz, "Pioneer Women," unpublished essay excerpted in *Hostiles and Friendlies,* ed. Virginia Faulkner (Lincoln: Univ. of Nebraska Press, 1959), p. 59.

20. Dawn Lander, "Eve among the Indians," in *The Authority of Experience: Essays in Feminist Criticism,* ed. Arlyn Diamond and Lee R. Edwards (Amherst: Univ. of Massachusetts Press, 1977), pp. 195–96. Subsequent references in the text are to this edition.

21. Mary Austin, *Earth Horizon* (New York: The Literary Guild, 1932), pp. 14–15.

22. Susan Armitage, "Western Women's History: A Review Essay," *Frontiers* 5, no. 3 (Fall, 1980): 71–73. In the past few years western historians have hotly debated how the West affected pioneer women. Many have shared Sandoz's view that although western women were heroic in making the best of limited circumstances, they were generally oppressed, leading lives which allowed for little personal freedom. Another group, headed by Sandra Myres, argues that the West did indeed provide women with liberating opportunities, did open the proverbial new horizons. Ironically, both groups seem to assess women's lives through the monocled viewpoint of Turner's premises, premises derived from men's and not from women's lives. It does not seem worthwhile to attempt to define the "female West" simply by its exclusion or inclusion in the "male West." The "female West" should be defined and judged on its own terms; Austin's effort to understand what her ancestors "discovered" about their own achievements and values is a fine model.

23. Armitage made this point in a keynote address to the first Women's West Conference in Sun Valley, Idaho, in August, 1983, and subsequently in a published essay, "Through Women's Eyes: A New View of the West," *The Women's West,* ed. Susan Armitage and Elizabeth Jameson (Norman: Univ. of Oklahoma Press, 1987).

24. Annette Kolodny, *The Land before Her* (Chapel Hill: Univ. of North Carolina Press, 1984), pp. xiii and 8. Subsequent references in the text are to this edition.

25. Gerda Lerner, "The Challenge of Women's History," in *The Majority Finds Its Past* (New York: Oxford Univ. Press, 1981), pp. 168–80.

26. Elaine Showalter, "Feminist Criticism in the Wilderness," *Critical Inquiry* (Winter, 1981): 203. Subsequent references in the text are to this edition.

27. Elinore Pruitt Stewart, *Letters of a Woman Homesteader* (Boston: Houghton Mifflin, 1914), and Agnes Morely Cleaveland, *No Life for a Lady* (1941; reprint, Lincoln: Univ. of Nebraska Press, 1977).

28. David Potter, "American Women and the American Character," in *The Character of Americans,* ed. Michael McGiffert (Homewood, Ill.: Dorsey Press, 1970), p. 319.

29. Richard Slotkin, *Regeneration through Violence* (Middletown, Conn.: Wesleyan Univ. Press, 1973).

30. Owen Wister, *The Virginian,* (1902; reprint, New York: Popular Library, n.d.), p. 302.

31. Cleaveland, *No Life for a Lady;* Austin, *Earth Horizon;* Smedley, *Daughter of Earth;* Le Sueur, *The Girl;* and Olsen, *Yonnondio.* The quote is from Sandoz, *Old Jules* (1935; reprint, Lincoln: Univ. of Nebraska Press, 1962), p. 412.

32. Carol Gilligan, *In a Different Voice: Psychological Theory and Women's Development* (Cambridge, Mass.: Harvard Univ. Press, 1982), p. 8. Gilligan sides with nurture over nature, but sociobiology may also provide interesting ways to speculate on the images of women and men in the West, as is suggested by William Bloodworth's paper on the popular western, "Testosterone Dramas: Sociobiology in the Western" (delivered at the Western Literature Association Convention in Reno in October, 1984).

33. Mary Austin, *The Young Woman Citizen* (New York: The Woman's Press, 1918), p. 19.

PART FIVE
Genres

Nature Writing and the American Frontier

PAUL BRYANT

The landscape of the high, dry, spacious American West has been established in the American mind as our ultimate frontier of settlement, and therefore a key factor in the development of our national literature. Our sense of the landscape was first developed by those who wrote about it, the explorers, the naturalists, the soldiers – the nature writers – primarily in the nineteenth century. As they learned to write about that special landscape, they taught us ways of thinking about America, and about ourselves as Americans.

A starting point, perhaps, would be to define nature writing. It is a specific genre of non-fiction prose about nature, written in a way that remains faithful to the objective scientific facts, includes those facts as a significant element of content, and at the same time presents a human response and relationship to those facts. Significant modern American writers in this tradition include Ann Zwinger, Joseph Wood Krutch, Edward Abbey, Annie Dillard, Sally Carrigher, John Muir, Aldo Leopold, and Loren Eiseley, to name only a few of a legion of skilled nature writers in American literature. From the eighteenth and nineteenth centuries, the tradition would include a long list of explorers, naturalists, travelers, and settlers, some of whom will be considered here.

Nature writing as a literary genre in English began in the eighteenth century. Before that time, wild nature, particularly mountain wilderness, was commonly regarded as uncontrolled, hostile, abhorrent, certainly not a fit subject for the aesthetic contemplation that might give rise to literature. The classical Greek and Roman writers had sometimes shown an awareness of nature, but usually as a place of threats and obstacles to be overcome. In their eyes, wild nature, particularly in the unsettled mountains and the open sea, was a source of danger and adventure, but seldom of aesthetic appreciation. Biblical writers thought in terms of the oasis, the garden, cultivated areas insulated from the chaos of nature.[1] Christ went into the wilderness as a trial and preparation for his ministry, and there he was tempted by Satan. For people in the Middle Ages, with their contempt for this world in contemplation of the next, nature might provide a symbolic basis for didactic writing on spiritual subjects, but there was little objective writing about wild nature.

Roderick Nash points out that the very etymology of the word *wilderness* derives from the idea of a place of wild beasts, a place out of control, and therefore a place of danger.[2] Without our modern understanding of biological systems and ecological relationships, nature appeared to be random, disorderly, without rules, uncontrolled.[3]

These generalizations, for which, of course, one may find exceptions, have been supported and documented in a good many studies, including the works of Paul Shepard, Roderick Nash, and, before them, the careful scholarly work of Marjorie Hope Nicolson.[4] Space here does not permit a thorough review of the arguments developed by these and other authors in support of these generalizations about classical and biblical attitudes toward nature. These ideas have become commonplaces among students of the aesthetics of nature, but, to paraphrase a remark of Nicolson's, they are commonplaces only because, like many clichés, they are basically true (p. 4).

The change began in the Renaissance. The discoveries of Renaissance explorers, and a shift in interest from the next world to this one, focused the attention of western civilization upon great tracts of wild nature to be explored, mapped, understood, sometimes ransacked, but in some way come to terms with. Explorers, empire builders, colonizers, merchants, adventurers of all kinds looked at wilderness with new interest. As they began to write about what they were seeing, they had to develop a new vocabulary and a set of conventions for describing and reacting to it. As Nicolson notes, "Like men of every age, we see in Nature what we have been taught to look for, we feel what we have been prepared to feel" (p. 1).

In America, that was true even in the earliest days of exploration along the Atlantic coast, where Europeans were encountering landscapes not markedly different from the less settled regions of Europe. The problem became more distinctly American, however, when exploration and settlement reached the American West. There they found a landscape, climate, plants, and animals far different from anything Europeans or their American descendants had written about before. The nature of the frontier changed, and this change had profound consequences for Americans' view of themselves and of their native landscape. The purpose of this essay is to examine briefly how explorers, naturalists, and nature writers responded to this new need for conventions and vocabulary, how that response has shaped our vision of the West today, and the resulting view of ourselves.

Besides the shift in viewpoint brought about by Renaissance explorations, there were more immediate and often very practical reasons for the new-found interest of Renaissance explorers in writing about the natural world. Their reports were composed under pressures both practical and imaginative. First they were operating with a geography of wonder, an imaginative predisposition to make fabulous discoveries in worlds unlike that from which they had come. Thus they sometimes saw more than was there and believed the fabulous stories of native Americans who, to get rid of the troublesome strangers, might tell them of wonders beyond the next mountain range or across the next narrow sea.

Added to this imaginative predisposition was a very practical consideration: they needed to bring a good report home to those who had financed the expedition. A queen or king who had drained the treasury to pay for ships and supplies did not enjoy being told there were no prospects for a payoff. A lackluster report could be hazardous to the reporter's health. In a sense, the returning explorer had to offer at least some promise and conclude with that standard closing of the modern sponsored research report from universities all across the land: "More research is needed." As an illustrative example, see *The Letter of Columbus on the Discovery of America.*[5]

Unfortunately, Renaissance Europeans had no literary tradition to guide them in the description of the wild new lands. As Conron observes, they could fall back on Old Testament imagery either of savage wilderness or Edenic garden, on the one hand, or on mere lists of the things they were seeing on the other.[6] Columbus could report encountering Caribbean natives who, going naked and possessing no metal weapons, seemed simple, ingenuous, timid, like Adam and Eve before the fall. The lands they inhabited were invariably fertile, and there was certainty of gold in the hills beyond. Verrazzano could describe the landscape of our East Coast as Edenic and the natives as if in a prelapsarian state of innocence.[7] Among the English explorers, Arthur Barlowe in 1584 could describe the area around the Roanoke colony as one where "The soile is the most plentiful, sweete, fruitfull and wholesome of all the worlde."[8] Beyond the Edenic images, however, these explorers could only list the trees, herbs, animals, and minerals they encountered, with greater or lesser accuracy, as did Barlowe, for example:

> This island had many goodly woodes full of deere, conies, hares, and fowles, even in the middest of summer in incredible abundance. The woods are not such as you finde in Bohemia, Moscovia, or Hyrcynia, barren and fruitless, but the highest and reddest cedars in the world, farre bettering the cedars of the Azores, of the Indies, or Lybanus, pines, cypress, sassaphras, the lentisk, or the tree that beareth the masticke, the tree that beareth the rine of blacke cinnamon, . . . and many other of excellent smell and qualitie. (P. 105)

This wonder could result from seeing forests much like those of Europe that were still relatively untouched wilderness. By contrast, we might expect far greater wonder, and greater difficulty in description, when European explorers encountered the West.

As Walter Prescott Webb observed, the Spanish were the Europeans best prepared as explorers for the conditions of the high, dry West,[9] so it is fitting that they were the first Europeans to encounter and attempt to describe it. Like the others, however, they did not have either the literary traditions or the vocabulary to describe their experiences adequately. The soldiers regarded the landscape only as ground to be gotten over. The great empty spaces of the West were obstacles between them and El Dorado, not matters for aesthetic contemplation. For example, Pedro Castañeda gave a very matter-of-fact description of the Grand Canyon, even though he was the first European explorer to see it:

After they had gone twenty days they came to the banks of the river, which seemed to be more than three or four leagues in an air line across to the other bank of the stream which flowed between them. . . . They spent three days on this bank looking for a passage down to the river, which looked from above as if the water was six feet across, although the Indians said it was half a league wide. It was impossible to descend, for after these three days Captain Melgosa and one Juan Galeras and another companion, who were the three lightest and most agile men, made an attempt to go down at the least difficult place, and went down until those who were above were unable to keep sight of them. They returned about four o'clock in the afternoon, not having succeeded in reaching the bottom on account of the great difficulties which they found, because what seemed to be easy from above was not so, but instead very hard and difficult. They said that they had been down about a third of the way and that the river seemed very large from the place which they had reached. . . . Those who stayed above had estimated that some huge rocks on the sides of the cliffs seemed to be about as tall as a man, but those who went down swore that when they reached these rocks they were bigger than the great tower of Seville.[10]

There is here no wonder at the vastness of the canyon, no awe at the majesty of nature, merely a report of how they encountered an obstacle and finally were unable to surmount it. The reference to the great tower of Seville is an early example of what was to become a tradition in describing the Western landscape – the reference to architectural forms. The jagged, blocky erosional forms common to arid regions led Western explorers, settlers, and nature writers to resort to architectural images for description, as evidenced by the names found so many places in the West: Courthouse Rock, Castle Rock, Chimney Rock. Prince Maxmilian, in *Travels in the Interior of North America,* describes rock formations on the upper Missouri as resembling a "blown-up fortress," and speaks of Citadel Rock.[11] Nathaniel Pitt Langford, in *The Discovery of Yellowstone Park,* describes geyser deposits as a "castle," and a miniature colosseum.[12] Earlier Langford had described a stream course as having been worked "into spires, pinnacles, towers and many other capricious objects. Many of these are of faultless symmetry, resembling the minaret of a mosque" (p. 19). Finally, he refers to Yellowstone as "the handiwork of the Great Architect" (p. 122).

John Wesley Powell, describing the Green River country in the latter part of the nineteenth century, says, "The fantastic carvings, imitating architectural forms and suggesting rude but weird statuary, with the bright and varied colors of the rocks, conspire to make a scene such as the dweller in verdure-clad hills can scarcely appreciate."[13] It was the beginning of a tradition that has served nature writers well in the West throughout the nineteenth century, and still serves today.

But even confronted with the Grand Canyon, Castañeda does not mention the sublime, as have many encountering the same scene since his time. The concept of the sublime in scenery had not yet been invented. Castañeda did not have the literary tradition for dealing with the Western landscape that has served writers in the last two centuries or so. The English, and their American descendants, came to the West much later, and, as a result, although they were less well prepared culturally to explore and settle it than were the Spanish, they were much better prepared to write about it.

What gave them that advantage was a profound cultural shift late in the seventeenth and early in the eighteenth centuries. This change has been described by Nicolson: "During the first seventeen centuries of the Christian era, 'mountain gloom' so clouded human eyes that never for a moment did poets see mountains in the full radiance to which our eyes have become accustomed" (p. 3). Like people of every age, she says, we see what we have been taught to look for in nature, and in response to what we see, we feel what we have been taught to feel. What Europeans and their descendants in America saw in wild nature before the late seventeenth century was barren waste and disorder.

But in the years from the mid-seventeenth century to the early eighteenth century, there came a change. The reasons for the change were several and will not be explored here–Nicolson does so quite convincingly and thoroughly. But during that time there was a shift in taste, a moving away from treatment of wild nature only in the traditional forms of the Latin poets. There was a discovery of the aesthetic, as distinct from the rhetorical, sublime.

In America, this shift came in time to provide explorers and naturalists on the western frontier with a new and more positive way of seeing and describing the landscape they were encountering. As exploration moved on westward, to the high, dry West, concepts of the sublime and the beautiful became the stock-in-trade of writers about the wilderness.

With the acceptance of wild nature as a fit subject for aesthetic contemplation, there arose conventional distinctions among the picturesque, the beautiful, and the sublime in describing scenery. These standard concepts developed in a context of seeing nature as picture, as object from which the observer is separated, as in the popular landscape paintings of Salvator Rosa and Claude Lorraine. Claude glasses became fashionable in the eighteenth century. These were spectacles with heavy, square frames that "framed" the wearer's view. The glass in those frames was tinted to give the view the rosy-golden color for which Claude Lorraine's paintings were famous.

As landscape architecture transformed the face of the English countryside in the eighteenth century, under the direction of such architects of Lancelot ("Capability") Brown and Humphry Repton, emphasis grew on discovering or developing "prospects."[14] These were set, formal viewpoints at which the cultivated gentry stepped briefly out of their coaches and "took the view," sometimes with the assistance of a large picture frame held up by the footmen so that the gentry could enjoy their view properly framed. This of course was not necessary if they were equipped with Claude glasses. On some of the great estates, whole villages were moved and rebuilt, streams diverted, waterfalls created by pumps, lakes dug out by hand, solely to provide a properly composed view.

This tradition survives today in the official U.S. government viewpoints in the national parks, at which one is supposed to park one's car (leaving the motor running and the air-conditioner on), for a brief step to the constructed stone wall to "take the view." Landscape becomes picture, the color slide or postcard one takes home as evidence of the refining experience of the Grand Tour. Thus the second of the three questions which, according to Edward Abbey, the rangers at the gates of our national parks answer hundreds of times each day: "How long's it take to see this place?"[15] Our whole concept of experiencing an area is reduced to one sense, the sight, and made static by the limitation on how much time can be devoted to using that sense. How long would it take to "see" Grand Canyon? All the viewpoints along the road on the South Rim can be visited in less than a day, but one could spend a lifetime fully experiencing the canyon.

Thus this tradition of landscape as picture has been preserved, and even made official by the Park Service, particularly in the American West. Nineteenth-century artists such as Bierstadt and Moran reinforced this literary tradition by giving the populated East vividly romantic pictures of the Western landscape. And, of course, the beginning of photography further encouraged us to see the West as picture, particularly after the advent of the simple box camera and dry film emulsions. Eastman, after all, may have done as much as Bierstadt or Moran to freeze the Western landscape of our consciousness into a static and limited picture from which we have become conceptually isolated.

By putting Americans into automobiles, Henry Ford also contributed significantly to this isolation. A countryside "experienced" through the rolled-up windows of an air-conditioned or cozily heated car is far different from countryside experienced on horseback or on foot.

Of course this tradition of nature as a static picture was well established before the frontier reached the 98th meridian. William Bartram writes of "A most enchanting prospect of the great Lake George, through a Grand Avenue, if I may so term this narrow reach of the river, which widens gradually for about two miles, towards its entrance into the Lake, so as to elude the exact rules of perspective and appears of equal width."[16] Bartram, a naturalist primarily, thus speaks of the sublime and shows a clear concept of the painterly rules for appreciating landscape.

Still, the greater scale of the Western landscape, and its novelty, gave greater impetus to the perception of it as a special object for aesthetic contemplation. We find Meriwether Lewis, in his journal, not merely giving us the size of the Great Falls of the Missouri, and their effect on the progress of the expedition, but also considering their aesthetic merit and concluding finally that the lower falls are "sublimely grand" while the upper falls are "pleasingly beautifull."[17] This is obviously self-conscious reporting within an established and shared literary and artistic tradition. By this time the tradition is clearly romantic, reveling in vastness, mystery, irregularity, difficulty of access, terror, awe, all the characteristics of the sublime enumerated in the eighteenth century by Burke, and all suiting the Western scale much better than the smaller landscapes of the East.

A few years after Lewis and Clark, John Charles Fremont, in his *Report of the Exploring Expedition to the Rocky Mountains,* can compare his first view of the Wind River Mountains with expectations built on comparisons made by others with the Alps, and he can comment that, "In the scene before us, we feel how much wood improves a view." Clearly he had a conventional concept of the requirements of the picturesque. On climbing what was to be named Fremont Peak, he speaks of a "view of the utmost magnificence and grandeur" and later of its "romantic beauty."[18]

The redoubtable Isabella Bird, in *A Lady's Life in the Rocky Mountains,* continued this tradition into the latter part of the nineteenth century. Traveling by wagon from Greeley, Colorado, to Fort Collins, along the Poudre River Valley, she compared the view of the Front Range of the Rockies with the Alps: "The lack of foreground is a great artistic fault, and the absence of greenery is melancholy. . . . Once only, the second time we forded the river, the cotton-woods formed a foreground, and then the loveliness was heavenly."[19]

Even so strict a scientist as John Wesley Powell operated under the romantic tradition, although he explored in the West and wrote about it after the Civil War, during the so-called Age of Realism in American literature. In much of his *Exploration of the Colorado River and Its Canyons,* Powell is the observant field scientist or scientific explorer, telling us of river courses, canyon depths, and rock strata. Or he is the adventurer narrating the perils through which he and his followers have passed. But on occasion, in little set-pieces scattered throughout his book, he is the conscious describer of the beauty of a landscape. For example:

> The traveler in the region of mountains sees vast masses piled up in gentle declivities to the clouds. To see mountains in this way is to appreciate the masses of which they are composed. But the climber among the glaciers sees the elements of which this mass is composed,—that it is made of cliffs and towers and pinnacles, with intervening gorges, and the smooth billows of granite seen from afar are transformed into cliffs and caves and towers and minarets. These two aspects of mountain scenery have been seized by painters, and in their art two classes of mountains are represented: mountains with towering forms that seem ready to topple in the first storm, and mountains in masses that seem to frown defiance at the tempests. Both classes have told the truth. The two aspects are sometimes caught by our painters severally; sometimes they are combined. Church paints a mountain like a kingdom of glory. Bierstadt paints a mountain cliff where an eagle is lost from sight ere he reaches the summit. Thomas Moran marries these great characteristics, and in his infinite masses cliffs of immeasurable heights are seen. (Pp. 387–389)

This shows substantial consciousness of the tradition of nature as picture. Consider the following, which please note, results from Powell's standing on a high point and taking the view:

> Standing on a high point, I can look off in every direction over a vast landscape, with salient rocks and cliffs glittering in the evening sun. Dark shadows are settling in the valleys and gulches, and the heights are made higher and the depths deeper by the glamour and witchery of light and shade. Away to the south the Uinta Mountains stretch in a long line,—high peaks thrust into the sky, and snow fields glittering like lakes of molten silver, and pine forests in somber green, and rosy clouds playing around the borders of huge, black masses; and heights and clouds and mountains and snow fields and forests and rocklands are blended into one grand view. Now the sun goes down, and I return to camp. (P. 125)

This emphasis on nature as picture, as contrasted with nature as milieu, creates a perception of nature as something "other" to be observed from a distance, something static, two-dimensional, involving only sight, not hearing or smell or taste or touch. Benton MacKaye has said that the only way to become familiar with the landscape is to engage in some activity in harmony with it. Nature as picture—something that can be hung on a wall or projected on a screen—requires no action, no participation, offers no direct relationship with the viewer.

Even John Muir, a nature writer leading into the modern, ecologically sophisticated tradition, used the scenic set-piece frequently, as in the following view of the South Dome in Yosemite:

Fancy yourself standing beside me on this Yosemite Ridge. There is a strange garish glitter in the air and the gale drives wildly overhead, but you feel nothing of its violence, for you are looking out through a sheltered opening in the woods, as through a window. In the immediate foreground there is a forest of silver firs, their foliage warm yellow green, and the snow beneath them is strewn with their plumes, plucked off by the storm: and beyond a broad, ridgy, canyon-furrowed, dome-dotted middle ground, darkened here and there with belts of pines, you behold the lofty snow-laden mountains in glorious array, waving their banners with jubilant enthusiasm as if shouting aloud for joy. They are twenty miles away, but you would not wish them nearer, for every feature is distinct, and the whole wonderful show is seen in its right proportions, like a painting on the sky.[20]

This tradition of seeing the Western landscape as picture still persists, but with greater ecological sophistication there has developed a group of nature writers in the twentieth century who present nature as milieu, as something to be "lived into" rather than observed with detachment. Muir, of course, wrote much in that vein (see for example his account of climbing Mount Ritter), but Aldo Leopold was perhaps the most consistent pioneer of that approach. In his *Sand County Almanac* and other essays he insists upon meticulous notice of detail, understanding of relationship and process, and sympathetic participation. Seldom does he give a static picture of nature, but rather narrates a running series of events and discoveries. Nature is presented as dynamic and intricately interrelated.

Most contemporary nature writing is in this ecological tradition. Some—Carrigher, Leopold, Peattie—focus more on the detail of natural structure and processes, while others—Annie Dillard, Peter Matthiessen—emphasize what the human observer/participant may learn about self in coming to terms with nature. Still others, such as Joseph Wood Krutch and Sigurd Olson, add the historical dimension of how our culture relates with nature and the consequences of that relationship. But all go beyond nature as picture to a sense of participation. Thus those at the forefront of twentieth century nature writing have outgrown its eighteenth-century roots. The same development can be seen in the poetry, fiction, and drama of the West. For our best writers in the twentieth century, the Western landscape is not a two-dimensional painted backdrop, but a three- (or more) dimensional milieu that contributes to the depth and complexity of the work.

So what can we conclude from this skimming of the literary tradition of nature writing in the American West? Let me suggest four conclusions that I believe have significance to the student of Western writing.

First, that shift in taste back in the eighteenth century, from fearing wild nature as chaotic and threatening to enjoying it as sublime, beautiful, or picturesque, came just in time to play a major role in the exploration and opening of the American West. The conventions were developed in time to glorify the typical Western landscape. Our sustained concept of the West as a heroic landscape and our cultural tradition of the sublime landscape grew up together. Without the Rockies and the Sierra Nevada, Bierstadt would have been limited to the Catskills. Without Yellowstone and the Grand Canyon, what would Thomas Moran have painted? The West has become established in our national consciousness as our frontier land, as that which makes America special, and the West is a sublime landscape. Thus America is, imaginatively, on a sublime scale–in many things beyond only landscape.

Second, this dual development of the sublime and the description of the western landscape gave our culture a focus on landscape in the West that has permeated its history and its treatment in literature. Thomas Hornsby Ferril has observed that the heroic scale of Western scenery sometimes leads writers to people that landscape with giants.[21] By the same token, this preoccupation with scenery may in some part account for the tendency of Eastern establishment critics to assume that significant human stories by serious writers are not likely to be set in the West, where scenery is the only real topic.

The other side of this critical coin, of course, is that inferior writers have indeed tended to use the grandeur of the landscape to prop up stories that do not adequately present the human situation. They count on their readers to assume that any figures on such a grand stage must themselves be grand, without the writer having the skill to show the qualities of the characters through their behavior. In a sense, this grand Western landscape may have encouraged and sustained some bad Western writing. Even for the best Western writers, the landscape in the West is a presence in the writing that always must be dealt with.

Third, we might conclude that the aesthetics of the sublime are essentially Romantic, and nature writing about the West, with its emphasis on the sublime, has remained romantic through not only the Romantic Age of the nineteenth century but also through subsequent ages of Realism, Naturalism, Surrealism, or whatever. John Muir's writing, considered with the time in which he wrote, serves as sufficient illustration of the persistence of romanticism in nature writing. This strong romantic element has also remained, imbedded perhaps in the setting, in fiction and poetry about the West. Even a realist like Frank Norris had to create a mystical Vanamee, whose powers evolved in his years of wandering the southwestern deserts.

Finally, the tendency to see the Western landscape as picture rather than as milieu has created one of the central problems for environmentalists today. The famous remark made a few years ago by a prominent California political figure—something to the effect that when you've seen one redwood tree you've seen them all—illustrates this problem. Such an approach assumes that if we can preserve one specimen of each kind, and a few points at which we can take the official Park Service view, we will have done enough conservation of nature. If the nature we wish to preserve is indeed only a selection of picturesque vistas for leisure-time appreciation, this approach might seem justified. Wendell Berry has observed the irony of our setting aside a few officially beautiful spots and then heedlessly devoting the rest of our land to ugliness.[22]

In sum, we might conclude that many of the roots of literature of the American West lie in the tradition of nature writing and the aesthetic conventions out of which nature writing has grown. Further investigation of the nature writing tradition may offer increased understanding of the whole Western literary tradition.

NOTES

1. Paul Shepard, *Man in the Landscape: A Historic View of the Esthetics of Nature* (New York: Alfred A. Knopf, 1967), discusses this at length. See especially chap. 3, "The Image of the Garden," pp. 63–118.

2. Roderick Nash, *Wilderness and the American Mind* (New Haven, Conn.: Yale Univ. Press, 1967), pp. 1–3.

3. There is a whole complex of philosophical and theological questions concerning whether or not nature was corrupted when humans became corrupt, whether wilderness therefore represented creation in Jehovah's original perfection or the inherently corrupt stronghold of Satan, where God's control was withheld (Chaos and Old Night). These questions provide fascinating insights into our present-day disputes between the developers and builders—who would bring God's order to the realms of Satan by building highways, dams, and subdivisions—and the preservationists, who would save God's uncorrupted nature from the pollution of fallen humanity. But these matters lie beyond the scope of this essay.

4. Marjorie Hope Nicolson, *Mountain Gloom and Mountain Glory: The Development of the Aesthetics of the Infinite* (Ithaca, N.Y.: Cornell Univ. Press, 1959). Subsequent references in the text are to this edition.

5. Christopher Columbus, *The Letter of Columbus on the Discovery of America,* ed. Wilberforce Eames (New York: The Lenox Library, 1892). Note especially pp. 4–5.

6. John Conron, *The American Landscape* (New York: Oxford Univ. Press, 1974), pp. 86–88. Subsequent references in the text are to this edition.

7. Giovanni da Verrazzano, "Letter to the King," in Conron, *The American Landscape,* pp. 95–99.

8. Arthur Barlowe, "First Voyage to Virginia," in Conron, *The American Landscape,* pp. 104–107.

9. Walter Prescott Webb, *The Great Plains* (New York: Grosset and Dunlap, 1931), p. 96.

10. Pedro Castañeda, *The Journey of Coronado* (1904; reprint, Ann Arbor, Mich.: University Microfilms, Inc., 1966), pp. 35–36.

11. Prince Maxmilian, *Travels in the Interior of North America,* in Conron, *The American Landscape,* pp. 326–29.

12. Nathaniel Pitt Langford, *Diary of the Washburn Expedition to the Yellowstone and Firehole Rivers in the Year 1870* (St. Paul, Minn.: J. E. Haynes, 1905), p. 110. Subsequent references in the text are to this edition.

13. John Wesley Powell, *The Exploration of the Colorado River and Its Canyons* (1895; reprint, New York: Dover Publications, Inc., 1961), pp. 124–25. Subsequent references in the text are to this edition.

14. For a useful summary of eighteenth-century landscape architecture in general, and of the work of Lancelot Brown and Humphry Repton in particular, see Edward Hyams, *Capability Brown and Humphry Repton* (New York: Charles Scribner's Sons, 1971).

15. Edward Abbey, *Desert Solitaire: A Season in the Wilderness* (New York: McGraw-Hill, 1968), p. 45.

16. William Bartram, *Travels* (1791; reprint, New Haven, Conn.: Yale Univ. Press, 1958), p. 64.

17. Meriwether Lewis, *Original Journals of the Lewis and Clark Expedition, 1804–1806*, ed. Reuben Gold Thwaites (New York: Antiquarian Press Ltd., 1959), p. 154.

18. John Charles Fremont, *Report of the Exploring Expedition to the Rocky Mountains* (Ann Arbor, Mich.: University Microfilms, 1966), pp. 174–75.

19. Isabella L. Bird, *A Lady's Life in the Rocky Mountains* (1873; reprint, Norman: Univ. of Oklahoma Press, 1960), p. 83.

20. John Muir, *The Yosemite* (1912; reprint, Garden City, N.Y.: Doubleday, 1962), pp. 55–56.

21. Thomas Hornsby Ferril, "Writing in the Rockies," *Rocky Mountain Reader* (New York: E. P. Dutton, 1946), pp. 395–96.

22. Wendell Berry, *The Unsettling of America: Culture and Agriculture* (San Francisco: Sierra Club Books, 1977), pp. 1–26.

"Home Sweet Home": Deconstructing the Masculine Myth of the Frontier in Modern American Drama

LINDA BEN-ZVI

"What is American about the American Drama?" One answer to that question is the repeated use playwrights have made of the frontier, both as a theme and structuring principle in modern American drama. Less concerned with the historical reality of American pioneering–confronting the wilderness, cultivating and securing areas, moving frontiers continually westward across large expanses, subduing peoples and nature while establishing communities from which to launch yet further forays against a rapidly retreating geographical frontier–American playwrights usually invoke the myth of the frontier that subsumed, altered, and embellished these historical facts after the closing of the geographic west, at the beginning of the century.

Richard Slotkin begins his exhaustive, six-hundred-page study *The Fatal Environment: The Myth of the Frontier in the Age of Industrialization* with several chapters detailing the construction of the myth of the American frontier, which he says, is experienced "less by maps than by illusions, projective fantasies, wild anticipations, extravagant expectation."[1] As "mythic space," the frontier is an aggregation of fears, wishes, expectations, exaggerations, and ultimately frustrations that produces, Slotkin argues, the "fatal environment" of his title. This false "web of Myth" tangled the feet of General Custer, trapping him in a jingoistic-induced fantasy, and continues to hold sway over us into the present, in which the myth's "fictive fatalities" are still at work in the world we inhabit. Slotkin outlines the process involved in the mythmaking: narratives formed which preserved fact and were themselves, through repetition, traditionalized, then conventionalized and abstracted until they became "powerfully evocative and resonant 'icons'" able to move people with their power (p. 16). Over time, in the process of conflating fact and fantasy, the range of mythic reference grew, since, as Slotkin observes, "each new context in which the story is told adds meaning to it, because the telling implies a metaphoric connection between the storied past and the present" (p. 16). Ironically, as actual roots in history become confused–tangled, to use Slotkin's word–the power of the myth expands, bearing as myths do "the encoded set of metaphors that may contain all of the lessons we have learned from our history and all of the essential events of our world view" (p. 16).

I have quoted Slotkin at length because most literary studies of the frontier–from D. H. Lawrence's *Studies in Classic American Literature* to Henry Nash Smith's *The Virgin Land,* Leslie Fiedler's *Love and Death in the American Novel,* Edwin Fussell's *Frontier: American Literature and the American West,* and Annette Kolodny's *The Lay of the Land* and *The Land before Her*–are predicated on the mythic use of the term "frontier" and, more specifically, on its metaphoric nature, which allows for constant reappropriation of the myth through the substitution of items assumed to have like properties. For example, such elasticity allowed panelists at a recent American Studies convention, using the generic umbrella "frontier," to give papers on topics ranging from early twentieth-century Western and religious novels, to John F. Kennedy's New Frontier and its connection to *Rambo: First Blood Part II,* and to the "Feminine in Space" in the films *Alien* and *Aliens.* Kennedy's political and social agendas were shown to be commensurate with the frontier myth of expansion, renewal, and change, just as Rambo, a panelist argued, could be seen as both an antiestablishment Kennedy disciple bringing progress and promise to a pastoral Vietnam, as well as a reconstituted frontiersman, saving comrades. Another panelist, Janice Hocker Rushing, saw Sigourney Weaver's character Ripley, in *Alien/s,* as frontiersman–not woman–reinscribing the myth as she did battle in the most recent frontier terrain–outer space–wielding the weapons of the military-industrial complex against the forces of evil, here the alien monster, thus playing out yet another variation on the mythic search and destroy missions of the original pioneers.[2]

Each of these metaphoric substitutions was shown to have exactly or nearly commensurate meanings, fitting neatly into the allotted slots in the mythic equation, where meanings associated with the mythic frontier stories easily transfer to the modern avatars imposing on the new tales predetermined readings and associations. Conversely, any attempts to rescript the tale–for instance, seeing the fact of Ripley's gender in *Alien/s* as a significant alteration –are, Rushing argued, often subverted, as in the film, in order to comply with the familiar configuration of the myth. "When the going gets tough, the tough get masculine," she noted. Ripley does not redefine the myth as a female quest story, but becomes masculine in order to function as predictable frontier persona, that is, as male.

It is this tendency to fit American history and politics and films into predetermined, scripted tales–a predilection that could make possible the equations of the Vietnam War with playing "Cowboys and Indians," Asian pacification with western conquest and settlement, that could allow Henry Kissinger to cast himself as the "Lone Ranger of foreign policy" and that understands SDI preparedness as a galactic equivalent to circling the wagons–which causes Americans to relive events, since history tends to collapse into the same familiar tale whose outcome often seems both predictable and inevitable, like that old story we know so well.

The same can be said for certain literature: the appropriation of the frontier myth and the metaphoric substitutions of events often produce works in which the frontier experience is once more played out, consciously or unconsciously, by the writer, and inferred, consciously or unconsciously, by the reader. The effect is to replicate the basic patterns of the myth, with little variation and little hope of alteration. What this means in simple terms is that the constitutive elements in the frontier myth have shaped much of the American canon and critical reaction to it. Let me cite at least four of those elements in the myth and then relate them to modern drama.

First, the frontier myth is a patriarchal story. It is gender related. It is *his* story, since the conquest of the continent has been encoded as a male adventure. Clearly, then, metaphoric replacements for the protagonist are always male, or when female, the values associated with the male are reinscribed in the myth, as in *Alien/s,* and the *she* becomes "as if" *he.* In his conquest of the land, he often seems to play out his own masculine identity. As Annette Kolodny has shown in her impressive gathering of materials of actual frontier writings, the land itself is metaphorically identified as feminine, "she," with man wishing to merge with it–to return to the sexually undifferentiated, pastoral state of infancy and the body of the mother, at the same time desiring to conquer, penetrate and defile it, become its lover, its owner, its husbandman. The myth of the frontier, then, becomes not only the historical account of conquest, but also the psychological tale of masculine individuation, separation, and schism.[3]

Second, this male is of a particular type. D. H. Lawrence first described him in terms of Cooper's Leatherstocking hero, whose soul, Lawrence said, is "hard, isolate, stoic, and a killer, it has never yet melted." "Of course," Lawrence noted, "the soul often breaks down into disintegration." Yet he quickly countered, "What true myth concerns itself with is not the disintegration."[4] While every historical account of the actual frontier experience indicates the inherent oppositions in the experiences–the fear of the unknown, the challenge of the new; the yearning for the pristine wilderness, the need to conquer and settle it; the desire to escape civilization, the compulsion to recreate it; the pastoral hope, the profitable goad–the hero in his mythic shape seems to emerge as monolithic, seemingly resolving the dichotomies of the actual experience and transforming any possible doubt into the positive values he espouses: independence, individuality, courage, coldness, acquisitiveness, aggression, violence. The myth, if it is to function, disallows the tensions of doubt and offers instead a solitary, univocal voice and set of values. In the same way, applying Kolodny's model, while the hero is often torn between maternal passivity and sexual activity, impregnation, and possession, his need to deny the schism often results in violence, against himself, Woman, and the surrogate for her–the land. This violence is also powerfully evoked in Susan Griffin's book *Woman and Nature: The Roaring inside Her.*

Third, while the hero is conventionalized, so too are those with whom he identifies, most particularly Woman. She is clearly *other.* If he is actor, she is passive recipient of his action; if he breaks new frontiers, she secures familiar ground; if he seeks adventure, she seeks security. Such are the familiar lineaments of the familiar frontier myth. He becomes allied metaphorically with the new, she with the traditional, that is with home, family, security. Since to conquer the wilderness he must venture forth, she often becomes an impediment, the force which stands in his way, the other who initially must be overcome if he is to meet his Manifest Destiny. Hers is a double bind; she is the female who keeps him from the land, and she is the female embodiment of the land. Metonymically she becomes home and mother; metaphorically she stands for all he fears and all he desires. In either manifestation, she can't win.

Having sketched these general elements in the frontier myth, I would like to briefly indicate how they function in modern American drama. Obviously, I will only be able to cite a few examples; the subject rightly requires a book. What I do want to point out, however, is that recognition of these generalized metaphors may aid in rethinking the limits and the inevitabilities of the tale the myth encodes. Seeing how easily we subscribe to the familiar stories may allow us, as both Slotkin and Kolodny hope, to reformulate the myth and free ourselves from forever rereading and reliving it.

I begin with Eugene O'Neill, the father of American drama. Having said that, I have said it all. As father, the patriarch, he has a patriarchal tale to tell. Since shapers of the canon have banished the mother of American drama, Susan Glaspell, we have only the masculine version of the frontier myth to read. When, however, Glaspell is read as a balance to O'Neill, just as when the histories of women are read as balance to the experiences of men on the frontier, a more even, less fragmented, picture may emerge, a myth that incorporates both genders rather than subsuming the female into the male script.

O'Neill's plays *do* make an excellent starting point for my investigation of the repetition of the basic frontier elements of myth in American writing and of the critical tendency to gloss experience and fit material into predetermined mythic patterns. In another paper, I called the dichotomy in O'Neill's plays the pull between freedom and fixity.[5] In the confines of this discussion, I would say that he clearly follows the Kolodny model: a writer who gives lip service to freedom and conquest, but whose works repeatedly illustrate the pull toward the opposite–a longing for home, for return, for the mother, for fixity. By placing O'Neill's works within the familiar myth, critics tend to overlook the tensions and aporias that actually give power to the plays, preferring to read the myth as if it were an unquestioned given in the text.

For example, the first poem that appears in the *Collected Poems of O'Neill* may proclaim (in some of the worst poetry ever written), "Then it's ho! for the plunging deck of a bark, the hoarse songs of the crew / With never a thought of those we left or what we are going to do" and end "And at last be free, on the open sea, with the trade wind in our hair,"[6] yet O'Neill's plays show something far different. Despite the sea locales of his early works and the mythic possibilities such images should convey, in none of the *Glencairn* cycle is an expanse of sea actually shown. Instead, the playing spaces tend to be closed, cramped quarters, small, crowded bunks, foreshortened areas. Instead of "plunging decks" O'Neill gives us roomlike, womblike enclosures which inhabitants seem to accept without question, as alternatives to life on land. In fact, in his sea plays as well as *The Hairy Ape,* O'Neill actually has his male figures reconstitute the lost home in the new setting. "Dis is home see," Yank tells his stokehole mates.[7] Home becomes the preserve of males, a land without wife or family, a new frontier, a self-willed terrain. And it is also seen as female; Yank's stoking of the ship's furnaces is clearly sexual, just as the frontier thrusting into the wilderness is a replication of sexual defilement and control: "Let her have it! All togedder now! Sling it into her! Let her ride! Shoot de piece now!" (p. 189). A mechnical gang bang, a metaphoric act of violent control of territory.

Yet Yank is displaced from this domain and home in a reenactment of his original displacement from the mother, again by a woman–Mildred, an iconic image appropriately wearing the white of virginity, a nautical Eve destroying the Edenic, albeit horrific, world of the stokehole.

The imagery indicates, I believe, conflicting needs in O'Neill–the need to espouse the frontier myth of escape and freedom apart from wife and family, to assert masculine control through violence and sex, to make a new home, alone and unencumbered by the past (certainly one element in the pioneering myth, at least as Leslie Fiedler describes it)[8] and the commensurate pull back to the home, to the female, to fixity, to the passivity that Kolodny illustrates in male writing of the frontier experience. Rather than situating the dichotomies and ruptures within the psyche of the persona, O'Neill presents the schism as external, played out both in the gendered world of man and woman, and in the political world of the haves and have-not's. Similarly, critics often fix on these external forces and read the myth as univocal, replicating in their criticism the very conflicts dramatized in the text, within the consciousness of the persona.

In O'Neill's later plays, the tensions between an espoused escape or freedom and a desired return or fixity become too obvious to ignore. Running through his cycle plays of possessors self-dispossessed–as well as the late plays–is the recognition that freedom, if possible at all, comes not from flight but from return, not in a promising future but in a redeemed past. "There's no present or future–only the past happening over and over again–now," James Tyrone says in *Moon for the Misbegotten,* while he rests in the arms of Josie Hogan.[9] His monologue traces a movement not outward–westward–but eastward, back to home with the body of his mother, the mother he has irretrievably lost. Such recognition culminates in the explicit pain of *More Stately Mansions,* in which O'Neill directly tells of the son's desire to merge with the mother in the garden she has cultivated, giving up all pretense of conquering the frontiers of business or territory, desiring instead, Simon Harford tells his mother Deborah, "this safe haven, where we could repose our souls in fantasy, evade, escape, forget, rest in peace."[10] Yet again, much of the criticism of the play sees Deborah and her mirror image Sarah as the causes of Simon's destruction–he, the mythic frontier hero, who desires freedom from women in some world "beyond the horizon." O'Neill's dichotomous heroes of the earlier play by that name may trace the tensions between those who stay and those who go; the later characters illustrate that it is not woman as much as the tensions within themselves that cause them to seek reabsorption into the undifferentiated world of the mother and of home. Simon speaks for many of them when he says, "I have become so weary of what they call life beyond the wall, mother" (p. 103).

O'Neill's plays are not the only ones in American drama that are often seen as replications of the myth of the frontier; Arthur Miller's plays are also read as reenactments of the frontier story. Particularly in *Death of a Salesman,* he clearly inscribes the frontier myth within the play, showing its gradual demise. Willy's father, a man with a white beard, who once lived in Nebraska, South Dakota, and Alaska–names that resonate with the frontier, especially for a man who lives in Brooklyn–made flutes, sold what he made, crisscrossing the country in a wagon, his children with him. Willy has a less open frontier, riding in a car up and down the New England territory, selling what others make, leaving his family behind. Happy, his son, is fixed in place, an assistant to an assistant, doing unspecified work, unmarried and childless. The youngest generation does not appear in the flesh. Howard's unnamed son is a disembodied voice, coming over a tape recorder, that 1949 marvel of a material society, and he repeats state capitals by rote, reducing the landscape and the frontier to an alphabetic game: "The capital of Alabama is Montgomery"[11]–prophetically pointing to the dehumanized "voices" of the computers of today that tell us the weather, the time, the price.

In many ways Miller seems to be critiquing the frontier myth and its debacle in the modern world of commerce. In fact, in an essay entitled "*Salesman* Has a Birthday," Miller describes Willy's tragedy as his failure to meet "the qualifications laid down for mankind by those clean-shaven frontiersmen who inhabit the peaks of broadcasting and advertising offices."[12] Such words would indicate that Miller is deconstructing the myth; and one might I suppose argue that he is. Yet, by the compelling reinscription of the metaphoric frontiersman, Ben, and the reshaping of the myth in 1949 terms and in words which have themselves become as familiar as gospel– "When I was seventeen I walked into the jungle, and when I was twenty-one I walked out. And by God I was rich" (p. 48)–Miller leaves ambiguous whether this variation, the materialist American dream, is being critiqued or being reified, whether Ben is the ideal or the debasement of it, or an ambiguous blend of both in the confused skull of Willy.

Such ambiguity often leads critics to see the Ben dream as the metaphoric equivalent to the frontier myth. Jeffrey D. Mason, for example in an essay entitled "Paper Dolls: Melodrama and Sexual Politics in Arthur Miller's Early Plays," says that Willy cannot risk the stability of his home to pursue the quest, implying that the quest is positive.[13] Linda Loman, that paper doll from a melodrama, who is never allowed to do more than carry the laundry, becomes the spoiler, the force who keeps Willy from his goal, replaying the role of frontier woman as encumbrance for the harried spouse, seeking to draw him into what Leslie Fiedler called "the facts of wooing, marriage, and childbearing."[14] Even more pointedly, Lois Gordon, a critic cited in Mr. Mason's paper, notes that Linda "encourages Willy's dream yet she will not let him leave her for the new continent."[15] To be fair, these comments reflect one aspect of the play which Miller himself posits. After all he writes the scene in which Linda keeps Willy from going after Ben. "You're doing well enough, Willy!" she says to her husband, and to Ben she counters, "Why must everybody conquer the world?" The scene and her words are exactly a reenactment of the frontier myth as read by Fiedler: Willy is the misunderstood man seeking escape from the clinging woman, the wife keeping the adventuring husband from his dream of the frontier or, as Nina Baym has ironically labeled such tales, "melodramas of beset manhood." Yet were that scene omitted from the play–were Linda Loman omitted–would Willy have pursued Ben? Would Willy have succeeded? Such questions go unasked because Miller fails to script them explicitly, creating instead a more familiar tale of gendered roles. Willy places the blame on Linda–for after all this memory is in the inside of his head–and I would argue that Miller in *Salesman* and in every one of his plays at some point indicts woman. Think of John Proctor faulting both the young girl he seduced *and* his wife for his adultery. Abigail was too sensual, his wife not sensual enough; thus he fell.

Unfortunately, instead of questioning this mythic pattern and revealing its structure, or Miller's appropriation of it, some critics tend to replicate the same indictments. "John Proctor is trapped between a wife and a whore who have woven the circumstances around him," Mr. Mason notes. On *Salesman* he says categorically, "Linda Loman dominates the situation that engulfs Willy." He does not say that Willy sees her this way, or that Miller has Willy see her this way, or that Miller sees her this way, but that she *is* this way. Such a reading recreates the very biases of the play, making the critic one more who falls prey to the generalized script of the myth. Mr. Mason does conclude that Linda is either "a confusingly contradictory role . . . or the product of Willy's uncontrollable imagination." I would say that she is both. But she is also the product of Miller's imagination and, ultimately, the embodiment of society's perception of woman–a perception that continually inscribes woman and man, as well, in the traditional frontier myth.

If we are ever to free ourselves from the sway of these roles and allow more than metaphoric reincarnations of the original, we must first recognize the existence of the myth. In the same way, if we as a society are to free ourselves from the frontier mentality which reduces all situations to Cowboys and Indians, good guys and bad guys, and all gender situations to heroic males and passive or destroying females, we must begin to resist the power of self-inscribed icons and attempt, as Slotkin and Kolodny do, to return to the historical evidence, and to rehistoricize our heritage on a less fanciful, tangled, and gendered path.

NOTES

This paper was originally prepared for presentation on a panel entitled "Gender and Family Relationships in Twentieth-Century Drama," at the 1987 meeting of the Modern Language Association.

1. Richard Slotkin, *The Fatal Environment: The Myth of the Frontier in the Age of Industrialization, 1800–1890* (New York: Atheneum, 1985), p. 11. Subsequent references in the text are to this edition.

2. Janice Hocker Rushing presented a paper entitled "Mythic Evolution of the 'New

Frontier' in Cinema: The Feminine Strikes Back," for a panel entitled "Old Frontiers/New Frontiers: Creating and Recreating the Western," at the 1987 American Studies Association meeting.

3. See Annette Kolodny, *The Lay of the Land: Metaphor as Experience and History in American Life and Letters* (Chapel Hill: Univ. of North Carolina Press, 1975) and *The Land before Her: Fantasy and Experience of the American Frontier, 1630–1860* (Chapel Hill: Univ. of North Carolina Press, 1984).

4. D. H. Lawrence, *Studies in Classical American Literature* (New York: Thomas Seltzer, 1923), p. 92.

5. See Linda Ben-Zvi, "Freedom and Fixity in the Plays of Eugene O'Neill," *Modern Drama: Special Issue on Eugene O'Neill* 31 (1988): 16–27.

6. Eugene O'Neill, *Collected Poems: 1912–1944* (New Haven, Conn.: Ticknor and Fields, 1980), p. 1.

7. Eugene O'Neill, *The Hairy Ape: Nine Plays by Eugene O'Neill* (New York: The Modern Library, 1941), p. 170. Subsequent references in the text are to this edition.

8. Leslie Fiedler, *Love and Death in the American Novel* (New York: Stein and Day, 1975).

9. Eugene O'Neill, *A Moon for the Misbegotten* (New York: Vintage, 1941), pp. 82–83.

10. Eugene O'Neill, *More Stately Mansions* (New Haven, Conn.: Yale Univ. Press, 1964), p. 103.

11. Arthur Miller, *Death of a Salesman* (London: Penguin, 1949), p. 77. Subsequent references in the text are to this edition.

12. Arthur Miller, "The *Salesman* Has a Birthday," in *The Theatre Essays of Arthur Miller*, ed. Robert A. Martin (New York: Viking Press, 1978), p. 15.

13. Mr. Mason presented this paper at the Modern Language Association meeting, December 28, 1987, on a panel on which I also appeared: "Gender and Family Relationships in Twentieth-Century American Drama." Subsequent citings of Mr. Mason refer to the contents of this paper.

14. Leslie Fiedler, "The Novel in America," in *A Fiedler Reader* (New York: Stein and Day, 1977), p. 133.

15. Lois Gordon, "*Death of a Salesman:* An Appreciation," *The Forties: Fiction, Poetry, Drama,* ed. Warren French (Deland, Fla.: Everett/Edwards, 1969), p. 105.

Western Film and the American Dream: The Cinematic Frontier of Sam Peckinpah

JOHN H. LENIHAN

The perpetuation of America's frontier myth throughout this century owes much to the motion picture and particularly the Western genre. From *The Great Train Robbery* in 1903 to *Pale Rider* and *Silverado* in 1985, countless Westerns have conjured vivid images of a late-nineteenth-century trans-Mississippi West, where the interaction between civilization and wilderness ultimately produced the modern social order of the twentieth century. Central to the Western is the ongoing conflict between individual freedom and social constraint that has engaged so many of America's literary and intellectual figures, from James Fenimore Cooper and Ralph Waldo Emerson in the nineteenth century to Ernest Hemingway and David Riesman in the twentieth century. How that conflict has been defined and resolved has varied considerably, reflecting not only the talent and predisposition of a particular filmmaker but also the diversity and fluctuation of ideas, assumptions, and concerns that mark the course of modern American culture.

To John Cawelti in *The Six-Gun Mystique,* the Western is a kind of social ritual "that reaffirms certain basic cultural values, resolving tensions, and establishing a sense of continuity between present and past."[1] But as those values and tensions change over time, the film industry and individual filmmakers have altered or adapted conventional elements in the Western to deliver an entertainment with which a given audience can identify. Such adaptability has been important from a sheer commercial standpoint. A Western that is out of date in terms of audience values and expectations is unlikely to attract paying customers. This is not to diminish the importance of creativity and artistic vision in a screenwriter or director but to suggest that he or she operates in a commercial medium that caters to a projected audience.

Joseph Kane, who had directed Gene Autry and Roy Rogers in many of their early Westerns, in later years expressed his envy that Sam Peckinpah could in the 1960s direct a film that he (Kane) had always wanted to do but could not because audiences of the 1930s and 1940s would not have been so receptive. How fortunate for Peckinpah, Kane added, that the times were right for the themes and point of view he wished to express.[2]

In the 1960s and early 1970s, Sam Peckinpah emerged as the one film-maker to rank with the likes of John Ford, Howard Hawks, Anthony Mann, and Budd Boetticher as a distinguished director of Western films. Like the aforementioned, Peckinpah mastered the genre to produce works of considerable force and artistry. At the same time, Peckinpah modified certain conventional elements in the genre and explored themes that were characteristic of other films of his time and relevant to the society around him.

From *Ride the High Country* (1962) to *Pat Garrett and Billy the Kid* (1973), Peckinpah went to the heart of the Western genre to explore the meaning and implications of an emergent or already entrenched urban civilization supplanting the nineteenth-century frontier.[3] In the traditional Western, the hero was a freedom-loving individualist who bridged the two worlds of civilization and wilderness, employing natural instincts and talents–including the use of violence–to help build a progressive society. If the process of creating a social order with all of its necessary laws and constraints implied an eventual loss of unfettered freedom for the frontier hero, his efforts were nonetheless deemed admirable and worthwhile–as long as the resulting society was indeed virtuous and progressive. Thus the sadness one feels for Alan Ladd in *Shane* (1953) as he is shut out of the society he has saved is offset by our conviction that his sacrifices have been socially beneficial. This kind of reconciliation, or synthesis, of individualism and the collective good was an emotionally satisfying prospect in the Western, provided that such a prospect retained credibility with the audience.

In the 1960s, however, an increasingly younger movie audience had serious misgivings about the America they had inherited. The liberal center that had prevailed through the 1950s and into the early 1960s appeared to unravel as both the political right and left decried the bureaucratization of American life and the consequent loss of individual freedom. The decade reverberated with campus protests, civil rights demonstrations, the antiwar movement, and a veritable explosion of urban tensions. The turbulence extended into the early 1970s, with revisionist intellectuals and the young counterculture attacking the injustices, imperialist aggressions, and technocratic dehumanization wrought by an ill-defined but powerful "establishment." The civil rights and Vietnam issues served to galvanize much of this criticism, disillusionment, and protest–which by the late 1960s involved direct confrontations between the state and its dissenters, confrontations that in places like Chicago in 1968 and Kent State in 1970 reached violent proportions. In the process, violence itself became an issue, whether it involved the use of armed force against the adversaries in Vietnam and against dissenters at home, the assassinations of Martin Luther King and John and Robert Kennedy, or the graphic depiction of brutality in movies and television.

It is unlikely that the Western could have survived these times as a marketable genre without some modification of traditional assumptions about the merits of civilization and without some modification of the kind of hero that would generate audience empathy. In Westerns of the sixties the process of civilizing a savage frontier remained, but the meaning and quality of civilization was redefined, as was the hero's relationship to that civilization. Where once the introduction of a progressive society had been a desirable result of the hero's actions, in Westerns of the 1960s that society spelled a vacuous middle-class status quo, technology that was more intrusive, or even deadly, than humanly purposeful, and a powerful corporate establishment, all of which threatened the freedom and dignity of the individual. Films of the 1950s like *High Noon, Johnny Guitar,* and *The Broken Lance* had already been heading in this direction, beginning a revisionist trend in the Western that Peckinpah and his contemporaries would bring to fruition.

When Peckinpah introduced Steve Judd (Joel McCrea) and Gil Restrum (Randolph Scott) in *Ride the High Country* as once-admired lawmen who are out of step with the modern America they helped make possible, he struck a theme more typical than unique for Westerns of the early 1960s. *Lonely Are the Brave* and *The Man Who Shot Liberty Valence,* released that same year (1962), conveyed the same nostalgic sense of loss for the aging Westerner no longer rewarded or appreciated by modern society. Likewise, the leading characters of *The Misfits* (1961) and the grandfather in *Hud* (1963) are the discards of modern progress, Western variations of "the other America" Michael Harrington wrote about in 1962: people deprived of meaningful employment or otherwise excluded from what was supposed to be a land of opportunity for the worthy individual, people locked into a perpetual struggle not just to survive physically, but to retain a sense of human dignity.[4] Hence Gil Restrum in *Ride the High Country* is reduced to working carnival circuits and eventually betraying his best friend for money. When Steve Judd rides into town at the opening of the film, he is nearly run down by a camel and horses racing down the street and then by an automobile, while a policeman abruptly tells him to get out of the way. The automobile becomes a deadlier artifact of civilization in Peckinpah's *The Wild Bunch* (1969) when used by Mexican federales as an instrument of torture (dragging Angel about on the rough ground of Agua Verde). And in *The Ballad of Cable Hogue* (1970), Peckinpah's protagonist is run over by an automobile —a fatal accident that occurs not long after Cable realizes that his business of selling water at a desert way station will eventually disappear as horses and stagecoaches are replaced by gasoline-operated vehicles.

Most of Peckinpah's Westerns focus on individuals trying to survive the modern age with their freedom of dignity intact. Changing times have rendered obsolete their way of life, leaving them little more than memories of better days. Only in *The Ballad of Cable Hogue* does Peckinpah's hero achieve a satisfying accommodation with the society that will eventually envelop him. With the financial backing of the town bank and stagecoach company, Hogue builds a prospering business selling water at his desert way station. Having spent much of his life as a desert rat, Hogue prefers living (and for a while with his beloved Hildy, the town prostitute) apart from the busyness of the community, but he feels neither alienated from nor bitter toward the emerging civilization. The automobile, which in this film is the most visible sign of modern progress, does inevitably threaten Hogue's enterprise and, at the film's conclusion, becomes the accidental instrument of his untimely demise. Peckinpah thus concludes his tale with a profound sense of the loss that progress brings in its wake, but without at the same time casting the kind of harsh portrait of modern corruption and dehumanization that characterizes his other Westerns.

In his lengthy analysis of Peckinpah's Westerns, Paul Seydor has argued that *Pat Garrett and Billy the Kid* is a departure from the director's earlier laments about the decline of frontier America. By virtue of setting his story in the 1880s instead of the early twentieth century, Peckinpah, according to Seydor, is suggesting that the good old days about which his major characters reminisce in *Ride the High Country* and *The Wild Bunch* were not so good after all.[5] Seydor's interpretation certainly applies to Tom Gries's *Will Penny* (1968) or Blake Edwards's *The Wild Rovers* (1971), which portray the nineteenth-century cowboy as less of a free spirit than a meager wage earner with little to show for years of hard labor but what he'll squander on a single Saturday night. The same cannot be said of Peckinpah's characters in *Pat Garrett and Billy the Kid.* Like Steve Judd and Gil Restrum in *Ride the High Country* or Pike Bishop in *The Wild Bunch,* Garrett and the Kid were once free agents who must either accommodate the modern order (taking root in the 1880s) or remain alienated from it. The old West, for all of its violence, vulgarity, and disorder, is clearly preferable to the modern legalized violence of the business-political establishment, represented in *Pat Garrett and Billy the Kid* by the Santa Fe Ring that governs New Mexico. Garrett has chosen to compromise with the power structure, to include enforcing its mandate to rid the territory of recalcitrants like Billy the Kid. While Garrett is understandably tired of the chaotic, rootless existence he once shared with the Kid and now opts for a quieter, settled life, his accommodation with the status quo brings with it guilt and betrayal.

The casting of Kris Kristofferson as Billy and Bob Dylan as a kind of groupie reporter provides an added touch of relevance to the theme of non-conformists bucking the status quo. At the same time, Peckinpah does not use these real-life idols of the young counterculture to symbolize values of peace and communal harmony. On the contrary, Billy and his gang are in many ways unattractively violent and anarchistic. Yet they embody the only remaining semblance of freedom and spontaneity in a world that is being put under wraps.

In *The Wild Bunch* Peckinpah presented his most damning indictment of the new order and elaborated with consummate skill and complexity both his love for the misfit and the prevailing violence that underlies the freedom-loving Westerner, and in a more horrific way, civilization. What distinguishes *The Wild Bunch* from a similarly plotted *Butch Cassidy and the Sundance Kid,* which was released the same year (1969), is the complexity and fallibility of Peckinpah's characters. In Peckinpah's world (at least after *Ride the High Country*) there are no innocents. Men are not simply victims of civilization but are also victims of their own personal failings. Pike Bishop, the leader of the Bunch, is an outlaw-killer, his behavior rendered sympathetic only because he subscribes to a code of honor and at least tries to compensate for his own violations of that code (his desertion of Deke Thornton and later Angel). In contrast are the forces of civilization–represented primarily by Harrigan, the unscrupulous railroad boss who for the good of the corporation sets into motion the terrifying slaughter at the beginning of the film. Harrigan proceeds to hire a bloodthirsty rabble to track down the Bunch and cruelly enlists Deke Thornton, a former friend and colleague of Pike Bishop's, to lead this bounty-hunting expedition. When Thornton berates Harrigan for his ruthlessness, Harrigan coldly reminds Thornton that he'll either do what he is told or go back to prison (a horrifying prospect that Peckinpah underscores with a brief flashback of the imprisoned Thornton being whipped).

Set on the eve of World War I, the film refers to technological developments that promise far greater devastation than the small-arms massacre at the beginning of the film. Members of the Bunch talk of how there are now airplanes armed with machine guns that can shoot from the sky. The destructiveness of the new era's technological progress is most vividly illustrated at the end of the film as Lyle Gorch and then Pike Bishop fire a machine gun in an almost orgiastic release of their violent instincts. It is significant that the machine gun is introduced to an otherwise primitive Mexican environment by German attachés–representatives of a presumably more advanced culture. Finally there is the automobile–again introduced by the Germans–which the federales eventually use to brutally drag the hapless Angel through the streets of Agua Verde. The only respite from this increasingly ugly, repressive modern world is Angel's tree-shaded, serene village where there is a warmth and childlike joy that contrasts with both the federale stronghold of Agua Verde and the Texas town (shown earlier in the film) with its starch-collared citizens and temperance reformers.

Mexico in the throes of turmoil and oppression was also the context (albeit the 1860s) for Peckinpah's earlier Western, *Major Dundee* (1965). Again, the older village culture of Mexico is threatened by national militarism–in this case that of France and the United States. In portraying the destructive impact of foreign intervention, Peckinpah's *Major Dundee* touched upon a particularly timely issue. A few months prior to the release of this film in April, 1965, President Lyndon Johnson had initiated the escalation of America's military role in Vietnam. Antiwar protests were erupting on the nation's campuses, while revisionist scholars were critically reassessing America's interventionist policies, whether in Latin America, the Middle East, or Southeast Asia.

In *Major Dundee* a grimly determined Union army officer, Maj. Amos Dundee (Charlton Heston), leads an unstable conglomerate of Confederate prisoners and civilian reprobates on a search-and-destroy mission against Apache renegades. He violates diplomatic protocol by crossing into Mexico and shortly thereafter invades a poor Mexican village to confiscate supplies for his troops. When in the process Dundee forcibly displaces a small garrison of French occupational forces, the villagers welcome him as a liberator. But Teresa (Senta Berger), who has carried on her deceased husband's work of servicing the medical needs of the villagers, suspects that Dundee's American army is just another aggressor, come to steal food from the already starving peasants: "We've been attacked by Apaches, by local bandits, by freebooters from Texas, then liberated by the French, and now the United States cavalry." Taken aback by her verbal assault, Dundee orders that the food commandeered by the French be distributed to the people. After a night of merriment and congenial intermingling between liberators and liberated, the cavalry unit leaves amidst fond waves and farewells–a scene that parallels the Wild Bunch's departure from Angel's village. Not long thereafter, Dundee receives word that the French army has conducted a reprisal against the village, killing or driving off the helpless people. Thus good intentions produce disastrous consequences, not for the American liberators but for the people they thought they were helping.

Later in the film Teresa and the Major become romantically involved, but she is bothered with his single-minded preoccupation with fighting a senseless and futile campaign against the Apaches and possibly the French. Why is fighting so important to you, she asks. In the traditional Western, this would have prompted from the hero an eloquent treatise about fighting for peace and defending the defenseless. But Dundee's reply is typical Peckinpah in affirming the violent nature of man: "Men can understand fighting. I guess maybe they need it sometimes. Truth is, it's easy."

More pertinent to the earlier clash between the ideal and reality of Dundee's liberation efforts is the farewell scene between Dundee and Teresa. She has found him with another woman when he is supposed to be recovering from an arrow wound in his leg. Afraid of losing Teresa, Dundee reminds her that "the war won't be forever." She replies, "It won't be for you, Major." Her point is that while he and his fellow Americans can depart to their homeland the people here will continue to suffer the tragedies of war, a war that the American presence has exacerbated rather than relieved. This same disturbing note would underlie President Nixon's policy of Vietnamization in the early 1970s as American soldiers returned home, leaving behind a people ravaged by war.

Unlike most Westerns since the early fifties, Peckinpah refrains from making the Indians in *Major Dundee* into noble, peace-loving victims of white prejudice. Sierra Charriba and his Apaches fight and destroy savagely. Yet Peckinpah suggests that the Apaches' behavior is not altogether different from that of Dundee and his troops and is less ruthless than that of the French. Dundee turns out to be wrong in his suspicion that the unit's Apache guide, Riago, is untrustworthy and may be collaborating with the renegade Charriba. Are we supposed to believe that an Apache would turn against his own people, Dundee asks his one-armed scout, Sam Potts (James Coburn). Potts replies, "Why not? Everyone else seems to be doing it," referring to America's civil war and the dissension within Dundee's own ranks. Also undercutting the righteousness of Dundee's mission as well as America's campaign against the Indian in general is a scene in which Dundee asks an elderly Indian why he has participated in the Apaches' bloody raids. The old Indian replies through an interpreter: "Why not? It's their land, all of it." Beyond this brief statement on the Indian's perspective, Peckinpah refuses to preach—a refreshing alternative to the three hours of John Ford's belabored translation of Mari Sandoz's *Cheyenne Autumn,* a film released the previous year.

As suggested earlier, there was nothing unique about Peckinpah's identification of civilization with war and oppression or with the entrenchment of a commercial, dehumanizing social order. This critical perspective of America's frontier epoch became in itself conventional in the 1960s and early 1970s, largely because this perspective was so timely and relevant. Directors Robert Altman and Arthur Penn, better known for their critical commentaries on modern America, utilized the Western genre (Altman in *McCabe and Mrs. Miller* [1971] and *Buffalo Bill and the Indians* [1976], Penn in *Little Big Man* [1970] and *Missouri Breaks* [1976]) to make similarly critical statements about America's frontier heritage. Clint Eastwood achieved stardom in both Italian and American Westerns that juxtaposed his cynical, violent individualism with a decayed, corrupt social environment. Eastwood has referred to Ernest Tidyman's screenplay for *High Plains Drifter* (1973) as having been inspired by the Kitty Genovese incident, when New York apartment dwellers witnessed a woman's murder without lifting a finger to save her.[6] Even John Wayne stands conspicuously aloof from and often in contempt of society in his sixties Westerns. Whether a cattle baron (*McLintock* [1963], *Chisum* [1970]), marshal (*True Grit* [1969]), or mercenary (*El Dorado* [1967], *The Train Robbers* [1973]), Wayne's personal integrity contrasts with the hypocrisy and duplicity of public officials and citizenry. Missing is the prospect of reconciliation between individual fulfillment and social progress that had characterized earlier Westerns, including most of Wayne's.

Pat Garrett and Billy the Kid was Sam Peckinpah's last Western. His subsequent films contain many of the same themes of innate human violence, the importance of personal honor, and the malevolence and constraints of modern society. With their rugged desert landscapes, *Bring Me the Head of Alfredo Garcia* (1974) and *Convoy* (1978) have very much the look of Westerns. Similarly, though Westerns in general have declined in number since the mid-1970s, many of the familiar plots and character types have appeared in other genres. Film critic Pauline Kael noted the resemblance of Clint Eastwood's Harry Callahan in *Dirty Harry* (1971) and especially Joe Don Baker's Buford Pusser in *Walking Tall* (1974) to the frontier hero. "The Western is dead," she pronounced in 1974. "But the Western hero hasn't disappeared: he's moved from the mythical purity of the wide-open spaces into the corrupt modern cities and towns."[7] Other critics have found Western themes in the immensely popular *Star Wars* trilogy and especially in the science-fiction thriller *Outland* (1981), in which space marshal Sean Connery, like Western marshal Gary Cooper in *High Noon,* refuses to be pressured into compromising with lawbreakers. Aside from adaptations of Western elements into other entertainment formulas, the genre itself has ceased to be a commercially attractive prospect for film producers. Rising production costs, combined with the box-office disaster of *Heaven's Gate* in 1980 and the disappointing returns of lesser efforts such as *Comes a Horseman* (1978), *The Long Riders* (1980), and *Barbarosa* (1982), have discouraged the financing of additional Westerns. Neither *Pale Rider* nor *Silverado,* both released in the summer of 1985, fared well enough at the box office to spark a revival of Westerns.

Some argue that the Western no longer retains credibility with today's young audiences who, instead of looking to the past, seek their action entertainment in the form of contemporary crime melodramas or futurist space fantasies. It is misleading, however, to infer from this that the Western was ever simply a retelling of stories about America's frontier past. What made the Western viable as popular entertainment was its current meaningfulness, its relevance to the contemporary scene. This was true in the Depression-era sagas of the James brothers driven to outlawry to avenge the exploitation of poor rural folks; in the 1950s, when the Indian conflict became a metaphor of America's cold war and racial problems; and in the 1960s when disillusioned nonconformists felt alienated from an oppressive civilization. It was in the latter context that Sam Peckinpah attained considerable recognition as the foremost cinematic interpreter of the American West.

In breaking with the nationalistic, progressive themes of earlier Westerns, Peckinpah was likewise omitting an important part of Frederick Jackson Turner's theory–that the existence of a frontier accounted for the evolution of free, democratic institutions in America. Yet Peckinpah did retain something of Turner's belief that the frontier had elicited "that restless, nervous energy, that dominant individualism, working for good and for evil, and withal that buoyancy and exuberance which comes with freedom."[8] Peckinpah also shared one of Turner's misgivings about modern America: "the concentration of economic and political power in the hands of a comparatively few men," who are, in Peckinpah's terms, the Harrigans and Santa Fe politicians (p. 25). Turner of course adhered to the hope that the spirit and idealism associated with settling a wilderness would enable Americans to confront twentieth-century challenges. Peckinpah, like many of his contemporary artists, offered the more despairing vision that not only the frontier but the rugged individualism it came to symbolize were incompatible with and overwhelmed by the forces of modernization. What remains in the twentieth century is not the legacy of a brave new world, but an idyllic myth of frontier heroism and community, much like the frozen, receding image with which Peckinpah concluded *The Wild Bunch:* having perished in the bloody, desert stronghold of Agua Verde, Peckinpah's ill-fated Bunch reappear on screen in a moment frozen in time–when they rode proudly amidst the peace and tranquillity that in reality had finally eluded them.

NOTES

1. John Cawelti, *The Six-Gun Mystique* (Bowling Green, Ohio: Bowling Green Univ. Press, 1971), p. 73.

2. Joseph Kane, interview with author, June, 1973, Malibu, Calif.

3. Peckinpah's first theatrical Western, *The Deadly Companions* (1961), was not available for viewing. For an analysis of this film, see Paul Seydor, *Peckinpah: The Western Films* (Urbana: Univ. of Illinois Press, 1980), pp. 16–24.

4. See Michael Harrington, *The Other America: Poverty in the United States* (Baltimore: Penguin Books, 1981).

5. Seydor, *Peckinpah,* pp. 183, 215–16.

6. Clint Eastwood, interview with Arthur C. Knight, March 15, 1973, Special Collections, Doheny Library, University of Southern California, Los Angeles.

7. Pauline Kael, "The Current Cinema: The Street Western," *New Yorker,* February 25, 1974, p. 100.

8. Roy Allen Billington, ed., *The Frontier Thesis: Valid Interpretation of American History?* (New York: Holt, Rinehart and Winston, 1966), p. 19. Subsequent reference in the text is to this edition.

The Lost Frontier: American Myth in the Literature of the Vietnam War

JOHN CLARK PRATT

We'll bring peace to this land if we have to kill them all.
GENERAL CUSTER
(GI latrine graffito, Saigon)

Now that the substantial body of Vietnam War literature (more than three hundred novels, an equal number of short stories, dozens of plays, hundreds of poems) is receiving serious scrutiny, more and more critics are placing much of this corpus squarely in the American mythic mainstream. Most notable are the dissertation by Margaret Stewart, "Death and Growth: Vietnam War Novels, Cultural Attitudes, and Literary Traditions" (1981), and two books, Philip Beidler's *American Literature and the Experience of Vietnam* (1982) and John Hellmann's *American Myth and the Legacy of Vietnam* (1986). Despite understandable differences, each critic would agree, I suspect, that throughout the war what might be called the "Little Big Horn" mindset obtained. As Richard Slotkin puts it, "The Frontier in whose real geography [General] Custer moved and acted was already in his own time a space defined less by maps and surveys than by myths and illusions, projective fantasies, wild anticipations, extravagant expectations."[1] Slotkin could, of course, have been describing the American attitudes toward the "New Frontier's" legacy–the war in Vietnam.

For Stewart, the warrior-hunter stories and captivity narratives provide a background for what she sees as a major theme in Vietnam War fiction, "the contest between civilization and savagery,"[2] and she believes that "ultimately, this literature is a powerful attack not only on the war in Vietnam but also on the American myths of innocence and mission which underlay it" (p. i).

To Vietnam-veteran Beidler, despite the use of models from Cooper's

Natty Bumppo, Melville's Starry Vere, and Twain's Hank Morgan, most writers show that "Vietnam became its own bizarre, hermetic mythology." "The silent suffocating truth," Beidler continues, "is that [Vietnam] was surely the biggest game there was: cowboys versus gooks,"[3] and the attitudes of Americans toward this war had their "prophecy there in the gliding, shadowed forms of an unseen enemy, the wily inscrutable foe, the specters of the forest, the multitudinous host born of a whole Western world's own best demonological imaginings" (p. 22).

Admitting the Vietnam War novelist's dependence on traditional American myth, John Hellmann goes further, noting that some of the novels' protagonists "uneasily sense that they themselves are the enemy of the population that they have ostensibly come to save, successors not to their own mythic forebears but rather to the Europeans against whom their forebears defined themselves."[4] The result, Hellman shows in his discussion of Robert Roth's *Sand in the Wind,* is "the destruction, not of [America], but of the myth that gave it life and in which [Americans] once believed" (p. 127). Using the *Star Wars* trilogy as the ultimate statement on Vietnam, Hellman believes optimistically that Luke Skywalker comes to an understanding (denied to most protagonists of Vietnam War fiction) that "the American Adam has learned that his parentage ties him to a fallen past, that he is not an exception to history and the fallen world of time, but is rather a limited, fallible person whose destiny is in profound doubt" (p. 217).

Each of these critics is of course correct in noticing the use and subversion of traditional American myth in the literature about the Vietnam War, but there are four limitations to these otherwise excellent assessments. First, none of them examines the entire canon (Beidler is the most comprehensive). Second, none distinguishes between those few authors who consciously examine American myth and those who, in their attempts to "tell it like it was," in fact merely record American attitudes possessed by characters who have unconsciously assimilated our mythic heritage. Writers such as Robert Roth, Stephen Wright, Larry Heinemann, Tim O'Brien, Asa Baber, David Winn, and James Crumley, for instance, not only served in the armed forces during the war but also went on to graduate school and studied literature. Many others, however, such as David Halberstam, the brothers Kalb, Jean Larteguy, and Robin Moore are basically journalists with a story to tell. Third, no one has yet examined the *sources* of the fictional characters' beliefs in American myths. Although a few of these characters are seen to read, most have been profoundly influenced only by the modern media, and it is ironic to note that just as the media formed modern America's mythic view of itself, so did the media serve during the war to provide precisely the "real geography" that Slotkin's Custer-watchers lacked. Finally, although most of the critics have shown *how* the frontier myth functioned for good and ill, no one has considered the one novel, *Into a Black Sun,* written not by an American but by a Japanese survivor of Hiroshima, that purports to show *why* the American myth became lost in Vietnam.

Basically, the literature of the Vietnam War is filled with American characters who enter Vietnam as traditional frontier huntsmen, then become men trying merely to survive in a wilderness they do not understand. There are constant references to Cowboys and Indians, often with some startling reversals of roles. (In Saigon, for instance, the Vietnamese motorcycle thieves were known as "Cowboys.") The most predominant cowboy mentioned in the literature is of course John Wayne, who is seen in the early fiction as a role model, then later as a figure of derision, his fall from grace mirroring the average American's change from optimism through doubt to despair about an eventual American victory.

Philip Beidler and John Hellmann both identify Norman Mailer's *Why Are We in Vietnam?* (1967) as being one of the earliest works to show how American frontier myths created our attitudes toward Vietnam. Beidler notes how a group of American hunters, aided by technology and a "storehouse of exquisite weaponry," attempts to conquer the Alaskan wilderness in "a collective national frenzy of overkill" (pp. 44–45). The paradigm of this ravaging of nature is to be the ravaging of Southeast Asia, but only at the end of the novel is Vietnam ever mentioned, as two of the characters, Tex and D.J., are about to be drafted and expect to "see the wizard in Vietnam. . . . Vietnam, hot damn."[5] We see the quintessential Texan and the Disc Jockey, the machismo and the media freak, about to go off happily to Oz to fulfill America's destiny.

Similar attitudes appear in many works. Lawrence Ferlinghetti's poem "Where Is Vietnam?" (1966) shows Colonel Cornpone (Lyndon Johnson) expounding: "I can see . . . Western Civilization still marching Westward and the New Frontier now truly knows no boundaries."[6] Likewise in Barbara Garson's play *MacBird* (1966), President Johnson is portrayed as the American who will inflict peace on the world no matter what the cost. After asking "Lord" McNamara where Vietnam is, MacBird exclaims:

> Since when do we permit an open challenge
> To all the world's security and peace?
> Rip out those Reds! Destroy them, root and branch!
> Deploy what force you think we need!
> Eradicate this noxious, spreading weed![7]

Although Mailer, Ferlinghetti, and Garson depict Americans at odds with the values they so loudly trumpet, other writers show Americans who are less offensive but just as dangerous in their dispensation of morality and justice. Jean Larteguy, for instance, presents in *Yellow Fever* (1965) an American colonel (based on the real Edward Lansdale) whose "advice" to a South Vietnamese president causes him to be "represented as a new Lawrence of Arabia."[8] Graham Greene, in his novel *The Quiet American* (1955) has a young CIA agent, Alden Pyle, attempt to win the East for democracy by trying to install a "Third Force" in Vietnam. All he causes is death, his own and others'. The narrator, a jaded English journalist, believes that Pyle has "the caution of a hero in a boy's adventure story" who has been "quite unaware of the absurdity and improbability of his adventure."[9] "They killed him because he was too innocent to live. He was young and ignorant and silly and he got involved. He had no more of a notion than any of you [Americans] what the whole affair's about, and you . . . said, 'Go ahead. Win the East for Democracy'" (p. 32).

The source of this American "innocence" is, of course, the traditional attitude that Americans can accomplish anything–and the pop culture hero of Western pulp novel and film was nowhere better embodied than in the characters played by John Wayne (who was appropriately selected to play the lead in the first major movie made about Vietnam, *The Green Berets*). In Larry Heinemann's *Close Quarters* (1977), Pfc. Philip Dosier has been raised "on 'the thou-shalt-nots' and willow switches and John Wayne (even before he became a verb)."[10] Introduced to drugs in Vietnam (as are so many other characters in the novels) and traumatized by the war, Dosier is unable to resume a normal life after he returns home. In a similar vein, Stephen Wright's *Meditations in Green* (1983) shows South Vietnamese Lieutenant Phan telling American Captain Raleigh, "You number one John Wayne Western man,"[11] indicating that the Wayne concept has been embraced even by America's Asian allies. And in James Crumley's *One to Count Cadence* (1969), Sgt. Slag Krummel, a man who seems identical to Mailer's Tex, awakens from a dream to find that his sheets are wet. "I wonder if John Wayne ever peed his bed?" he remarks sardonically.[12]

Interestingly, Crumley's novel contains scenes of the earliest American full-scale combat in Vietnam (1961–62), but *One to Count Cadence* also presents the most faithfully depicted frontier hero of any of the Vietnam novels. Slag Krummel, believing that he has been bred to be a warrior, fighter, and brawler, claims when drunk to be "the last survivor of an Apache attack on Fort Dodge, Iowa" (p. 53). Telling people that his grandmother was a Comanche (p. 93), he attributes his belief that "killing the enemy was a good and beautiful thing" to "the millions of comic books and B-movies" that he has seen (p. 146). A friend characterizes Krummel: "If you can't fight it or fuck it or drink it, it don't make sense" (p. 148). Krummel's credo? Obsessed by his thoughts of Indians fighting and dying, he believes war to be "perhaps the last noble thing" (p. 149). That Slag Krummel survives not only Vietnam but also a subsequent CIA assignment to Laos shows Crumley's belief that the American frontier spirit was still operational during the Vietnam War's early years.

Indeed it was, but as the war dragged on, more and more Americans began to question whether or not even the John Waynes or Slag Krummels of this world could effect a permanent change in Southeast Asia. Shortly after the 1963 coup that toppled South Vietnamese President Diem, Americans generally believed that the war could be won, as expressed by an Army major in Thomas Fleming's *Officers' Wives* (1981), by bringing "in our own guys."[13] What "our guys" found in Vietnam caused them more and more to feel like Custer's soldiers in Montana. As Philip Beidler notes, actual operations maps showed Vietnamese villages codenamed "Dodge City" that "marked the way to 'Indian Country'" (p. 8). Similarly, the opening line of Robin Moore's *Green Berets* (1965) describes a U. S./South Vietnamese command post that "looks exactly like a fort out of the old West."[14] Later, Moore's Americans show an "epic western" movie to their allies: "The strikers [South Vietnamese] loved the action and identified themselves with it. When the Indians appeared the strikers screamed 'VC,' and when the soldiers or cowboys came to the rescue, the Nam Loung irregulars vied with each other in shouting out the number of their own strike-force companies" (p. 127).

Again and again, novels about the Vietnam War use the cowboy-Indian motif, usually echoing words and phrases that were actually part of the Vietnam vernacular. In Michael Herr's nonfiction *Dispatches* (1977), a captain says to Herr just before a patrol, "Come on . . . we'll take you out to play Cowboys and Indians."[15]

This exuberance, also found in Moore's *Green Berets,* seemed not to last long, however. One of the actual–and most deadly–battle zones was called "The Arizona" and is featured in many novels, as well as in David Rabe's play, *The Basic Training of Pavlo Hummel* (1971). Tobey Herzog notes that in Winston Groom's novel *Better Times Than These* (1978), Col. James Patch "views Vietnam as just another Indian uprising," but Herzog misses the irony in the codename of the unsuccessful mission that Patch leads into an area much like the Arizona: "Operation Western Movie."[16] Even Philip Beidler succumbs to the habit of associating things Vietnamese with the American West. In discussing David Halberstam's *One Very Hot Day,* Beidler describes Captain Beaupre's base camp as "Alamo West", (p. 33) a term that Halberstam does not use.

It is James Crumley, however, who best shows why this frontier association had so much appeal. Sitting outside in the warm afternoon sun, Sgt. Slag Krummel watches some Vietnamese digging bunkers while others cook dinner:

> Inside the outer perimeter, children played, wives gossiped, and their soldier husbands and fathers sat in shaded places and cleaned their old Springfields. . . .

In spite of the activity, the compound, the scene, seemed essentially peaceful; perhaps because work is a peaceful occupation, whatever you're building. I was reminded of the American West, of building a fort against the hostile land, of peaceful treaty Indians camped about the stockade walls; out-riders, woodcutters, and scouts moving out and back across the parched grass hills. And over all this, controlling each contraction of muscle in this new land, the confident, foolish idea that . . . we shall be masters, . . . never fearing . . . that the aborigines who came before us can stand against us, feathers and paint and leather shields no hope against a Sharps or a Henry. (P. 237)

Unfortunately for the Americans, however, the Vietnamese "aborigines" demonstrated that they could stand up well against the modern cowboys. In David Halberstam's *One Very Hot Day* (1967), American Captain Beaupre (who never shows knowledge of his French heritage) comments on the aftermath of a successful Viet Cong attack: "Most likely a massacre," he says, to which his Vietnamese counterpart, Captain Dang replies, "Yes . . . that is the word, massacre. From your Indian films."[17] We may remember Dien Bien Phu, but Beaupre does not. And as the Viet Cong/North Vietnamese resistance showed no signs of letting up, the expressions of optimism that characterized most Americans' initial attitudes toward the war began to produce serious questions. Set in 1970, Donald McQuinn's *Targets* (1980) shows a newly arrived American officer being scolded by a Vietnamese woman: "What did you think? Did you expect to spend your time in an American war film, no real pain, only healthy excitement? Everyone lives happily ever after?"[18] In a similar vein, an experienced American pilot in Charles Larson's *The Chinese Game* (1969) comments to another new arrival: "You know what's wrong with this fouled up hemorrhoid of a war? . . . There's no ruttin' villains."[19] The pilot adds, "Captain, this isn't a nineteen forty-three movie. Don Ameche isn't going to win the girl" (p. 187).

Their expectations created by an often unconscious acceptance of frontier values presented by "comic books and Grade-B movies" where pioneers settle and prosper and the cowboys subdue the Indians, the fictional Americans who arrive in Vietnam after the war has gone on for a while have experiences that contradict their basic beliefs. In Donald McQuinn's *Targets,* for instance, the Army colonel who has become disillusioned by the war expresses a widely held opinion. Having noticed how the attitudes and tactics of the Americans are becoming more like those of their enemy, Colonel Winter observes, "We're getting to be more and more like the savages we're up against" (p. 324). Similarly, in James Webb's *Fields of Fire* (1978), an appropriately named lieutenant, Robert E. Lee Hodges, comments on the death of one of his buddies: "The super-hero assaulted a North Vietnamese bunker and caught a grenade in the stomach (it had never happened to John Wayne)."[20]

The cause of this change in attitude was not only the length of the war but also the increasingly impersonal war-as-routine impression that the U.S. government gave to the draftees as well as to the "lifers." To have been on the frontier was traditionally to have been an individual, but as the protagonist in Charles Durden's *No Bugles No Drums* (1976) puts it:

> We were a pain in the ass, and just so many numbers on some dude's board in Saigon, the Pentagon, and the international desks of the networks. Once a week the voice, for thirty seconds, became somber and the announcements seeped into the ether: Forty-five Americans were reported killed in Vietnam this week. The Dow Jones industrial average was off today, down three points to 983. No one loved us for bein' their clay'n'spirit. They were grateful to those of us who went away quietly, without makin' too big a fuss 'r screamin' Hell no, we won't go."[21]

To those Americans who experienced the later years of the war, if John Wayne was not dead, his ruggedly individual spirit was at least noticeably absent from the scene.

To many of the GIs who had entered the war with the conventional American frontier ideals of individualism, courage, and ingenuity, the increasingly mechanized and impersonal nature of the American presence seemed to cause an ironic reversal of motives. As Margaret Stewart puts it, novels such as John Briley's *Traitors* (1969) become "part of a more recent counter-tradition that portrays the American military itself as a threat to civilization" (p. 10). As a result, some later novels show that the enemy, the North Vietnamese or the Viet Cong, possesses precisely the attributes normally given to the traditional American frontier hero. In Steven Smith's *American Boys* (1975), for instance, a single North Vietnamese soldier has survived numerous ground and air attacks and always emerges from the shattered trees to fire his rifle at helicopters, gunships, and fighter-bombers. Says Smith,

> At chow the talk was only of the man. He had earned everyone's respect, was almost a hero, but one who had to be killed. He seemed to excite the imagination like some Jesse James or Billy the Kid whose daring caused envy and admiration in those whose great satisfaction would be to kill him. For Chambers the man assumed heroic proportions. He hoped he was indestructible.[22]

Even at home, as John Hellmann so brilliantly points out, the frontier myth became inverted as the "hippies" protested the war, and with their drugs, buckskins, and beads took on "the guise of the Indian" (p. 76).

Whether the basic reason was the length of the war, the depersonalization of the American individual, or the failure to win with traditional American dispatch, most of the novels show the innocent, well-meaning American soldier not only losing his belief that he can prevail but more significantly embracing a more pragmatic goal, that of mere survival. As Tim O'Brien's *Going After Cacciato* (1978) shows, Pfc. Paul Berlin wishes only "to live long enough to establish goals worth living longer for."[23] Drunk after a fierce battle, the men of William Pelfrey's *The Big V* (1972) sum up an attitude held by many draftees and even career military who had experienced the continuing war: "Fuck you . . . Kennedy! Fuck you, Kennedy! Fuck you, New Frontier."[24]

In reaction to not winning (to Americans, the equivalent of defeat), some characters in the fiction come up with a typically American can-do solution, one which I think derives directly from the concept of frontier "success," here seen satirized as the "ultimate solution." Says the newly appointed head of the Committee on Revolutionary Development (CORDS), American Ambassador Risher, in Derek Maitland's *The Only War We've Got* (1970), "In broad terms, we're going to uproot all the people–all sixteen million of them–and resettle them in a heavily-guarded reservation [the significance of this word should not be missed] outside Saigon. Then we're gonna defoliate the entire rest of the country and turn it into a free-fire zone, and anyone caught moving out there–V.C. or not–is going to get his ass shot off." Risher's plan for victory? "The only way we're gonna win this war . . . is to tow the goddam country out into the middle of the Pacific and bomb the shit out of it until it sinks."[25]

Perhaps the most bitter indictment of the American frontier myth can be seen in the epigraph to wounded veteran Ron Kovic's *Born on the Fourth of July* (1976):

> I am your yankee doodle dandy
> your john wayne come home
> your fourth of july firecracker
> exploding in your grave.[26]

Another overtly antiwar work, Emilio de Grazia's *Enemy Country* (1984), attacks an even more basic American myth. The chapter entitled "The Light at the End of the Tunnel" ends the book with an absolutely conventional (and, one hopes, a parody of) traditional allegory. The main character, Sam (who tears apart the picture of his niece and trades his cowboy hat for a "gook" conical one) apparently commits suicide while striding like John Wayne toward the enemy. The narrator alone senses what has happened; the other GIs never understand. Says one, "the 'rat of God killed that po' boy." Comments another, "Communism killed Sam."[27] No one, however, notices Sam for the symbol he is, and *Enemy Country* ends with the American soldiers bickering over why "Uncle" Sam has met his demise in Vietnam.

No intelligent reading of the literature published to date about the Vietnam War can support any other basic thesis than this one: that the United

States went into the war with highly principled ignorance (some may read innocence); then, when faced with the disillusioning fact that the traditional concept of American heroism and manifest destiny did not have the impact in Asia that it did in, let us say, mid-nineteenth-century Mexico, turn-of-the-century Cuba, the American West, or more recently, Grenada, Americans in Vietnam both in actuality and in fiction looked for a way to save face, ironically a traditional Asiatic gesture. In the "real geography" of the war, the concept was Vietnamization, the failure of which caused the death of the American Dream for Vietnam and the humiliating 1975 evacuation of Saigon.

Although many Vietnam War writers saw, and millions of Americans sensed, that the American frontier hero was not prevailing in Vietnam, only one novelist, himself not an American, has convincingly shown *why* things went wrong. Takeshi Kaiko's novel *Into a Black Sun* (1968; trans. 1980) examines our national myths at work in Vietnam with an objectivity perhaps denied to those Americans whose myths these are. A blend of fact and fiction (Kaiko was a Japanese correspondent in Vietnam during 1964–65, the setting of his novel), *Into a Black Sun* presents an Asian narrator's experiences quite similar to those of Robin Moore's *The Green Berets* (1965) and David Halberstam's *One Very Hot Day* (1967). The main American character is U.S. Army advisor Captain Wain (one wonders if his name intentionally echoes America's media hero), about whom the smaller Asian narrator observes, "I thought of the thousands and thousands of hamburgers, tens of thousands of cokes, that had been consumed to form his body."[28] Kaiko offers acute insights into the ruthlessness of the Communists and the naive militarism of the Americans; then, during the climactic battle that becomes surreal in its realism, the American advisors are killed, the South Vietnamese break and run, and the Japanese narrator flees deeper into the ominous rainforest.

Kaiko's assessment of the American captain's motives is compelling:

> There was some raw, insatiate energy . . . that drove him on. . . . It made me think of men in covered wagons, those ancestors of his who rode into the great plains and drove the Indians out. Moving, plowing, praying after killing, repenting and moving on, arriving at a goal and, once established, drinking hard and sometimes ending their own lives in violent ways. Men of excess, both heaven- and hell-bent. Wasn't it their strange, restless blood that flowed in him? (Pp. 198–199)

To this Asian who knows more about America than most Americans do, Americans are "all descendants of Captain Ahab, a strange, obsessive species, driven to fill their tormented souls with purpose and action. If Ahab had never found a whale, he would have borne one of his own and continued his pursuit, and if he'd lacked an ocean, he'd have invented one" (p. 165). Forced to fight in a culture far older than their own, one that possesses far more complex myths, Kaiko's American characters unfortunately do not dispute what the American Dr. Percy says:

> The peasants around here are shrewd, but they're so ignorant, no one's taken the trouble to educate them. They've had no experience of newspapers, magazines, the radio, television, anything. They've never seen neon lights; they don't know about running water. They're a forsaken people in a godforsaken country. (P. 29)

Significantly, Dr. Percy's concept of education considers only present, modern concerns, and it is here that Kaiko shows the reasons for the Americans' failure. Says one Vietnamese, "I must admit [Americans] try to learn, and they work hard at it. But they can sweat away at it for as long as they like, they're still too young. They're too young to understand people in old countries like Vietnam and Japan" (pp. 86–87).

Apparently, though, Kaiko believes that Americans are too "young" even to understand themselves—and the reason seems to be an act of omission, not of ignorance or innocence. In short, Americans know themselves no more than they know their allies or their enemies, and they do not seem to understand the basic sources of their motivation. "They don't mind to drop napalm, but can't stand seeing torturing," says Vietnamese Colonel Kiem. "They're hypocrites, sentimental hypocrites. . . . Americans are softhearted. But they're still devoted to war. . . . Strange people" (p. 47).

Kaiko, however, does understand because he has been reading Twain's *Connecticut Yankee in King Arthur's Court* during battle lulls. He chuckles as "The Boss" (like Ed Lansdale in the mid-1950s) becomes King Arthur's "Perpetual Minister and Executive" and begins to modernize the state, but Kaiko's humor pales as he reads about the deaths, the conflicts and the destruction that ensue despite "The Boss's" introduction of advanced technology. He becomes "deeply moved" at the final scene when the Yankee fortifies himself and a few men with minefields and barbed wire (the scene reminds me, belatedly, of the last Strategic Hamlet I saw), yet despite all the modern gadgetry, all die except Merlin the magician, the "Wizard" that Mailer's D.J. would never have been able to find.

Kaiko admits to having read widely in political science journals from all sides about Americans and American policy, "yet none had had the devastating reach of Twain's fantasy" (p. 46). Unlike most Americans who experienced the Vietnam War, Kaiko finds all his answers in Twain's

> amazing book. The Americans were spending astronomical amounts of money [in Vietnam], perhaps as much as six million dollars daily; and yet we'd known the outcome all along, from a novel written seventy-five years ago. The war—its

beginning and its end, its details and essentials, its accidents and its inevitable course—was all there, encompassed in this tale that combined Don Quixote and Gulliver. (P. 46)

Watching the snoring American Captain Wain sleeping in the cot next to his, Kaiko feels an "indescribable sadness," and with his knowledge, "lonely" (p. 46), having met Americans of all races and political persuasions who do not understand how myths reflect and cause national character and purpose. Why don't they understand? Because they have not read or examined them, then made the necessary contemporary connections.

Americans do know the "good" myths, yes, but so many know only the "Grade-B" white-hat variety. In the "real geography" of the past, Jesse James and Billy the Kid were no more admirable than are people like Theodore Bundy or any other serial murderer, yet these figures remain a part of our unexamined, hence misunderstood myths. (I am not surprised, for instance, that the vogue of the cinema Western began to decline only when Hollywood started trying to achieve verisimilitude by having roughly dressed good guys shoot the bad guys in the back.) Even if American policy-makers *had* read academic myth-makers like Crevecoeur, I suspect that most would have misapplied the Frenchman's notion, as quoted by Hellmann, that "Americans are the western pilgrims, who are carrying along with them that great mass of arts, sciences, vigour, and industry which began long since in the east; they will *finish* [italics mine] the great circle" (p. 5). As Hellmann so rightly notes, Crevecoeur's "great circle" started in the Far East, and for Americans to have seen southeast Asia as just another Montana of the 1860s, peopled with ignorant savages that could be subdued by modern technology and the American way, makes us ironically Adamic in quite an unusual way. Considered innocent by many, Adam was actually an extremely knowledgeable man; he knew everything *except* good and evil, a biblical fact that many who do not read closely have misunderstood. His fall was *not* caused by his innocence, but by an ignorance of the most massive kind.

Most of the Vietnam War writings show that Americans have also misunderstood their own myths and have applied them misguidedly, and if Richard Slotkin is right, that "myth is history successfully disguised as archetype" (p. 20), then I suggest that modern Americans had better follow Kaiko's advice and read Twain, then the literature of the Vietnam War, and ponder the roots of our so-called American mythos, especially in order to penetrate the disguise, to see the difference between history and archetype, and to determine whether it is our destiny, or just ignorant Ramboesque obstinacy, that is truly manifest at all.

NOTES

1. Richard Slotkin, *The Fatal Environment: The Myth of the Frontier in the Age of Industrialization* (New York: Atheneum, 1985), p. 11. Subsequent references in the text are to this edition.

2. Margaret Stewart, "Death and Growth: Vietnam War Novels, Cultural Attitudes, and Literary Traditions," Ph.D. dissertation, University of Wisconsin–Madison, 1981), p. 6. Subsequent references in the text are to this edition.

3. Philip Beidler, *American Literature and the Experience of Vietnam* (Athens: Univ. of Georgia Press, 1982), p. 15. Subsequent references in the text are to this edition.

4. John Hellmann, *American Myth and the Legacy of Vietnam* (New York: Columbia Univ. Press, 1986), p. 110. Subsequent references in the text are to this edition.

5. Norman Mailer, *Why Are We in Vietnam?* (New York: G. P. Putnam's Sons, 1967), p. 208.

6. Robert Bly and David Ray, eds., *A Poetry Reading against the Vietnam War* (Madison, Minn.: The Sixties Press, 1966), p. 16.

7. Barbara Garson, *MacBird* (New York: Grove Press, 1967), p. 55.

8. Jean Larteguy, *Yellow Fever* (New York: E. P. Dutton, 1965), p. 199.

9. Graham Greene, *The Quiet American* (London: Penguin Books, 1962), p. 145. Subsequent references in the text are to this edition.

10. Larry Heinemann, *Close Quarters* (New York: Farrar, Straus and Giroux, 1977), p. 53.

11. Stephen Wright, *Meditations in Green* (New York: Charles Scribner's Sons, 1983), p. 104.

12. James Crumley, *One Count to Cadence* (New York: Random House, 1969), p. 19. Subsequent references in the text are to this edition.

13. Thomas Fleming, *Officers' Wives* (Garden City, N.Y.: Doubleday, 1981), p. 471.

14. Robin Moore, *The Green Berets* (New York: Crown Publishers, 1965), p. 25. Subsequent references in the text are to this edition.

15. Michael Herr, *Dispatches* (New York: Alfred A. Knopf, 1977), p. 60.

16. Tobey C. Herzog, "Writing about Vietnam: A Heavy Heart-of-Darkness Trip," *College English,* 41, no. 6 (February, 1980): 691; Winston Groom, *Better Times Than These* (New York: Summit Books, 1978), p. 162.

17. David Halberstam, *One Very Hot Day* (Boston: Houghton Mifflin, 1967), p. 185.

18. Donald McQuinn, *Targets* (New York: Macmillan, 1980), p. 327.

19. Charles Larson, *The Chinese Game* (Philadelphia: J. B. Lippincott, 1969), p. 186. Subsequent references in the text are to this edition.

20. James Webb, *Fields of Fire* (Englewood Cliffs, N.J.: Prentice-Hall, 1978), p. 283.

21. Charles Durden, *No Bugles No Drums* (New York: Viking, 1976), pp. 142–43.

22. Steven Smith, *American Boys* (New York: G. P. Putnam's Sons, 1975), p. 357.

23. Tim O'Brien, *Going After Cacciato* (New York: Delacorte Press, 1978), p. 27.

24. William Pelfrey, *The Big V* (New York: Liveright, 1972), p. 10.

25. Derek Maitland, *The Only War We've Got* (New York: William Morrow, 1970), pp. 134–35.

26. Ron Kovic, *Born on the Fourth of July* (New York: McGraw-Hill, 1976), frontispiece.

27. Emilio de Grazia, *Enemy Country* (St. Paul, Minn.: New Rivers Press, 1984), p. 145.

28. Takeshi Kaiko, *Into a Black Sun,* trans. Cecelia Segawa Seigle (New York: Kodansha International, 1980), p. 9. Subsequent references in the text are to this edition.

Frontiers in Space

GARY K. WOLFE

My title is borrowed from a 1955 paperback science-fiction anthology, edited by Everett F. Bleiler and T. E. Dikty, which bears on its back cover the claim that science fiction has "opened new frontiers to the pioneer hero, given him new worlds to conquer and marvellous means to conquer them." Such claims were endemic among science-fiction publications of the period. A few years later, another paperback advertised, "Centuries have passed since man first set out across the uncharted seas of his own world. But the same urgent spirit that drove men on journeys from which they knew they might never return is still tugging and pushing. And now the restless questing of mankind has sent him out across the unknown seas of space."[1] Such comments might fairly be said to represent the marketing of science fiction rather than the fiction itself, but they do serve to illustrate a widely held popular belief concerning the relationship of science fiction with the concept of the frontier, a belief which has often been expressed by science-fiction writers and fans themselves.

The basic tenets of this belief are as follows. For centuries, such genres of fantastic literature as the imaginary voyage and the utopia had thrived upon people's fascination with the vast uncharted areas of the globe. In America, this fascination became focused upon the western frontier–not quite uncharted or even unsettled, but still an arena for the kind of heroic individualism that increasingly seemed to be disappearing in the urbanized and industrialized East. With the closing of that frontier, the popular audience sought promises of yet new areas to explore, and science fiction gained popularity as a kind of literature which not only offered new frontiers but did so without sacrificing the technological idealism that had equally come to characterize industrial America. Science fiction offered its audience both the machine and the wilderness–in fact made them interdependent–and thus opened for exploration the moon, other planets, and finally other stars. Popular fiction had, in fact, found itself an infinite frontier, or "the final frontier," as TV's "Star Trek" had it.

According to this view, science fiction almost inevitably became an outgrowth of frontier fiction. Indeed the growth of popular science fiction did coincide to some extent with the closing of the American frontier, and indeed there are a great many science-fiction works that portray frontier societies as arenas for individual heroism. The term "space opera," coined by science-fiction fan (and later writer) Wilson Tucker in 1941 to describe the cosmic adventure epics of pulp magazines in the 1930s, seems to insist on a relationship between such stories and the "horse operas" of the same period. And as if to demonstrate this relationship once and for all, a little-known pulp writer named Guy Archette (pseudonym of Chester S. Geier) was able to transform a Western into a science-fiction story by changing only a few key words and publishing it in *Amazing Stories* in 1953.[2]

Such a view necessarily oversimplifies the nature of science fiction and of popular literature in general. While it is true that much science fiction deals with the colonization of other worlds, most of it does not, and this theme is only one among dozens that have evolved during the long course of the genre's history. While it is true that popular science fiction in America developed close upon the end of the frontier period–around the turn of the century–so did the Western and the urban crime story. And while it is probably true that popular literature sought ways of dealing with the narrowing arenas for heroic adventure on earth, science fiction was far from the only response to this need. The "lost race" novel, the jungle adventure tale, the prehistoric romance–even the tale of universal cataclysm, which provides a kind of "frontier" by returning much of the earth to a depopulated wilderness–all enjoyed vogues during the late nineteenth and early twentieth centuries. Utopian fiction also began to appear with increasing frequency in America during this period, and at least one of the authors of such fiction–William Dean Howells–believed that the utopian story was late in coming to America because of the presence of a frontier to absorb and deflect utopian impulses.[3]

Nor is it entirely accurate to view the history of science fiction solely in terms of the pulp-magazine phenomenon which began around the turn of the century and eventually gave the genre its present name. In recent years, much research has been done on the science-fiction elements in works of Hawthorne, Poe, Melville, Fitz-James O'Brien, Thomas Wentworth Higginson, and others, and one curious observation that derives from all this work is that such early science fiction overlaps very little with the body of frontier literature that began with captivity narratives and became most clearly defined in the works of James Fenimore Cooper. While it might be argued that the appeal of such frontier literature has much in common with the later appeal of such science-fiction works as Ray Bradbury's *The Martian Chronicles* (1950)–the notion of settling a new land, of finding a new kind of democracy, of evolving a "natural aristocracy" based on assimilation with the new environment, of escaping the ills of urban life–it is also important to remember that works such as Bradbury's came relatively late in the history of science fiction, that Bradbury himself (at least) was deliberately attempting to recreate a frontier experience in his stories,[4] and that the science fiction of the nineteenth century expressed few such concerns.

In fact, it might well be argued that the first real confluence of science-fiction themes with the literature of the frontier did not occur until the advent of the dime novel. Edward S. Ellis's *The Steam Man of the Prairies* (1865; reprinted over the next forty years under such variant titles as *The Huge Hunter, Baldy's Boy Partner,* or *Young Brainerd's Steam Man*) is generally credited as the first of the dime novels to introduce the "marvelous inventions" theme which would later become such a staple of the genre in the "Frank Reade, Jr." series (which also virtually plagiarized this novel in the 1876 *Frank Reade and His Steam Man of the Plains*). As Everett F. Bleiler describes the formula of these early science-fiction adventures, "a boy genius invents something that is not too far removed from the science and technology of the day, and then has adventures which usually could have happened just as well without the invention."[5]

While this is generally true of Ellis's novel as well–most of the novel is given over to Indian chases, buffalo hunts, and mining expeditions–*The Steam Man of the Prairies* is nevertheless interesting both for what it does and doesn't tell us about the relationship of science-fictional ideas to the notion of the frontier. Ellis was a New Jersey school administrator whose 1860 *Seth Jones* had been one of the first works to prove the immense potential of the Western dime novel as a popular literary form. A popularizer of American history who apparently drew much of his inspiration from James Fenimore Cooper, he never experimented with science fiction before or after *The Steam Man.* But elements of the novel show some awareness of what the basic appeal of popular science fiction would eventually be, and there is some evidence that well-known modern science-fiction writers such as Robert A. Heinlein were familiar with this story in one of its many incarnations.[6]

The Steam Man concerns a ten-foot steam-driven iron robot (which looks suspiciously negroid in at least two of the illustrated editions) designed by a lovable but deformed boy-genius. (Already, echoes of the later Heinlein are apparent, since one of Heinlein's most popular stories for *Astounding Science Fiction,* "Waldo" [1942], also concerned a crippled boy-genius who invents remarkable devices for increasing his strength.) Some of the inspiration for the idea of the steam man becomes apparent when a New Englander, upon his first seeing the machine, claims he had had a similar idea "ever since [he] went through Colt's pistol factory in Hartford."[7] Despite the detail which Ellis lavishes upon his descriptions of the operation and maintenance of the robot, the machine is really good only as a substitute horse, pulling a specially designed wagon at speeds up to sixty miles an hour (although for safety's sake the boy seldom drives it above twenty). The boy makes friends with a "strong, hardy, bronzed trapper," who invites him to take the machine west. The machine is shipped to Independence, from where it is taken out upon the prairies to frighten Indians, assist in gold mining, and hunt buffalo. Even though the robot eventually proves of limited use–it can only go forward over flat terrain, and it can't work in the rain–the boy's ingenuity finally saves his party from a band of hostile Indians when he devises a means of converting the steam man into a moving bomb, which wipes out the Indians.

While there is little of frontier society as such in this tale, there might have been something naively appealing to Ellis's nineteenth-century audience about the idea of bringing a single item of technology to bear upon such disparate undertakings as Indian extermination, buffalo extermination, and gold mining. It would be easy to read the steam man as a metaphor for the railroad, but it seems unlikely that Ellis and his readers were as concerned with metaphor as they were with the fantasy of using technology as a way of bringing adventure into the life of a weak and disadvantaged urban youth. This appeal would later characterize much juvenile and pulp science fiction, from the Tom Swift stories of "Victor Appleton" to the "space operas" of the pulps in the 1930s. And the notion of a young technologist solving a problem by thinking of a new way to use his machine–turning it into a bomb–was a remarkable anticipation of the ingenious engineer-hero of much later science fiction. At the very least, the story is significant in showing how a dangerous wilderness may be conquered by an urban boy with technical training as well as by the traditional frontier hero.

At the same time, the story is a long way from modern science fiction, and a long way from presenting any substantial notion of a frontier other than the pop culture American West. It would take a long time for science fiction to translate the American frontier to other worlds and still longer for it to treat "outer space" or the galaxy as frontiers in themselves. In fact, the relatively sophisticated technique of exploring social issues through the presentation of frontier-like societies on other planets was rather late in coming to science fiction, and the young genre had to pass through a number of important transitions before the intellectual scaffolding for such a theme would be fully in place.

The first such transition involved the dislocation of the frontier from the American West into "science-fictional" settings, and for this no better example can be found than in the work of Edgar Rice Burroughs. Whereas Ellis and a few other writers (notably Luis Senarens in his "Frank Reade,

Jr." books) enthusiastically shipped marvels of technological invention westward, it was quite another thing to imagine entirely new frontiers. Burroughs, with his "interplanetary romances," represented an important shift from introducing imaginary machines into an existing wilderness to creating a completely imaginary environment. Other planets had been seen before in fiction, to be sure, but for the most part they were settings for utopian fantasies (as in Percy Greg's *Across the Zodiac* [1880]) or for confrontations between technological superpowers (as in Garrett P. Serviss's *Edison's Conquest of Mars* [1898]). Burroughs's "Barsoom," in contrast, was clearly intended as a setting for adventure. Burroughs, who had served for a time in the U.S. Seventh Cavalry and was familiar with the American West, found a way of returning the frontier hero to his roots, so to speak; rather than giving his characters technical superiority, he placed them in environments which served effectively as new kinds of frontiers. In a sense, it made little difference whether these environments were Mars, Africa, Venus, or the interior of the earth–Burroughs was almost certainly influenced by the "lost civilization" motif popularized by H. Rider Haggard and his imitators–but from the point of view of science-fiction history, his choice of Mars as a setting for his earliest successes was undeniably significant. As Paul A. Carter notes, "John Carter's initial impression–that Mars is a place not so very different from Arizona–has decisively influenced all subsequent interplanetary fiction. When Americans land on another world, it seems, they expect it to resemble the American West."[8]

Burroughs's John Carter first appeared in "Under the Moons of Mars" in *The All-Story Magazine* in 1912. In 1917, this was retitled *A Princess of Mars* for its book publication. Carter, a Virginia aristocrat and veteran of the Civil War, is an almost supernatural figure at the book's outset, never seeming to age and living over a hundred years by his own account. He undertakes a prospecting expedition with his friend Capt. James K. Powell in Arizona in 1866 (described as a professional mining engineer, Powell almost inevitably calls to mind John Wesley Powell). After the two of them strike gold, Powell is killed in an Indian attack and Carter is pursued to an isolated cave, from which–perhaps with the aid of ancient Indian magic–he somehow projects himself to Mars by simply staring at it in the Arizona sky. Burroughs's description of the moonlit Arizona landscape is telling: it is "as though one were catching for the first time a glimpse of some dead and forgotten world, so different is it from the aspect of any other spot on earth."[9]

The Mars to which Carter transports himself is indeed such a "forgotten world," and if it is not dead, it is dying. Remnants of a once-great technological society struggle to keep the atmosphere intact with great machines, while warring races of various colors dominate the mostly barren landscape. If Burroughs was borrowing from the literature of the frontier, it was not from later myths of the West as a garden but from earlier visions of a Great American Desert which, as Henry Nash Smith writes, "throws the hero back in upon himself and accentuates his terrible and sublime isolation. He is an anarchic and self-contained atom – alone in a hostile, or at best a neutral, universe."[10] John Carter's Mars is not a land fit for settlers, and no settlers will follow him. It is not a new land, but a decaying one, and in most conventional senses it is not a frontier at all. But his adventures there – a repeating cycle of pursuit, capture, escape, and trial by battle – bear a noticeable resemblance to the adventures of the early fictional frontier heroes; and some of the races he encounters – notably the fifteen-foot-tall, bellicose "green men," seem suspiciously like the Plains Indians of early Western lore. Onto this basic frame, Burroughs has grafted elements of the "lost race" novel, with its beautiful princesses, and elements of the "marvelous invention" story, with its atmosphere generators and flying machines. The mixture proved enormously successful for the next several decades, and if it did not quite treat outer space as a "new frontier" it at least opened it up as a likely arena for frontier-like adventures and as a means of keeping alive some of America's favorite myths about its self-sufficient frontier heroes.

Popular genres may evolve in many ways: formulas may become more variable, style more refined, characters and themes more complex. Early pulp science fiction seems to have evolved through a simple process of accretion. To the basic adventure-story template were added marvelous inventions, interplanetary settings, lost races and princesses, scientists, aliens, spies – practically everything popular fiction had to offer, each piled on anew with none of the older conventions retired to make way. The formulaic, episodic adventure structure of Burroughs' novels resembles the structure of such earlier dime-novel series as Frank Reade and Tom Swift, but whereas the latter concerned young scientific geniuses using their wits to escape perils on Earth Burroughs reinstated the traditional masculine hero and moved the setting to other planets. From here it was only a series of steps to combine all these elements into the figure of a young, masculine, scientific genius-hero whose domain was not merely other planets but the entire universe. This almost uncontrolled proliferation of devices and character types culminated in the "space opera."

Less than three years after "Under the Moons of Mars" appeared in magazine form, E. E. Smith (who would later sign his name "E. E. Smith, Ph.D." to lend credibility to his fantastic tales, even though his doctorate was in food chemistry and he was a doughnut-mix specialist by profession) began writing the first of what would eventually become known as science fiction's "space operas." Unable to find a market for his story of a brilliant scientist who ranges throughout the universe destroying whole planets to spread civilization and win the hand of his sweetheart, Smith did not publish *The Skylark of Space* until after the advent of the first pulp science-fiction magazine, Hugo Gernsback's *Amazing Stories,* in 1926. The novel was serialized in 1928 and immediately spawned a host of sequels and imitators. (The subtitle of the first sequel, *Skylark Three* [1930], was "the tale of the galactic cruise which ushered in universal civilization.") While there is much of a Wild West flavor about Smith's astonishingly naive (and, according to some, crypto-fascist) tales, he did little to add to the science-fiction myth of the frontier beyond expanding the scope of Burroughs's other planets to include whole galaxies, and Burroughs's multiple races to include endless varieties of alien civilizations. Nevertheless, his "space opera" helped outline the broad canvas upon which future science fiction would draw its increasingly sophisticated portraits of colonization and conflict.

Space opera dominated pulp science fiction of the 1930s, but the genre as a whole began to undergo a widely documented sea-change when John W. Campbell, Jr., assumed the editorship of *Astounding Stories* in September, 1937. Arguably, it was Campbell's strong editorial hand that eventually forced science-fiction writers to think more systematically and rationally about what "frontiers in space" might be like. Although Campbell himself had written space operas in his youth, as an editor he demanded narratively realistic treatments of carefully worked-out scientific and social concepts, with (in most cases) the science dominant. Stories began to appear that seemed to share common assumptions about future human expansion into the universe, and authors such as Robert A. Heinlein were encouraged to place their stories in the context of an overall "future history." Eventually such tales became sufficiently codified that at least one historian of the genre, Donald A. Wollheim, was later able to identify what he called a consensus "cosmogony," or future history, underlying much of the science fiction of the forties and fifties. This future history involved voyages to the moon and planets, followed by interstellar flights, the rise of a "galactic empire," the dominance and later decline of this empire, a period of "interregnum" or reversion to barbarism, the evolution of a more stable galactic civilization, and finally a "Challenge to God." If many stories of the Campbell years were so codified, the *codex* for them was almost certainly Isaac Asimov's series of "Foundation" stories which appeared in *Astounding* between 1942 and 1950. Asimov's ambitious borrowing from Edward Gibbon provided a context for science fiction which incorporates all sorts of opportunities for frontier narratives, even though Asimov's own series hardly falls under this rubric.

This "consensus future history" provides the next major transition leading toward modern science-fiction frontier narratives. If Burroughs moved the frontier hero to other planets, and Smith crossbred him with the superscientist and moved him across the universe, these *Astounding* stories provided him with the essential context for all real frontier narratives—a history. The myths about American history that underlay the fiction of the American frontier could not be adapted wholesale to the needs of science fiction, and it took the genre some twenty or thirty years to construct its own historical myth, drawn loosely not only from Gibbon but from parts of Toynbee and Spengler as well. Ironically, this development gave science fiction an opportunity to speculate intelligently upon the meaning of the frontier at the same time that it isolated the genre from other types of popular fiction and made it appear inaccessible to all but the most devoted readers; while a Western enthusiast could follow Burroughs with no trouble, and could read space opera with only an extended effort at suspending disbelief, this same reader might have more difficulty with stories whose common assumptions about scientific and technical advances seemed to be shared only with an initiated readership. Confined by the magazine format to short stories, series, and serial novels, popular American science fiction provided its authors few opportunities to construct an extended epic of space frontiers, and the epic evolved instead as a series of what Patrick Parrinder called "epic fables"–short tales depicting episodes in an unfolding galactic epic whose broad outlines were only familiar to regular readers of the genre.[11]

To examine one of these "epic fables" is to discover in large measure what was happening to the idea of the frontier within the emerging historical myth of Campbellian science fiction. A widely anthologized story that is often cited as a "touchstone" for such fiction–Tom Godwin's "The Cold Equations" (*Astounding Science Fiction*, 1954)–is also coincidentally (perhaps) written by a Western native and former prospector who lived in Nevada. Little else is known about Godwin, and his science-fiction output was limited to few other stories and novels, but if ever an author can be said to have established a reputation based on a single short story, it is he. What is more curious about the story is its reputation as the archetypal "hard science-fiction story"–the kind of science-fiction story built around real physical laws and accurate calculations–even though there is very little "hard science" in it. In fact, it is a frontier story which attempts to find in science a rationale for some cherished traditional myths that are not too far removed from those of Burroughs or even Edward Ellis. It attempts to tell us that it is the nature of the universe itself, and the "cold equations" which describe that universe, that determine a value system based on masculine ideals and stoic behavior.

Much of the popular impact of the story undoubtedly derives from its disarmingly simple plot: a young girl stowaway aboard a spaceship learns she must be jettisoned because her additional weight will exhaust the carefully calculated fuel supply before the ship can safely land. The spaceship in this case is a one-man "Emergency Dispatch Ship" on a rescue mission bearing serum to a frontier outpost on a remote planet. Barton, the pilot of the ship, is a fair example of what had become of the frontier hero in science fiction: he is "inured to the sight of death, long since accustomed to it and to viewing the dying of another man with an objective lack of emotion."[12] Thus it is without hesitation that Barton, upon detecting the presence of a stowaway, prepares to jettison his unknown passenger in accordance with strict regulations.

The story is set up in such a way that the law of the frontier becomes a law of physics, and the values of the frontier become principles of science: environmental determinism is carried to such an extreme that no one is really responsible for his or her actions. The interweaving of frontier and scientific imagery underline this world view: "It was a law not of men's choosing but made imperative by the circumstances of the space frontier" (p. 247); "she was of Earth and had not realized that the laws of the space frontier must, of necessity, be as hard and relentless as the environment that gave them birth" (p. 250); "H amount of fuel will not power an EDS with a mass of m plus x safely to its destination" (p. 261); and so on. And, within the context of the story's contrivances, there is little arguing with this bleak and deterministic view. Frontier settlements are visited by large space cruisers only according to fixed schedules, and any emergencies must be handled by the small EDS craft dispatched from the larger ships, which then speed on their way. Using liquid rocket fuel rather than the complex atomic mechanisms of the cruisers, these ships are given only sufficient fuel for a one-way mission (the pilots, presumably, must wait for the next scheduled cruiser stop to return), and that fuel is carefully allocated by computer. Additional weight will result in insufficient fuel for landing, and the ship will crash. No rescue of a stowaway is possible, and the only solution is jettisoning. Much of the appeal of the story, in fact, may derive from the apparently scientific cast it gives to the familiar hardboiled line, repeated by Barton, that "That's the way it is."

Godwin's complication is making the stowaway a young girl, which permits him to exploit the sentimental potential of this world view while at the same time reasserting its masculine values. "She belonged in that world of soft winds and warm suns, music and moonlight and gracious manners and not on the hard, bleak frontier" (p. 258). The girl is a poor teenager hoping to visit her brother, who has been sending money home to help her take courses in linguistics which, presumably, will make her employable on the settled planets. Her brother–one of six men in a settlement whose disease serum had been destroyed, significantly, by a tornado from the "Western sea"–is like Barton, one of the "men of the frontier" who "had long ago learned the bitter futility of cursing the forces that would destroy them for the forces were blind and deaf" (p. 261). By sentimentalizing his woman character, Godwin can easily proceed to show how she has no place in a harsh Newtonian universe. The myth of coldly rational science has been merged with the myth of the boys' book; the whole universe becomes an heroic, masculine arena, and it's nobody's fault. The Western desert is made infinite.

Like the American frontier, however, the space frontier is as much a creation of economics as of environment. Godwin reveals little of the economics of a society that would institute such draconian regulations regarding fuel (it is never clearly explained why no emergency supply is allotted), but we can pick up enough hints to discover that it is an essentially capitalist society which exploits its frontier in familiar ways: the girl's parents can barely eke out a living from their small shop, she has to pay for the education that will make her employable, and the money is sent back by her brother. She wears sandals made of cheap imitation "Vegan leather," and practices her language on a "native girl" who works as a cleaning lady on the space cruiser. In a later story, "The Last Victory," Godwin postulates an oppressive society founded in "Technogration" (a portmanteau of "technology" and "integration") from which rugged individualists called "Outlanders" seek to escape on the space frontier. The fear of racial mixing in the latter story is as evident as the fear of women in "The Cold Equations"; in both cases, space is the last hope of white male hegemony, and in both cases this doctrine is heavily disguised through sentimentality and the appeal to science.

No one claims Godwin as one of the great writers of science fiction, but he is interesting precisely because he lacks the distinguishing idiosyncrasies of more familiar writers like Robert A. Heinlein or Isaac Asimov, who have also dealt with frontiers in their fiction.[13] While it is probably unfair to characterize his work–as some have–as purely the outgrowth of editor John Campbell's beliefs or of a consensus future history emerging from science-fiction conventions, a story like "The Cold Equations" does have much in common with other science-fiction stories of its period in its view of frontier life and economics. It represents a view which, though harshly criticized in the fiction of relatively anomalous (in terms of the Campbell tradition) writers like Ray Bradbury, is in most ways characteristic of science fiction's view of other worlds once these other worlds came to be viewed as frontiers for colonizing rather than as merely arenas for swashbuckling action. Godwin's significant variation on the problem-solving formula of much Campbellian science fiction is that he posits a frontier so uncompromising that even the ingenuity of trained spacemen cannot provide a solution.

David Mogen (in *Wilderness Visions*) has observed that treatments of the frontier in modern science fiction tend to be either metaphorical or literal. Ray Bradbury, in *The Martian Chronicles* (1950), is an example of a metaphorical writer who pays little attention to the possible conditions of life on other planets, whereas the Campbell school of "hard" science fiction–

which includes Tom Godwin—views the movement into space as a kind of extension of the manifest destiny myth of American expansion, focusing largely on the problem-solving aspects of life in a hostile wilderness. A classic story of this type is Isaac Asimov's "The Martian Way" (1952), which deals with a conflict between Martian settlers and the Earth over water rights (the Martians import small amounts of water from Earth, and this leads to their being targeted by a demagogic politician clearly modeled on Joseph McCarthy). The "Martian way" of responding to this threat is to tow an enormous iceberg from the asteroid belt to Mars and offer to sell water to Earth. The industrious pioneer spirit exemplified by this dramatic and risky undertaking is, Asimov implies, the spirit that will eventually lead to the colonization of the universe.

Asimov's story is significant in that it introduces, albeit simplistically, an economic theme into its considerations of the frontier. Economic concerns had generally not been adequately addressed in Campbellian science fiction (as evidenced by "The Cold Equations"), and when they were addressed it was often in the context of a satirical utopia (such as depicted in Eric Frank Russell's ". . . And Then There Were None" [1951]). With the rise of *Galaxy* magazine in the early 1950s, economic satire became popular, largely through the works of Frederik Pohl and C. M. Kornbluth, most notably with their depiction of a world dominated by advertising agencies in *The Space Merchants* (1953; in *Galaxy* magaxine as "Gravy Planet," 1952). Even in this work, however, the view of the space frontier as safety valve for the industrious and independent-minded persisted.

This growing awareness of the necessary economic relations between the frontier and the Earth eventually began to evolve formulas of its own. One such formula, apparent in "The Martian Way" and in several other works by Asimov and Robert A. Heinlein, depicts fundamentalist or politically conservative groups opposing the idea of expansion into space either in principle or because of the need to address resource shortages on Earth. (Ironically, the argument that resources devoted to space travel could better be directed toward domestic problems emerged as a stereotype of right-wing thinking in science fiction at about the same time it was beginning to emerge as a liberal issue in American politics.) Another formula, almost the direct opposite of the first, sees the frontier as an arena for capitalist exploitation. In *The Space Merchants,* a project to colonize Venus is undertaken by corporations as a way of tempting settlers to relocate to a hostile environment in order to support an overexpanded economy on Earth (although eventually the project is co-opted by "Conservationists," who seek to colonize Venus in the name of the more traditional science-fiction virtues of freedom and human hegemony in the universe).

Selling the frontier became a fairly common theme in science fiction, one often used for bitterly satiric purposes; in C. M. Kornbluth's "The Marching Morons" (1951), for example, a future society threatened by overbreeding of imbeciles is "saved" when a businessman from the present awakes from suspended animation and concocts a vicious scheme to dispose of the excess population in space by convincing them they are immigrating to a promising new world. In Philip K. Dick's *Do Androids Dream of Electric Sheep* (1968), people are urged to relocate from a dying Earth by a massive advertising campaign that even promises personal slaves, or androids, to those choosing to immigrate to Mars (some of this propaganda is retained in the very different film based on the novel, *Bladerunner*). A few authors, such as Ursula K. Le Guin (in "The Word for World Is Forest" [1972]) focused on the alien societies subjugated under capitalist imperialism in stories clearly influenced by the American experience in Vietnam (as well as by the history of white/native-American relationships), and by the reevaluation of a number of cherished American myths in light of that experience.

In recent years, a growing awareness of complex economic and social issues has informed the work of a number of writers using frontier themes, including not only Le Guin, but Samuel R. Delany, Joanna Russ, James Tiptree, Jr., and others. Science fiction's "consensus" view of the space frontier survives primarily in the work of "hard" science fiction writers, but even among authors often classed in this group there has begun to emerge a greater degree of concern about the implications of such frontiers and the economic conditions that might underlie them. In fact, one of the most fully mature recent science-fiction novels set in a "space frontier" has come from an author often classed as a "hard SF" writer. Gregory Benford's *Against Infinity* (1983), drawing as it does on both the traditions of Campbellian science fiction and the broader traditions of the American *bildungsroman,* provides an interesting perspective on earlier science-fiction frontiers and is an excellent example of the "new" science fiction that neither entirely breaks free of its genre precedents nor is subsumed by them.

Against Infinity is closely modeled on William Faulkner's classic 1942 novella "The Bear," so much so that some readers have chosen to regard it as a *tour de force* of little significance on its own merits. To be sure, the ingenuity with which Benford transforms Faulkner's bear hunt into a search for an alien artifact on a moon of Jupiter is impressive, but the tale was archetypal even when Faulkner told it. Benford's use of this classic structure provides him with an opportunity to demonstrate how the resources of science fiction can enlarge upon and extend some deep-rooted American myths of maturation and confrontation with the wilderness.

Set on the moon Ganymede, the novel is organized in six parts, the first five of which roughly parallel the five parts of Faulkner's novella, and the sixth of which extends the theme of the frontier to incorporate broader "science-fictional" concerns–not only of the infinitely receding frontier represented by the physical universe but by the scientific and even metaphysical frontiers represented by the unusual nature of an alien artifact called "the Aleph." (In this latter regard, Benford borrows as much from Jorge Luis Borges as from Faulkner; Borges' 1945 story "The Aleph" also concerns an artifact which seems to contain infinity.) The basic story concerns the coming of age of a boy named Manuel Lopez, who first sees the legendary Aleph when he is thirteen. The Aleph itself is one of those marvelous inventions of pure alienness which science fiction is sometimes capable of producing–an apparently unstoppable "thing" which has for decades burrowed unpredictably throughout Ganymede, sometimes disrupting settlements and wreaking havoc with human attempts to "terraform" the satellite into a habitable world. ("Terraforming" is a concept borrowed from Campbellian science fiction, although the notion of altering planetary environments had been used earlier and may even have its roots in nineteenth-century dreams of turning the "Great American Desert" into a garden; the word itself was coined by Jack Williamson in a story published in 1942.) Over the next several years, Manuel repeatedly encounters the Aleph until finally, under the tutelage of an aging pioneer named Matt Bohles (who appeared as a teenager in Benford's 1975 novel *Jupiter Project,* set nearly a century earlier) and with the aid of a mechanically enhanced part-human animal known as Eagle, he is able to immobilize it. Benford's plot is so rich in science-fiction invention –terraforming, mechanically reinforced animals with enhanced IQ's, alien artifacts, space colonies, etc.–that it may seem daunting to readers not familiar with science fiction. But its significance derives in large part from the degree to which it does derive from the traditions of the genre. Apart from some passages of Faulknerian prose, the first two-thirds of the novel might easily be read as an interplanetary adventure firmly in the tradition of John W. Campbell, Jr.'s *Astounding Science Fiction.*

The last two parts of the novel, however, provide a perspective that is often lacking in such fiction. Part IV, like part IV of Faulkner's novella, is set some years later and provides historical and social background for what went before. Manuel has moved from the frontier settlement of Sidon to the city of Hiruko, where he encounters the effects of the socialist doctrines that have come to dominate Earth society when two men demand possessions from him as part of a legislated redistribution of wealth. A colleague explains to him that socialism on Earth evolved out of the contradictions inherent in capitalism, but that the socialist system itself–while efficient at handling the overpopulated condition of Earth–must expand into new worlds to maintain efficient production of goods, and this in turn breeds a new kind of capitalism at the frontier. "So we get humankind–with refined, humanitarian socialism in the older, crowded core. And capitalism sprouting up like weeds at the edge."[14] The frontier society of which Manuel has been a part, then, is less the product of a dream of conquering new worlds than of economic forces. Like Isaac McCaslin in Faulkner's "The Bear," Manuel learns that his inheritance is tainted. His mentor–the propertyless Matt Bohles who had lived more than a century in the colonies around Jupiter and who apparently had no family ties (the figure of Sam Fathers from "The Bear")–is a social anomaly rather than a harbinger of a regenerated society. And the Aleph itself has been reduced to an object of scientific research nearly resembling a museum piece. It is at this point, appropriately, that Manuel learns his estranged father has died.

Returning to Sidon, Manuel encounters Earthmen visiting Ganymede to conduct research on the Aleph, and comes to realize that "*They came here out of duty. Not from a yearning, but because their commonweal decided. They're priests, not explorers*" (p. 190). At Sidon, the frontier is giving way to civilization, even though the settlement's random sprawl still contrasts with the orderly grids of Hiruko. After the funeral, Manuel learns an odd fact about his military father: earlier in the novel, Colonel Lopez had seemed to represent the order of civilization in contrast to Matt Bohles's pioneering spirit of independence. Now Manuel learns that the hunts which eventually brought down the Aleph had been financed by his father for years at a loss to the settlement's economy, not only to give the men something to do in contrast to their oppressive settlement life but for "the thing itself." This "pioneering spirit," then, was alive in Manuel's father as well as in Bohles: perhaps it was not purely an anomaly.

The final section of the book begins, as did the first chapter, with an expedition from Sidon settlement in search of the Aleph. Now new domes have grown up, an atmosphere is becoming evident on the satellite, and there is talk of the mechanized animals creating a new underclass in society, "yet another source for the forward tilt of capitalism" (p. 213). Manuel accompanies an Earth scientist doing research on the Aleph and learns that the Aleph has revealed secrets as challenging to physics as the space frontier itself is to society: it continually rebuilds itself at the atomic level, "like something restlessly remaking itself, forever discontented" (p. 228). It reveals, in fact, that the physical laws governing the universe may themselves undergo evolutionary change. "Nothing remains, nothing is held constant," as the scientist explains to Manuel (p. 230). At the same time, the Aleph seems to contain all it has encountered, like the Aleph of Jewish legend: venturing inside it, Manuel finds images of Matt and of himself, stored from his earlier encounter with the artifact. Shortly after, an earthquake resulting from the stresses imposed by the terraforming process kills the scientist and nearly destroys the settlement. "The land ruled now, not men" (p. 248).

Manuel realizes that years earlier–at the time of Matt's death–"he had joined forever the other side–the wilderness, the opening-outward, the undomesticated, the country of the old dead time" (pp. 244–45). The "killing" of the Aleph not only accompanied the death of Matt, it prefigured the death of Manuel's father as well and committed the boy to a new way of thinking, dominated neither by the economic structures of his society nor by the scientific mode of its progress. "Out here, forging some understanding was not a matter of guessing and then testing, like a scientist, but of listening; waiting; witnessing the slow certain sway of worlds, the rhythms of gravity and ice. . . " (p. 249). The universe resolves itself into a series of dialectical frontiers at various levels: economic systems generate new patterns as a result of internal stresses, stresses in the crust of a planet build and rebuild it into a kind of ongoing dialogue between what humanity seeks with its terraforming and what nature will permit, and stresses at the subatomic level of matter itself–such as within the Aleph–suggest a universe forever remade and never completely understandable, but one that will always draw certain individuals into its vastness. *Against Infinity* suggests as few other novels have that "frontiers" in science fiction are multiplex and have the potential of encompassing such diverse themes as economic expansion, particle physics, planetary exploration, and the ancient myth of the hunt. If Burroughs's John Carter could not quite handle such frontiers, neither could John W. Campbell's scientists and engineers. But, Benford suggests, humanity seems to have a way of producing the individuals it needs for the new frontiers it encounters, and in the end it is this optimism that links his work most firmly with those earlier traditions. That perhaps is what is finally the defining characteristic of the genre's persistent return to the frontier.

NOTES

1. John Wyndham and Lucas Parkes, *The Outward Urge* (New York: Ballantine, 1959), jacket copy.

2. Brian Stableford, "Colonization of Other Worlds," in *The Science Fiction Encyclopedia,* ed. Peter Nicholls (Garden City, N.Y.: Doubleday Dolphin, 1979), p. 128.

3. Howells is quoted in James Gunn, *The Road to Science Fiction: From Gilgamesh to Wells* (New York: New American Library, 1977), pp. 312–13.

4. See, for example, my essay "The Frontier Myth in Ray Bradbury," in *Ray Bradbury,* ed. Joseph D. Olander and Martin Harry Greenberg (New York: Taplinger, 1980), pp. 33–54.

5. Everett F. Bleiler, ed., introduction to *Eight Dime Novels* (New York: Dover, 1974), p. xiii. This volume includes a facsimile of an 1882 reprint of Ellis's novel.

6. See, for example, H. Bruce Franklin, *Robert A. Heinlein: America as Science Fiction* (New York: Oxford Univ. Press, 1980), p. 11: "As a boy, Heinlein was an avid reader

of the Frank Reade, Jr., and Tom Swift science-fiction dime novels, and there are still copies of them in his library."

7. Edward S. Ellis, *The Steam Man of the Prairies,* in *Eight Dime Novels,* n.p.

8. Paul H. Carter, *The Creation of Tomorrow: Fifty Years of Magazine Science Fiction* (New York: Columbia Univ. Press, 1977), p. 62.

9. Edgar Rice Burroughs, *A Princess of Mars* (New York: Grosset and Dunlap, 1917), p. 20.

10. Henry Nash Smith, *Virgin Land: The American West as Symbol and Myth* (reprint, New York: Vintage, 1950), p. 97.

11. Patrick Parrinder, "Science Fiction as Truncated Epic," in *Bridges to Science Fiction,* ed. George E. Slusser et al. (Carbondale: Southern Illinois Univ. Press, 1980), p. 103.

12. Tom Godwin, "The Cold Equations," in *The Road to Science Fiction #3: From Heinlein to Here,* ed. James Gunn (New York: New American Library, 1979), pp. 246. Subsequent references in the text are to this edition.

13. For a discussion of how major science fiction writers such as Heinlein and Asimov dealt with frontier themes, as well as how later satirists such as Frederik Pohl and C.M. Kornbluth viewed them, see David Mogen, *Wilderness Visions: Science Fiction Westerns,* Vol. I (San Bernardino, Calif.: Borgo, 1982). Mogen's study (the second volume will be titled *New Frontiers, Old Horizons*) provides such a satisfactory overview of the frontier "myth" as adapted by science fiction (and later criticized by it) that I have taken some pains to avoid duplicating his effort in the present essay.

14. Gregory Benford, *Against Infinity* (New York: Pocket Books, 1984), p. 169. Subsequent references in the text are to this edition.

Contributors

Rudolfo A. Anaya, is a professor of English, University of New Mexico, and is the author of a number of creative works, including *Children of Atzlán* and *Tortuga,* and a nonfiction work, *A Chicano in China.* His novel, *Bless Me, Ultima,* a recognized classic among Chicano literature, won the prestigious Quinto Sol award.

Linda Ben-Zvi is an assistant professor of English at Colorado State University and is currently working on an extended analysis of gender in American drama.

Paul Bryant is dean of the Graduate College at Radford University in Radford, Virginia. He has published in *A Literary History of the American West, Twentieth Century Western Authors, Fifty Western Writers,* and *Teaching Environmental Literature.* He is the author of the Twayne U.S. Authors Series volume on H. L. Davis.

Mark Busby, an associate professor of English at Texas A&M University, has published *Preston Jones* and *Lanford Wilson* and is the author of *Ralph Ellison* in the Twayne U.S. Authors Series, scheduled for publication in 1990. He has published in *Western American Literature, MELUS, New Mexico Humanities Review, A Literary History of the American West,* and elsewhere.

Langdon Elsbree, chairman of the Department of English at Claremont McKenna College in Claremont, California, is the author of a book on ritual patterns in narrative.

James K. Folsom was a longtime member of the English department at the University of Colorado, Boulder, and the author of *The American Western Novel* as well as numerous articles on western literature. He was the editor of the *Western.* He died in 1988.

Melody Graulich teaches English at the University of New Hampshire. She is the editor of *Western Trails: A Collection of Short Stories by Mary Austin* and numerous publications and professional papers. In 1984 she won the Don D. Walker Prize for the best essay in western American literature.

Gerald A. Haslam, professor of English at Sonoma State University, has published several short-story collections and one novel, as well as booklets on Jack Schaefer and William Eastlake. He is the editor of *Forgotten Pages of American Literature, Western Writing, California Heartland,* and coeditor of *A Literary History of the American West.*

John Lenihan teaches history at Texas A&M University and is the author of *Showdown,* an analysis of social themes in Western films. He is currently at work on a study of cold war themes in film.

Mick McAllister, who took his Ph.D. in eighteenth-century English literature at the University of New Mexico, has written extensively on Western American writers, notably N. Scott Momaday and Frederick Manfred. He is also the author of two books on computer programming.

Charlotte S. McClure, associate professor of English, Georgia State University, is author of *Gertrude Atherton* in both the Western Writers Series and the Twayne U.S. Authors Series, and has published various articles on women writers. She is coeditor of *Feminist Visions: Toward a Transformation of the Liberal Arts Curriculum.* She directs the Honors Program, Georgia State University.

David Mogen teaches at Colorado State University in Fort Collins and is the author of *Wilderness Visions* and *Ray Bradbury* in the Twayne U.S. Authors Series. He has published in *American Literary Realism, Genre, Studies in Popular Culture,* and is currently finishing a study of science fiction, *New Frontiers, Old Horizons.*

Joan Penzenstadler completed her Ph.D. at Texas A&M University, where one of her areas of specialization was Chicano literature. She currently teaches at Louisiana State University at Shreveport.

John Clark Pratt teaches at Colorado State University at Fort Collins. He is the editor of a casebook on *One Flew Over the Cuckoo's Nest* and a collection of Vietnam literature entitled *Vietnam Voices.*

Wayne Ude was born in Minnesota but grew up in north-central Montana. He currently teaches creative writing at Old Dominion and is the author of two books of magical realist fiction, *Becoming Coyote* and *Buffalo and Other Stories.* From 1977 to 1984 he was the fiction editor of the *Colorado State Review.*

Ritchie D. Watson, Randolph-Macon College, Ashland, Virginia, is the author of a study on the image of the cavalier in Southern literature.

Gary K. Wolfe teaches science fiction at Roosevelt University in Chicago and has published a study of iconography in science fiction titled *The Known and the Unknown*.

Delbert E. Wylder is a professor of English at Murray State University in Murray, Kentucky, but has taught in the West at the University of New Mexico, Utah State University, and Colorado State University. He is the author of *Hemingway's Heroes* and *Emerson Hough,* and he has also published on Eastlake, Abbey, and Manfred. He helped found the Western Literature Association, was once its president, and is now the executive secretary.

Index

The Frontier Experience and the American Dream was composed into type on a Compugraphic digital phototypesetter in ten point Galliard with two points of spacing between the lines. Galliard was also selected for display. The book was designed by Jim Billingsley, typeset by Metricomp, Inc., printed offset by Thomson-Shore, Inc., and bound by John H. Dekker & Sons, Inc. The paper on which this book is printed carries acid-free characteristics for an effective life of at least three hundred years.

TEXAS A&M UNIVERSITY PRESS : COLLEGE STATION